Piwik Web Analytics Essentials

A complete guide to tracking visitors on your websites, e-commerce shopping carts, and apps using Piwik Web Analytics

Stephan A. Miller

BIRMINGHAM - MUMBAI

Piwik Web Analytics Essentials

First published: October 2012

Production Reference: 1270912

Published by Packt Publishing Ltd.
Livery Place
35 Livery Street
Birmingham B3 2PB, UK.

ISBN 978-1-84951-848-2

www.packtpub.com

Cover Image by Avishek Roy (roy007avishek88@gmail.com)

Credits

Author
Stephan A. Miller

Reviewers
Amir Shaked
Adrian Speyer
Deepak Vohra

Acquisition Editor
Usha Iyer

Lead Technical Editor
Kedar Bhat

Technical Editors
Farhaan Shaikh
Jalasha D'costa
Veronica Fernandes

Copy Editors
Aditya Nair
Alfida Paiva

Project Coordinator
Yashodhan Dere

Proofreader
Maria Gould

Indexer
Hemangini Bari

Production Coordinators
Nilesh R. Mohite
Manu Joseph

Cover Work
Nilesh R. Mohite

About the Author

Stephan A. Miller is a web and app developer, SEO expert, and blogger who lives in Kansas City, Missouri. He was head developer at All About Doors and Windows in Kansas City for six years and was a freelance developer and SEO expert for eight years.

In his career, he has worked with Wordpress, Drupal, Magento, osCommerce, ZenCart, and many other online applications, as well as developing sites from scratch in PHP and MySQL or using the Lithium PHP framework. But this is not all. Because his business was at times a one man show, he knows Linux, Apache, and Nginx well and has developed desktop applications in Python where PHP just won't work. He also knows search engine optimization techniques, web analytics software, and search engine marketing which he uses to promote his own handful of sites. He blogs semi-regularly at `http://www.stephanmiller.com` about his work.

I would like to thank Usha Iyer for contacting me with the idea for this book; Matthieu Aubry, the Project Leader at `Piwik.org`, for providing input on the book and the necessary screenshots I was missing and helping me with the Piwik Zen Cart plugin; Maarten Vonz for contributing and working with me on the open source project for the Piwik Zen Cart plugin; and Ruud Hein of Search Engine People, who published a post on Piwik for me. I would also like to thank all of my technical reviewers for making sure the book turned out as well as it did.

About the Reviewers

Amir Shaked is an R&D manager by day and software developer by night. He is proficient in several technologies, such as C#, WPF, PHP, Python, Java Script, Data Systems, Networks, and more.

In recent years, he has been working on several open source projects for Windows (including eLibrary: `openelibrary.org`), Android, and web applications. Through his work on open source and websites he discovered Piwik, and has since used, tweaked, and customized it for several projects.

He blogs on his website `amirshk.com` on various technical issues.

Deepak Vohra is a consultant and a principal member of the `NuBean.com` software company. He is a Sun Certified Java Programmer and Web Component Developer, and has worked in the fields of XML and Java programming and J2EE for over five years. He is the co-author of *Pro XML Development with Java Technology, Apress* and was the technical reviewer for *WebLogic: The Definitive Guide, O'Reilly*. He was also the technical reviewer for *Ruby Programming for the Absolute Beginner, Thomson Course Technology PTR*, and the technical editor for *Prototype and Scriptaculous in Action, Manning Publications*. He is also the author of *JDBC 4.0 and Oracle JDeveloper for J2EE Development, Packt Publishing, Processing XML documents with Oracle JDeveloper 11g, Packt Publishing*, and *EJB 3.0 Database Persistence with Oracle Fusion Middleware 11g, Packt Publishing*.

www.PacktPub.com

Support files, eBooks, discount offers and more

You might want to visit www.PacktPub.com for support files and downloads related to your book.

Did you know that Packt offers eBook versions of every book published, with PDF and ePub files available? You can upgrade to the eBook version at www.PacktPub.com and as a print book customer, you are entitled to a discount on the eBook copy. Get in touch with us at service@packtpub.com for more details.

At www.PacktPub.com, you can also read a collection of free technical articles, sign up for a range of free newsletters and receive exclusive discounts and offers on Packt books and eBooks.

http://PacktLib.PacktPub.com

Do you need instant solutions to your IT questions? PacktLib is Packt's online digital book library. Here, you can access, read and search across Packt's entire library of books.

Why Subscribe?

- Fully searchable across every book published by Packt
- Copy and paste, print and bookmark content
- On demand and accessible via web browser

Free Access for Packt account holders

If you have an account with Packt at www.PacktPub.com, you can use this to access PacktLib today and view nine entirely free books. Simply use your login credentials for immediate access.

I dedicate this book to my best friend Erin, who convinced me that I should write this book and for putting up with me while I did, and to my kids – Jared and Maddie – who I hope find even bigger dreams come true for them in their lives

Table of Contents

Preface

Web analytics is a necessity if you have a website. More and more websites are being constructed. Small niches have hundreds of competing sites. And those sites that won't listen to what their traffic is telling them will soon disappear or be buried in the search results under sites that do pay attention to their traffic. And that is why anyone who has any type of website needs web analytics software such as Piwik to help them hear what their visitors are saying.

Web analytics began as simple log parsing to determine how many hits a website would get in a day, and has evolved into a complex science that can give you minute details on the people and bots that visit your site. And while there are many third-party, open source solutions for tracking and analyzing your web traffic, Piwik stands at the forefront as the open source alternative to Google analytics.

Unlike third-party solutions, Piwik gives you total control of your code, the server it runs on, and the privacy settings of your tracking. Piwik can be downloaded and installed on your server in five minutes for free and Piwik has the same advanced features as other third-party analytics services.

Piwik started in 2003 with a little web statistics program called phpMyVisites. At the time, it was one of the modern open source web statistics programs available. In 2007, phpMyVisites was replaced by the new and improved Piwik. Since then developers from all around the world have contributed to its constant improvement and have made it the advanced application it is today.

Piwik offers real-time reporting that allows you to track visitors from the instant they land on your website. Piwik also provides a dashboard interface that is customizable to the reports, charts, and date ranges you want. Piwik does this through the use of widgets that can be added and removed with the click of a button. Piwik protects your visitors' privacy with advanced privacy features that you control from a unified dashboard. Piwik handles multiple users and multiple websites out of the box and users can have access to one or many websites. Piwik can track e-commerce traffic, file downloads, 404 pages, RSS feeds, clicks on external websites, and internal site actions such as video interaction. Piwik's API makes it easy to integrate into any website CMS or backend CRM you may use, and that is only a few of the features that Piwik provides.

What this book covers

Chapter 1, Installation and Setup, shows you how to set up Piwik on your hosting environment. It will teach you the requirements for running Piwik and how to meet them if your server does not currently support them. It will also walk you through adding the default tracking code to your first website and configuring analytics for that site.

Chapter 2, Using Piwik's Interface and Reports, will teach you how to use and manipulate Piwik's dashboard and widgets. It will also show you how to customize online reports and the PDF and HTML e-mail reports. You will learn how to use the real-time analytics features of Piwik and how to filter and search your visitor logs to target specific data sets.

Chapter 3, Tracking Visitors with Piwik, gives details about using the default tracking code and goes beyond that and shows you how to configure cookies, how to set up tracking for downloads and outbound links, and how to use multiple trackers at once. By the end of the chapter, you will also be up-to-date on using asynchronous tracking in Piwik.

Chapter 4, Setting Up and Tracking Goals, defines goal conversion tracking and teaches you how to measure and reach goals for your website and business using Piwik's goal conversion tracking features. You will discover how to set up goals in Piwik and how to read and use goal overview reports and goal detail reports. This chapter will also show you how to set up revenue tracking.

Chapter 5, Tracking Marketing Campaigns, explains how to use Piwik to track visitors, conversions and revenue from paid ads, display ads, e-mail campaigns, and other sources. You will learn how to track with URL parameters, how to create campaign URLs, and how to track paid search ads and keywords.

Chapter 6, Tracking Events, teaches you how to record and track user interaction with website elements such as flash, videos, and widgets. You will find out why event tracking is important and how to set up your Piwik installation to track interactions with the Flash, AJAX, and JavaScript elements of your web pages.

Chapter 7, E-commerce Tracking, is devoted to those of you who own or run an online shopping cart and it will go through the details of tracking your ecommerce visitors, sales, conversions, bounce rates, and more. You will learn the difference between standard and e-commerce tracking and how to set Piwik up to handle your chosen monetary unit. By the end of the chapter, you will be able to track orders, items purchased, shopping cart actions, product page views, category page views, and be able to read the e-commerce reports like an expert.

Chapter 8, Piwik Website and User Administration, is all about multiple domains and multiple users. You will discover how to create new users or make your Piwik installation open for user registration. You will learn how to set user access levels and other advanced user management topics. You will also find out how to add multiple websites and subdomains to Piwik.

Chapter 9, Advanced Tracking and Development, will help you move beyond the JavaScript tracking features of Piwik and into more advanced methods of tracking visitors. By the end of this chapter, you will have learned how to use image tracking, how to use Piwik's tracking API, how to build a simple Piwik Plugin, and how to debug any tracking issues you may have.

Chapter 10, Piwik Integration, explains how to integrate Piwik into various CMS and CRM platforms, how to access Piwik when mobile, and the basics of using the Piwik Analytics API to create custom tracking applications. You will also learn how to embed Piwik widgets on other websites and how Piwik can be embedded in your own projects.

Appendix A, Tracking API Reference, is a minimal glossary of the Piwik Tracking API calls, which is handy for a quick reference when that API call just does not pop into your head, or for you to print out and use beside your computer.

Appendix B, Analytics API Reference, is a minimal glossary of the Piwik Rest API calls, handy for the same reasons as *Appendix A, Tracking API Reference*.

What you need for this book

You will need to have a server installed either locally on your computer or on a web hosting account. For most of you this will mean a LAMP stack of Apache, PHP, and MySQL, but the Apache server can be replaced with other servers such as Nginx or lighttpd if needed. PHP should be version 5.1.3 or higher and MySQL should be version 4.1 or higher. For some of the graphing capabilities of Piwik, you will need to have the PHP GD extension installed.

You will need FTP access and an FTP client if you are installing Piwik on a remote web server. If you are installing Piwik for learning purposes locally on your computer, you won't need to use FTP.

You can get 90 percent of what you need out of Piwik without knowing how to code. But that extra 10 percent can help a lot. JavaScript and PHP knowledge is helpful but any coding knowledge should suffice. Two chapters in the book are devoted to interacting with Piwik via code and code will be sprinkled throughout the book.

Who this book is for

This book is for anyone who wants an open source solution for web analytics. It is suitable for bloggers, website owners, JavaScript application developers, or analytics professionals. It will benefit those new to web analytics as well as experienced users and developers. And it will take you from installing Piwik to creating custom code to tweak Piwik data and integrate Piwik with your own projects.

Conventions

In this book, you will find a number of styles of text that distinguish between different kinds of information. Here are some examples of these styles, and an explanation of their meaning.

Code words in text are shown as follows: "This function is the same as `_trackPageview(opt_pageURL)` in Google Analytics or `submit()` in Yahoo! Analytics".

A block of code is set as follows:

```
    [Tracker]
campaign_var_name="campaign"
campaign_keyword_var_name="keyword"
```

Any command-line input or output is written as follows:

```
chown -R www-data:www-data piwik
```

New terms and **important words** are shown in bold. Words that you see on the screen, in the menu or dialog boxes for example, appear in the text like this: "Navigate to the **Campaigns** menu in Piwik and check it out".

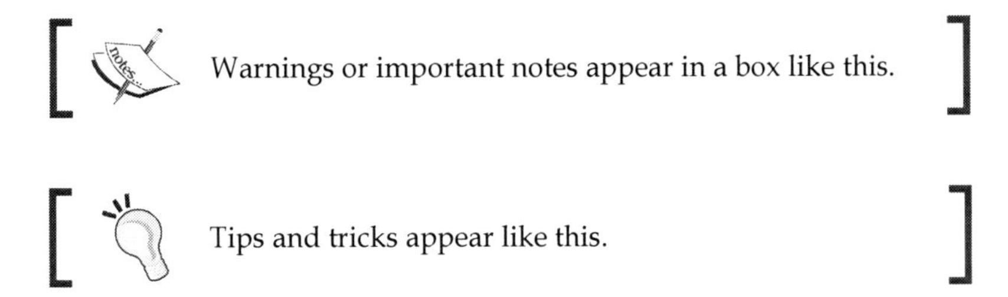

Warnings or important notes appear in a box like this.
Tips and tricks appear like this.

Reader feedback

Feedback from our readers is always welcome. Let us know what you think about this book—what you liked or may have disliked. Reader feedback is important for us to develop titles that you really get the most out of.

To send us general feedback, simply send an e-mail to `feedback@packtpub.com`, and mention the book title via the subject of your message.

If there is a topic that you have expertise in and you are interested in either writing or contributing to a book, see our author guide on `www.packtpub.com/authors`.

Customer support

Now that you are the proud owner of a Packt book, we have a number of things to help you to get the most from your purchase.

Downloading the example code

You can download the example code files for all Packt books you have purchased from your account at `http://www.PacktPub.com`. If you purchased this book elsewhere, you can visit `http://www.PacktPub.com/support` and register to have the files e-mailed directly to you.

Errata

Although we have taken every care to ensure the accuracy of our content, mistakes do happen. If you find a mistake in one of our books—maybe a mistake in the text or the code—we would be grateful if you would report this to us. By doing so, you can save other readers from frustration and help us improve subsequent versions of this book. If you find any errata, please report them by visiting `http://www.packtpub.com/support`, selecting your book, clicking on the **errata submission form** link, and entering the details of your errata. Once your errata are verified, your submission will be accepted and the errata will be uploaded on our website, or added to any list of existing errata, under the Errata section of that title. Any existing errata can be viewed by selecting your title from `http://www.packtpub.com/support`.

Piracy

Piracy of copyright material on the Internet is an ongoing problem across all media. At Packt, we take the protection of our copyright and licenses very seriously. If you come across any illegal copies of our works, in any form, on the Internet, please provide us with the location address or website name immediately so that we can pursue a remedy.

Please contact us at `copyright@packtpub.com` with a link to the suspected pirated material.

We appreciate your help in protecting our authors, and our ability to bring you valuable content.

Questions

You can contact us at `questions@packtpub.com` if you are having a problem with any aspect of the book, and we will do our best to address it.

1
Installation and Setup

This chapter will guide you through the setup and installation of Piwik Open Source Web Analytics on a web server or on your local computer in a test server environment. This is not a complicated procedure, but there are a few ways to set up your Piwik installation, and a couple of choices you will have to make during the installation procedure.

Piwik can be downloaded easily from its website at `http://piwik.org/`. It is a free and open source application, and is released under the GNU General Public License. This means you can download Piwik, modify it, and release new software using its code base as long as you agree to pass on the same rights to others who use your modified code.

In this chapter, we will cover the following topics:

- Meeting system requirements
- Uploading to your hosting account
- Creating a database for your installation
- Installing Piwik
- Retrieving and using the default JavaScript tracking code
- Securing your installation
- Setting up Piwik for high-traffic situations
- Updating your installation
- Backing up Piwik

Meeting system requirements

At the time of writing this book, the latest version of Piwik was 1.8; the following are the requirements for this version. A newer version of Piwik may have more or less the same requirements as those covered below.

Firstly, you need to make sure that your server and/or development environment is set up and ready for the install. Fortunately, the requirements of Piwik are not very hard to meet. Most hosting companies' standard PHP and MySQL packages will meet these requirements.

- First, you need a web server. The most common, Apache, is the standard for most Piwik installations. Piwik also runs well on light web servers like Nginx or lighttpd. In fact, for high traffic websites, a light web server is the recommended option. But if you are a beginner with Piwik or Nginx, it is best to stick with Apache.
- Piwik requires MySQL version 4.1 or greater to store its analytics data.
- Piwik also needs PHP version 5.1.3 or higher installed on your web server; version 5.3 or higher is recommended for less memory usage.
- You will also need to have either the `pdo` and `pdo_mysql` extension installed, or the `mysqli` extension installed. These MySQL extensions can use some of the more advanced features of MySQL 4.1 necessary for Piwik to run.
- You will also need the PHP `GD` extension to create the images for some of the graphs in Piwik.

Chances are that a web hosting company will have the required PHP extensions enabled on your account. They are standard on most modern servers. If they do not have it enabled, you can put in a support ticket to have the above requirements met. Editing the `php.ini` file to enable the correct PHP extensions yourself will be covered in the installation process.

Downloading Piwik

Once you have the environment for Piwik ready and you are waiting for a brand new Piwik installation, it is time to go to the Piwik website http://piwik.org and download the Piwik archive file. Just like the screenshot below, you should be able to see a big orange button containing the download link to the current version of Piwik. The current version, during the writing of this book, is 1.8.

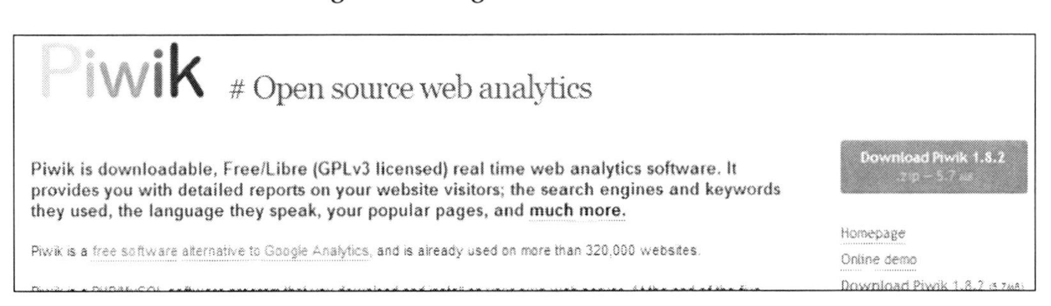

This button links to the zip file version of the download—something you might prefer on a Windows or Mac computer. If you are looking for other archive formats, like tar.gz, you can find a list at http://builds.piwik.org. The most current version of Piwik will be named either latest.tar.gz or latest.zip.

Download the zip file to a place you want to store it temporarily. If you are going to upload with FTP, use a tool like 7zip, Peazip, or the archive tool built into your operating system, to open up the zip file. You should be able to see a piwik folder in there, as well as a How to install Piwik.html file. If you are going to use cPanel's **File Manager** or some other web server administration tool, you don't have to unzip this file. You will be uploading it whole and extracting the files from the server.

You can now drag or extract this piwik folder to the location you want it in. This will be a temporary location if you plan on uploading the files via FTP. If you are only running a test server on your local machine, you can drag the folder to the document root of your local server. The document root is the directory on your web server where the files for your web site are held. The name of this folder varies depending upon your server configuration. Some common document root folder names are:

- HTTPDocs
- HTDocs
- HTML
- Public_HTML
- Web

Downloading Piwik with SSH

You can skip the steps of downloading, unzipping, and even the next step of uploading, if you are familiar with SSH. Just use the following steps and you don't have to worry about opening your FTP client. SSH is a network protocol that allows secure command execution between two networked computers. Using SSH can be quicker and easier once you get used to typing commands in a terminal window.

You will need an SSH client to do this. If you have an Apple computer, it will come with a program called Terminal. If you are using Windows, you will have to download Putty, which is available at `http://www.chiark.greenend.org.uk/~sgtatham/putty/`. These tools allow you to interact with your remote web server and execute commands via your server's command line interface.

1. Log in to your web server using Putty or Terminal. If you are logging in as `root`, this will put you in the `/root directory`. If you are logged in under a user account, you will most likely be at `/home/YOURUSERNAME`, where `YOURUSERNAME` is the same username you just logged in with.
2. Navigate from your home directory to the directory that Apache will be serving the documents from. On many servers, this will be `/var/www/` or `/var/www/vhosts/your-domain.com`. If you need to find the document root, you can run this command on the command line:

   ```
   grep -i 'DocumentRoot' httpd.conf
   ```

3. Once you know where your document root is, just use the `cd` command to get there:

   ```
   cd /var/www
   ```

4. Use `wget` or `curl` to grab the `tar.gz` from `http://www.Piwik.org`. `wget` is the more common of the two, but both will work similarly (if you are using `curl`, just replace `wget` with `curl`, in the following command):

   ```
   wget http://builds.piwik.org/latest.tar.gz
   ```

5. Now you will want to extract Piwik's files from the archive:

   ```
   tar -xvwzf latest.tar.gz
   ```

6. You can delete the archive file, as you will no longer be needing it:

   ```
   rm latest.tar.gz
   ```

7. You can stop right here if you want your Piwik installation in a folder called `piwik`. If you are running Piwik alongside an active site, putting your Piwik installation in a subfolder is the best choice.
8. If you want to move the location of your Piwik folder before you install, instead of browsing to the `piwik` subfolder of your domain or localhost, you can (from your current location at the document root):
    - Rename it or move it to another folder:

      ```
      mv piwik NEW_FOLDER
      ```

    - Move it to the document root:

      ```
      mv -r ./piwik/* ./
      ```

Uploading to a web hosting account

If you have put Piwik on a local web server or used `wget` to download Piwik to your Linux web host, you can skip this section. For those of you who still need to get Piwik to its home on a web server, it's time to decide how you are going to do that. If your web hosting company is running a web-based server administration software like cPanel, Plesk, or Webmin/Virtualmin, then you can probably upload through your browser and never have to use your FTP software.

Uploading using cPanel or other file managers

Many modern web hosts provide their users with administration tools that allow the users to do just about anything they can imagine with their servers. It's good to become familiar with the tools your hosting company provides you. There may be a few things hiding in there that you don't know about, like creating new e-mail addresses, new databases, and new name server records, and uploading files. cPanel is one of the most common and commercial web-based web server administration tools. If you plan on using one of these tools, you don't even need to unzip the file and upload each file one by one. You can unzip the zip file on the server after it's uploaded. Follow these steps to upload the file:

1. Browse to the **File Manager** utility in your cPanel installation.

2. This should bring up a pop-up window with your **Web Root** already selected. Click on the **Go** button.

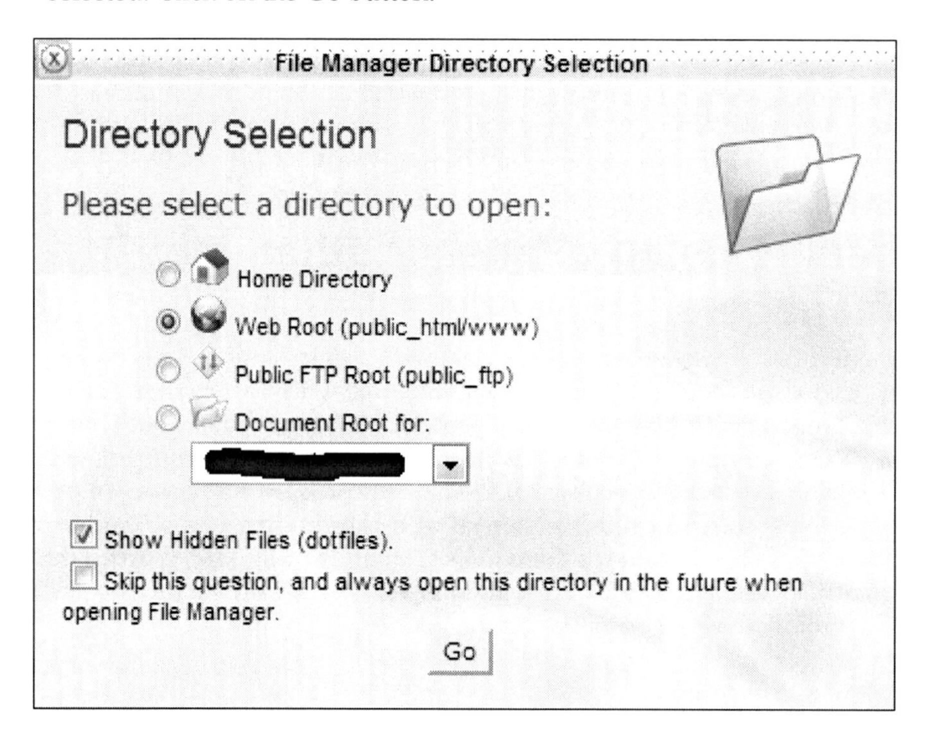

3. Click on the **Upload** link in the **File Manager** and you will be at the upload page. Click on the **Choose File** button and choose the **latest.zip** file you downloaded from `http://piwik.org`. Don't worry about any of the other checkboxes on the page. They can be left as is.

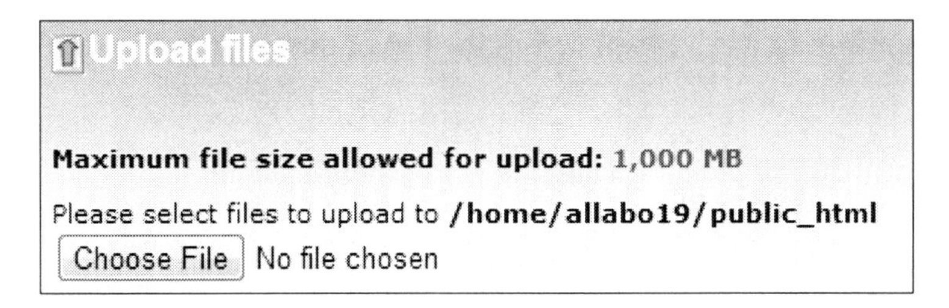

4. After the upload is done, return to the **File Manager** screen, right-click on the **latest.zip** file and choose **Extract**. This will put your Piwik installation inside a folder called `piwik` in your web root. If you want, you can rename this folder with some other name by right-clicking on the file and choosing **Rename**. Naming this folder something like `stats` may help you remember what type of software is in this folder.

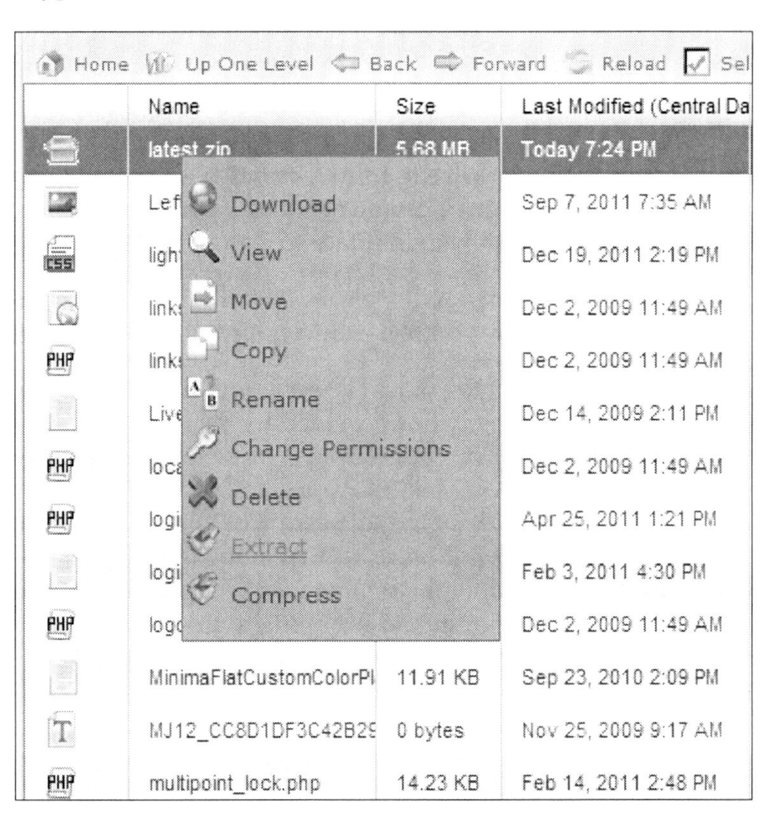

If you are using a web-based administration tool other than cPanel, you will use a process similar to this to upload the Piwik zip file to your web server. Look out for a help or knowledge base link or search Google if you have trouble finding your web-based FTP tool. Most web admin systems will name the tool you are looking for, as `File Manager` or `Web FTP`. Some may use the right-click method to bring up a menu and some may use a menu across the top of the page. It shouldn't be too hard to figure out.

Uploading using FTP

If you are running a barebones host without cPanel software, it's time to open your FTP software. If you don't have an FTP client installed on your computer—no problem. I can recommend two great free FTP tools that run on either Windows or Mac, and one that will run from a browser:

- **Filezilla**: Filezilla is a lightweight, free FTP software that has been around for years. It is open source and is in constant development. There is a client version and a server version. You will only need the client version. You can get Filezilla at `http://filezilla-project.org`.
- **CyberDuck**: This free FTP software has lots of features, but earlier versions of CyberDuck were only for Macs. It's very easy to use, and has recently become available to Windows users. You can find CyberDuck at `http://cyberduck.ch`.
- **Net2ftp**: This free service will run from a browser, so even if you have to upload the Piwik files with a Chrome notebook, you can get it done. Net2ftp has both a Java and a Flash web interface to choose from.

There are dozens of free FTP clients. A Google search will turn up a lot more than the three I have listed. Just choose one you feel comfortable with and let's get to work.

Using your FTP software, connect to your FTP server with the **Host**, **Username** and **Password** your hosting company has provided for you. For security reasons, it is better to use sFTP—a secure FTP connection. Browse to the folder you want to install Piwik in, with your FTP tool. Most FTP software, such as Filezilla, will show your local files on the left-hand side of the software window and your remote files on the right side of the software window, as shown in the following screenshot. But those like Cyberduck may show only the remote files by default, and all uploads and downloads are done by dragging from and dropping to the Cyberduck window.

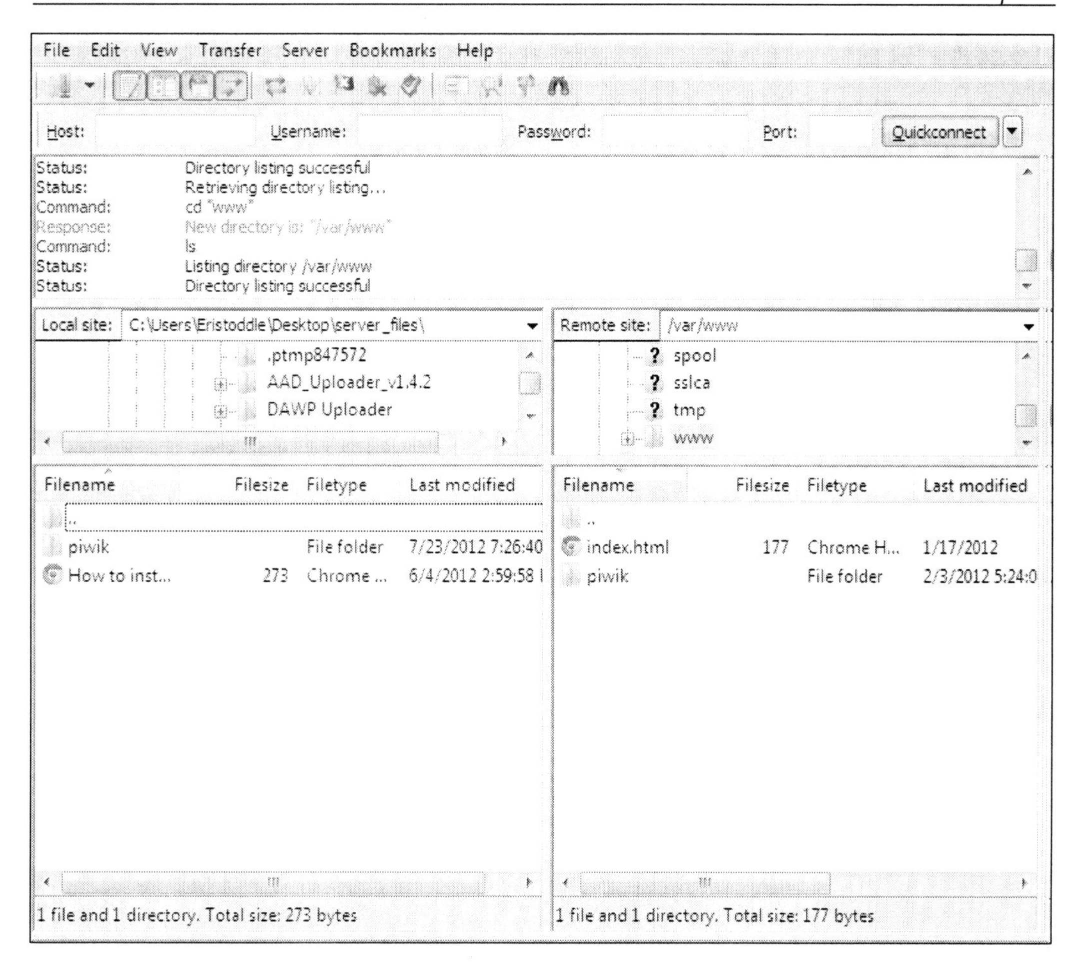

Now select all of your local Piwik files from inside the `piwik` folder in either the left pane of your FTP software or from an Explorer or Finder window to the remote folder you want them to reside in on the server in your FTP tool. It may take a minute or so to upload all the files, but once that is done, you are ready to create a database and then start the installation wizard.

Creating a database for your installation

Now it's time to create the MySQL database and admin user that your Piwik installation will be using. It is recommended that you create a user and database specifically for Piwik to use to keep your MySQL users and databases segregated.

Creating a user and database for Piwik in cPanel

Create a user and database for your installation, using the following steps:

1. Open your browser, browse to the location of your cPanel installation, and click on the **MySQL Databases** link in cPanel.

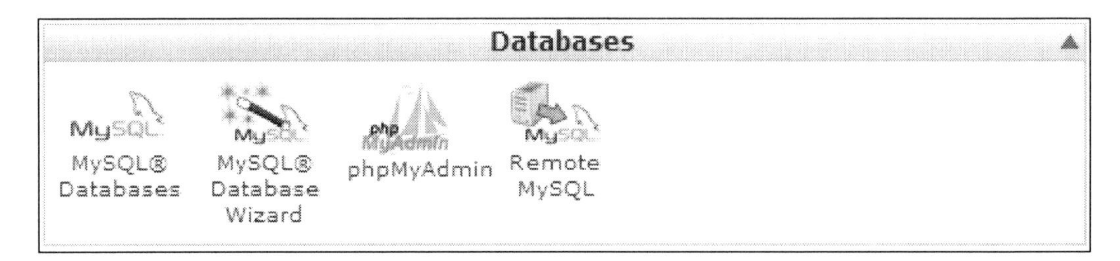

2. Enter a name for the database you will be using for Piwik, and click on the **Create Database** button. If you are on shared hosting, cPanel will add your username as a prefix. For example, if you chose `piwik` as the name of your database and your username is `username`, the actual name of the database created will be `username_piwik`. You will need to remember this database name for the web-based Piwik installation.

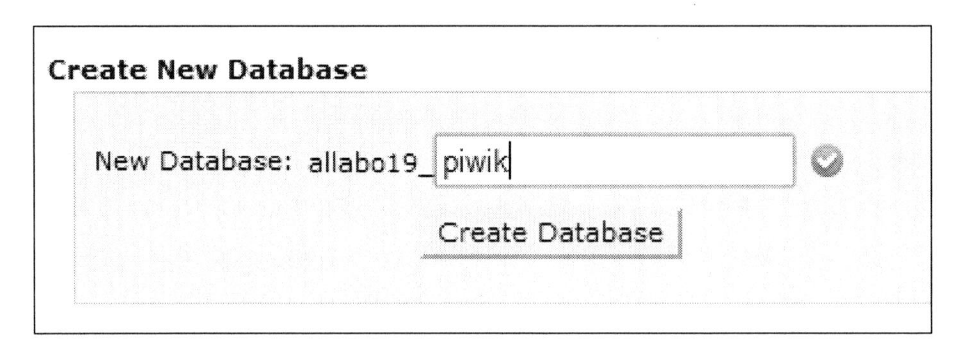

3. Now it's time to create a user and assign the user to our new database. Jump down to the **MySQL Users** section. Enter your desired username and password twice, and click on **Create User**. You will need to remember the username and password for the Piwik installation. With cPanel on a shared host, you will get a new MySQL username with your username as a prefix, like this: `username_mysqluser`.

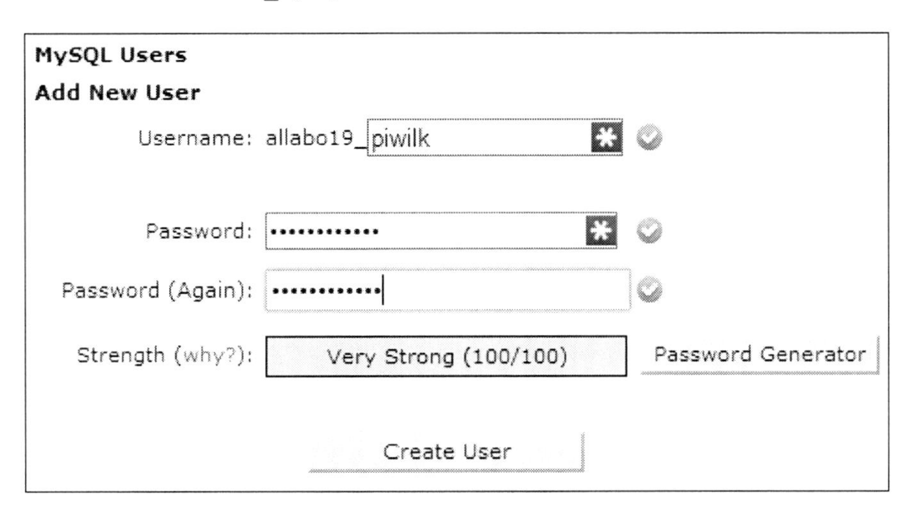

4. Now add the user to the database, by clicking on the **Add** button.

Add User To Database

User: allabo19_piwik

Database: allabo19_piwik

Add

5. Next, check the **ALL PRIVILEGES** checkbox for the user and click on the **Make Changes** button, so that the new user gets full control of the new database.

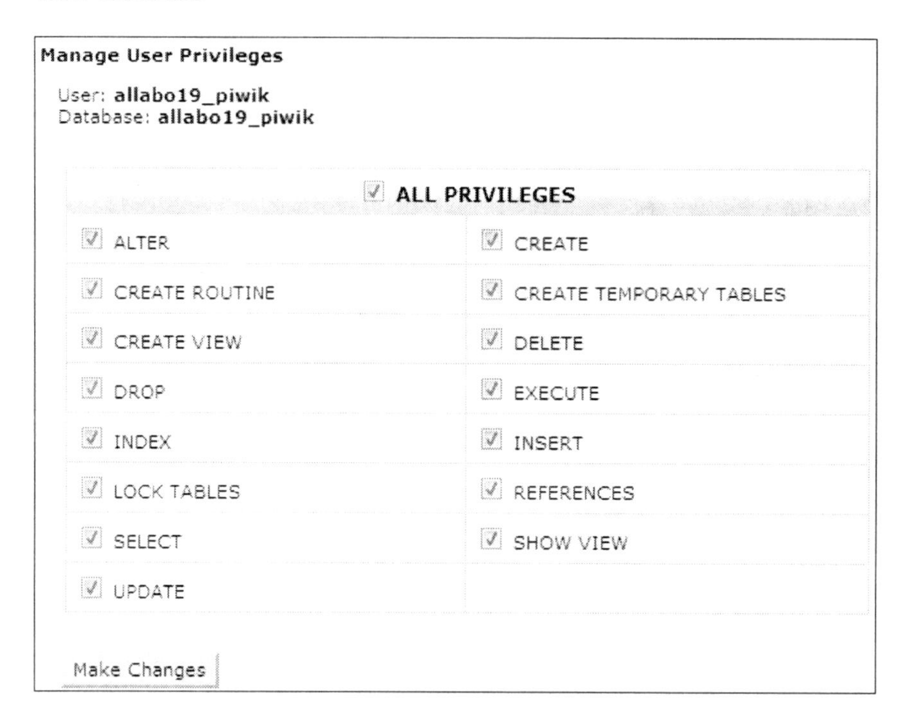

Creating a user and database for Piwik with phpMyAdmin

Some web hosts provide you with an installation of phpMyAdmin with your hosting account, and other hosts may give you a way to install phpMyAdmin with a one-click installation process. In either case, here is how we create a user and database in Piwik using phpMyAdmin:

1. Navigate to the folder where phpMyAdmin is installed. The location of this installation depends upon your hosting provider or the directory you choose in the phpMyAdmin one-click installation process.
2. Click on the **Databases** link.
3. There, you should see a textbox with the words **Create new database**. Enter the name of your database in the box and click on the **Create** button.

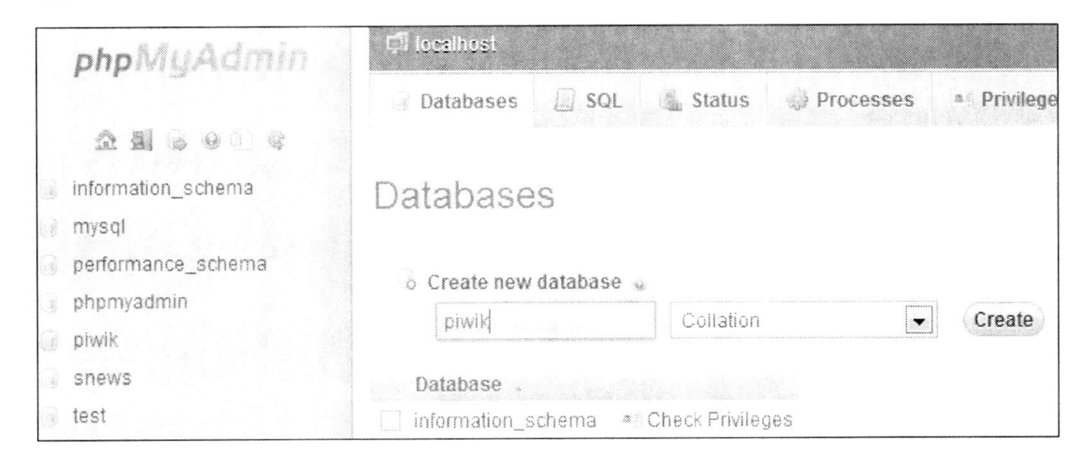

4. Now that your database exists, it is time to create a user. Click on the **More** link on the far right-hand side of the upper menu. This will bring up another menu. One of the items in that menu will be **Privileges**. Click on that link.

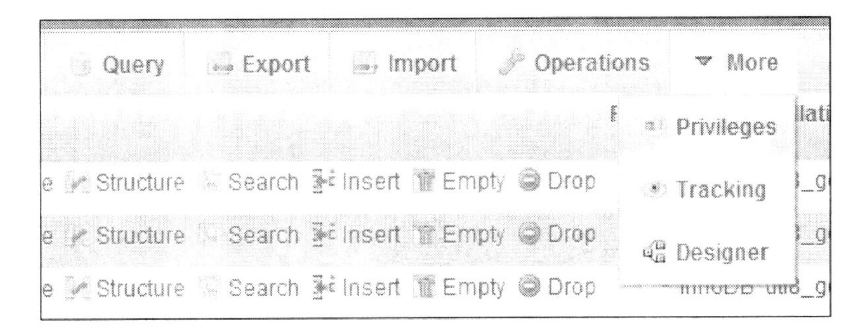

5. When the page loads, click on **Add a new User**.

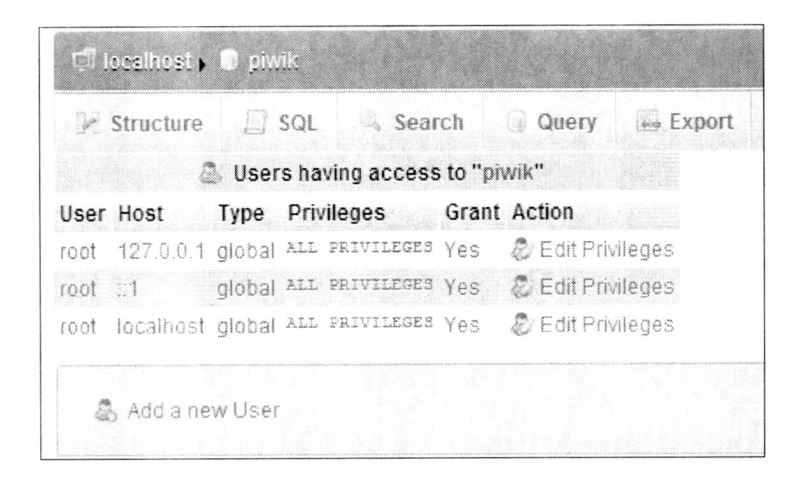

6. Enter a username, a password, and the same password again, in their designated boxes. Below that, in the **Database for user** section, make sure **Grant all privileges on database "Your_Database_Name"** is checked, where **Your_Database_Name** is the database you just created.

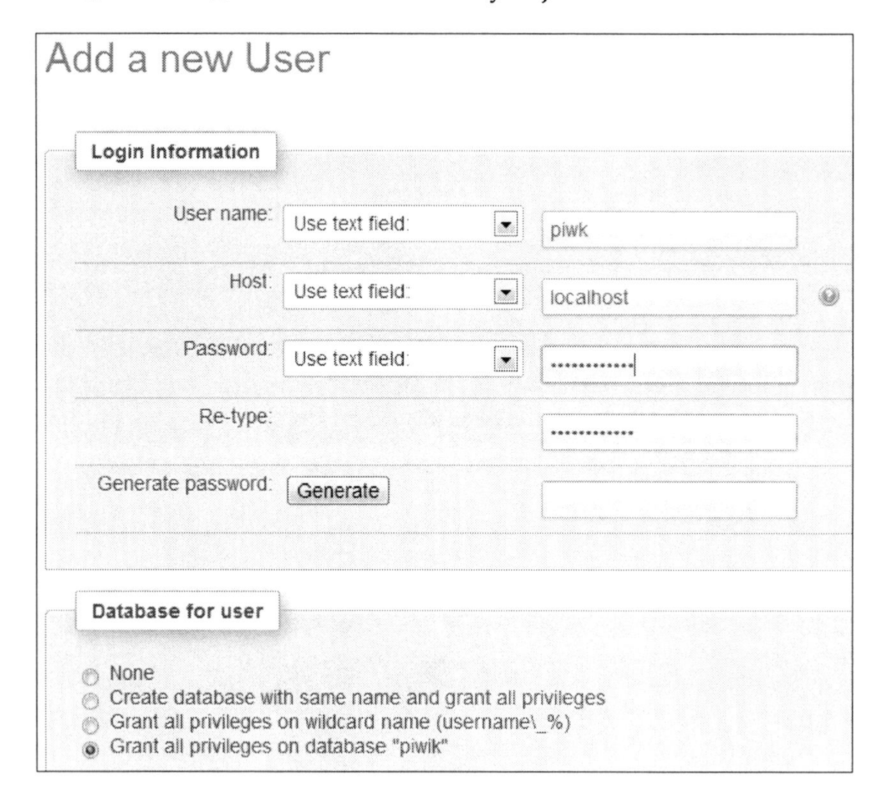

7. Click on the **Go** button at the end of the page. Once the page loads, you are done with the creation of a database section.

Creating a user and database for Piwik with SSH

For those of you who would rather use SSH to create your database for Piwik, you can use the following steps:

1. Log in to your web server via SSH, using Putty or Terminal.
2. Connect to the MySQL server, using the following command:

```
mysql -u root -p
```

   In this command, `root` is a MySQL user with full permission.

3. You will be prompted for this user's password. Enter it.
4. Run the following command:

   ```
   CREATE DATABASE piwik;
   ```

   In this command, `piwik` is the name of the database you are creating.
5. Run this command:

   ```
   GRANT ALL ON piwik.* TO piwik_user@'localhost' IDENTIFIED
   BY 'password';
   ```

   In this command, `piwik_user` is the MySQL username you choose and `password` is the password you choose for that user.

Your database will be ready, but you may have to run the last command for all the possible host names you will be using. You will also need to run the last command for localhosts such as 127.0.0.1, and the domain your Piwik installation will be running under, if any.

Using the Piwik installation wizard

Now that we are done making everything ready for the installation process, it's time to start the Piwik 5-minute installation. Browse to the location of your Piwik installation on your server. If you installed Piwik to a local server, this may be `http://localhost/piwik`. If you installed Piwik into a folder called `piwik`, you would browse to `http://your_domain_here.com/piwik`. You will be greeted by a page that looks like the one below. There will also be a handy little progress bar at the bottom of the page, which is cut out of these screenshots.

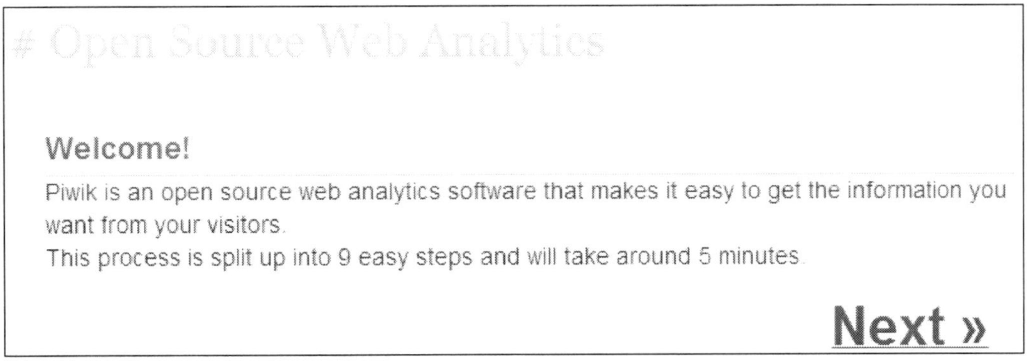

Open Source Web Analytics

Welcome!

Piwik is an open source web analytics software that makes it easy to get the information you want from your visitors.

This process is split up into 9 easy steps and will take around 5 minutes.

Next »

There is not much else to do here except click on **Next**. This will take you to the **Systems Check** portion of our installation. The following screenshot shows what this page will look like if you don't have the correct extensions for MySQL installed. This should not happen with most servers, but it could happen.

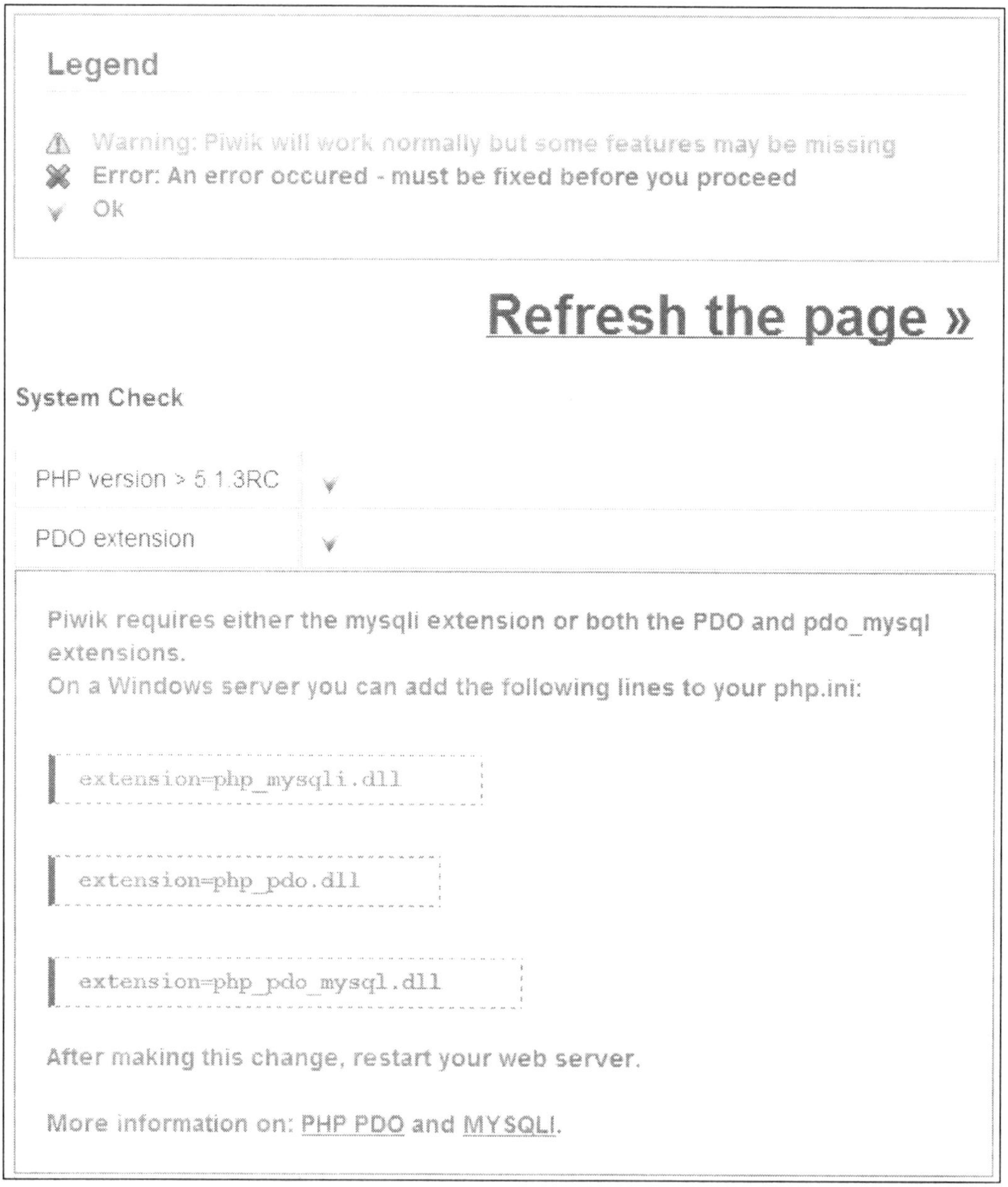

Legend

Warning: Piwik will work normally but some features may be missing
Error: An error occured - must be fixed before you proceed
Ok

Refresh the page »

System Check

PHP version > 5.1.3RC

PDO extension

Piwik requires either the mysqli extension or both the PDO and pdo_mysql extensions.
On a Windows server you can add the following lines to your php.ini:

```
extension=php_mysqli.dll
```

```
extension=php_pdo.dll
```

```
extension=php_pdo_mysql.dll
```

After making this change, restart your web server.

More information on: PHP PDO and MYSQLI.

In order to activate these extensions, you need to locate and edit your `php.ini` file. If you do not know where this file is located, you can upload a PHP file to your Piwik folder or to a location you can browse to on your server. In this file, which you can name something like `info.php`, you need to have the following PHP code:

```
<?php phpinfo(); ?>
```

Browse to the location of that file on the server, using your web browser. The page that loads will tell you just about everything you need to know about your PHP installation. You need to find the location of your `php.ini` file. It is usually located near the top of the page and will look something like the following screenshot:

Configuration File (php.ini) Path	C:\Windows

Once you have your `php.ini` file loaded in your text editor, it may be hard to find exactly where the extensions listing is, as the file could have thousands of lines. When you search the file for the term `Dynamic Extensions`, you should find a list like this:

```
;extension=php_bz2.dll
;extension=php_curl.dll
;extension=php_fileinfo.dll
;extension=php_gd2.dll
;extension=php_gettext.dll
;extension=php_gmp.dll
;extension=php_intl.dll
;extension=php_imap.dll
;extension=php_interbase.dll
;extension=php_ldap.dll
;extension=php_mbstring.dll
;extension=php_exif.dll
;extension=php_mysql.dll
;extension=php_mysqli.dll
;extension=php_oci8.dll
;extension=php_oci8_11g.dll
;extension=php_openssl.dll
;extension=php_pdo_firebird.dll
;extension=php_pdo_mssql.dll
;extension=php_pdo_mysql.dll
```

On a Linux server, these extension names will end in `.so` instead of `.dll`. To activate a PHP extension, all you need to do is remove the semicolon in front of the extension name. So, remove the semicolon from the front of either `extension=php_pdo_mysql.dll` or `extension=php_mysqli.dll`. Also, remove the semicolon in front of `extension=php_gd2.dll` on Windows or `extension=php_gd2.so` on Linux, or you will see the error pictured below and will be unable to see some of the graphs that Piwik provides.

GD > 2.x (graphics)	⚠ GD > 2.x (graphics) The sparklines (small graphs) and image graphs (in Piwik Mobile app and Email reports) will not work.

Another error you might run into with Piwik installations and/or updates is a file permission error. To fix this, you need to know the user your Apache or Nginx web server runs under. With Apache on an Ubuntu server, it is commonly `www-data`, but the specific username of your server depends on your installation. You can fix the issues with the automated install by doing the following in an SSH connection with your server, where `www-data` is replaced with the username of your running server:

1. Browse to the folder above your Piwik folder.
2. Use the full path to your Piwik folder, in the following commands:
    - Run the following command:

      ```
      chown -R www-data:www-data piwik
      ```

    - Run the following command:

      ```
      chmod -R 0755 piwik
      ```

What you are doing here is giving your web server the ownership of the Piwik files, and the ability to execute and write to them. FTP software may let you set these file permissions to `0755`, but may not have the ability to change the ownership of the files.

If you have fixed these issues or had no issues in the first place, you should see a long line of green check marks going down the page. Now that every requirement is satisfied, click on **Next** and move on to the next page, the **Database Setup** step.

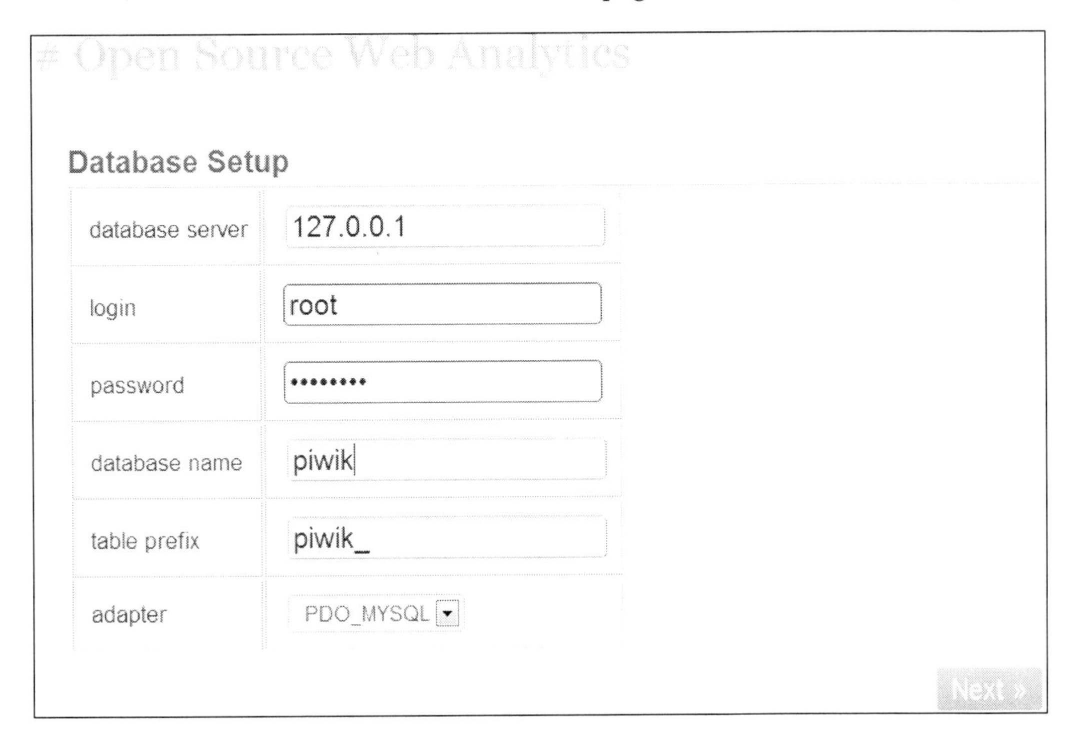

This is where you will enter the name of the MySQL database you created for Piwik, as well as the username and password that you created for the Piwik database. You may want to leave the **table prefix** alone. It doesn't hurt anything and will be necessary if you want to add plugins to Piwik or when you are installing Piwik in a **database** that is already in use by another software. You can leave the **adapter** drop down as is. Once you have filled out all the information, click on **Next**, and the installer will create all the necessary tables for your Piwik installation. You should see a page like the one below:

Open Source Web Analytics

Creating the Tables

Tables created with success!

Next »

Click on **Next** again and you will be taken to the page to create your **super user login**. You can create almost unlimited users in one Piwik installation, but there will only be one super user who controls everything. Pick a login name and a secure password, and enter your e-mail address in the correct box. If you want to receive notifications of Piwik upgrades and security alerts, you can check the box, and they will be delivered to your e-mail address. And if you want news about community updates, you can check that box too.

When you are done entering your login details, click on the **Next** button. You will be taken to the page where you will set up your first website to track.

Enter the name of your website in the correct textbox. This is nothing more than a label to identify the website you are tracking. In the next box, enter the URL of your website. If you are testing Piwik tracking on a website that runs on a local server like XAMPP, then this URL will start with `http://localhost` and end with the folder you have installed your test site into, like `http://localhost/wordpress/`. On a live website, this URL can be the WWW version or the non-WWW version. Either one will do, because Piwik will track both versions when you enter one. Next, to select the time zone, select a major city nearest to your location. If the website you are tracking is a shopping-cart website that takes payments, you will want to select the **Ecommerce** option. This option adds goal tracking features specifically geared to shopping-cart websites. When you are done with everything, click on the **Next** button.

This will take you to the page where you will find the JavaScript code that has to be included in the website you are tracking. The best place to paste this code in your web pages is right before the closing `</body>` tag. If you are using a PHP-based CMS, chances are that there will be a PHP file which generates the footer of all the pages in the website you will be tracking. In a Wordpress installation, this would most likely be the `footer.php` file in the theme you are using. So, you would find that file and paste this JavaScript before the `</body>` tag. In osCommerce, you would also look for the `footer.php` file, find the `</body>` tag, and place your JavaScript right before it. In a phpBB installation, you would find the `overall_footer.html` file and add this JavaScript before the `</body>` tag. It is pretty simple to add tracking to any site, if you know where to look for the closing HTML body tag.

There may also be a plugin or extension available for your CMS. We will cover all the other options you have for adding tracking code to your site in later chapters. For now, you have to start tracking. So get that JavaScript on your website.

Click on **Next** again and you are greeted with the **Congratulations** page. You can click on **Continue to Piwik** to view the Dashboard of your new Piwik installation.

Securing Piwik

The data that Piwik collects from visitors comes with responsibility. You are now responsible for the privacy of your visitors. While this responsibility may not be as big as storing encrypted credit card numbers, still, it shouldn't be taken lightly. The developers that work on Piwik are dedicated to providing users with a secure and bug-free application. But there are a few things you can do to make your Piwik installation more secure. Most of these would apply to any PHP and MySQL application.

- **Use a separate MySQL database for Piwik**: It is a good practice to do this with all of your databases. That way, if an attacker happens to be able to access one database, this database will not be linked to multiple applications.

- **Give your Piwik database its own username and password**: The first thing a hacker might try is to use one set of credentials that work on all of your databases. Giving each database a separate username and password limits the damage an attacker can do. To learn more about MySQL best practices, please visit: `http://dev.mysql.com/tech-resources/articles/mysql-administrator-best-practices.html`.
- **Always access Piwik over SSL**: With a standard HTTP connection, information is sent in plain text. This includes usernames and passwords. Choosing to always use the HTTPS connection guarantees that this data will be encrypted. This is a pretty simple process that gives a lot of added security.
    - Make sure your web server is configured to accept SSL requests. You can use a self-signed certificate, but a valid SSL certificate is recommended for a production installation of Piwik.
    - Find the section marked `General` in the `config/config.ini.php` file in your Piwik install folder and add `force_ssl=1` underneath the `General` heading, as follows:

```
[General]
force_ssl=1
```

- **Restrict access to Piwik files**: Only the `piwik.js` and the `piwik.php` files are required by external websites for tracking. You can use `.htaccess` to restrict the access of every other file in the Piwik installation to only those IP addresses you will be using to check your stats.
- **Keep backups**: Regular backups will protect your data in case of a disaster. First make sure that your Piwik MySQL database is backed up. There are plenty of free scripts or downloadable software to back up MySQL databases. Any one that works, should do. The only file you have to worry about backing up is `config.ini.php` in the `config` folder of your Piwik installation. Back it up to your computer or another location, regularly. This is all you need to restore a Piwik installation if your current installation is ever damaged. To learn more about backing up your MySQL databases, please visit: `http://dev.mysql.com/doc/refman/5.1/en/backup-methods.html`.
- **Keep your system up-to-date**: Your system is only as strong as its weakest link, and there are many links in its chain. Sometimes, software updates add features, but often these updates fix bugs and plug security holes. So, keeping Piwik, Apache, Linux, PHP, and MySQL up-to-date is an important part of the security of your Piwik installation.

- **Use the Piwik security plugin**: Piwik comes with a **SecurityInfo** plugin that will test your installation for any security issues and return a recommendation report. This plugin is not activated by default. First, you must activate the plugin in the **Piwik's Settings** | **Plugins** menu. You can then view the **SecurityInfo** plugin by going to **Settings** | **Security** in the Piwik admin interface. Anything marked green in the report is in good condition. Anything red should be checked out and fixed, if possible. Yellow is somewhere between both extremes, but not a dire threat.
- **Use strong passwords**: This is always a good practice. Another good practice is changing your passwords regularly. You can generate a strong password online at `http://www.pctools.com/guides/password/`.
- **Use SSH and secure FTP**: This is another general good practice. This will encrypt your connection to your web server—so no one snooping on your connection can capture data in any readable form.

Backing up Piwik

It is a good practice to regularly back up your Piwik installation, and you should definitely back up Piwik before you plan on doing an update. You can never be sure that everything will go as planned on your server. So, it is better to be safe than sorry. Fortunately, this is a simple process involving only two steps.

Firstly, you need to back up the `config.ini.php` file located in the `config` folder of your Piwik installation. This file contains your Super User credentials, your database connection details, and the list of plugins you have installed. All you need to do is open your FTP software, connect to the FTP server of your website, download the file, and store it in a safe place. This will ensure that you can get a new Piwik installation up and running using your old data, if anything bad should happen to your old installation.

The second thing you need to do to back up your Piwik installation is to back up the MySQL database that Piwik uses. This involves dumping the contents of the database to a SQL file. This is not as hard as it sounds either. You don't need to know any special database queries to do it. You can use the same tool, which you used to create the database, for creating backups.

In **phpMyAdmin**, just browse to your Piwik database, click on **Export** in the top menu, and when the page loads, click on the **Go** button.

When your browser asks you to save the SQL file, just choose a suitable location on your hard drive and wait for the download to finish. If you use cPanel, phpMyAdmin comes installed already, so you just browse to where your cPanel is located, find the **Databases** section, click on **phpMyAdmin**, and follow the instructions above. There are many other ways you can run a MySQL backup using various GUI-based MySQL tools. You can explore these other ways at `http://codex.wordpress.org/Backing_Up_Your_Database`. This page details how to back up a Wordpress database, but the same instructions will work for Piwik.

Once you have these two files some place safe, you have everything you need to rebuild your current Piwik installation from scratch. Now it is safe to update Piwik.

Updating Piwik

Every once in while, Piwik will notify you of an update—which is a good thing. Piwik updates always bring new features, bug fixes, and security fixes. During the writing of this book, I actually had to update from version 1.6 to version 1.7 and then from version 1.7 to 1.8. Piwik updates are a three-click process, if your file permissions are correct. Everything can be done in the browser.

If your Piwik installation requires an update, you will see the notification in the top right corner of the Piwik dashboard, as long as you are an Admin or a Super User of your Piwik installation. If you hover over the notification with your mouse cursor, you will see a link to the update page and to the changes page. The changes page will tell what is new in the update. Click on the **Please update now!** link to get started.

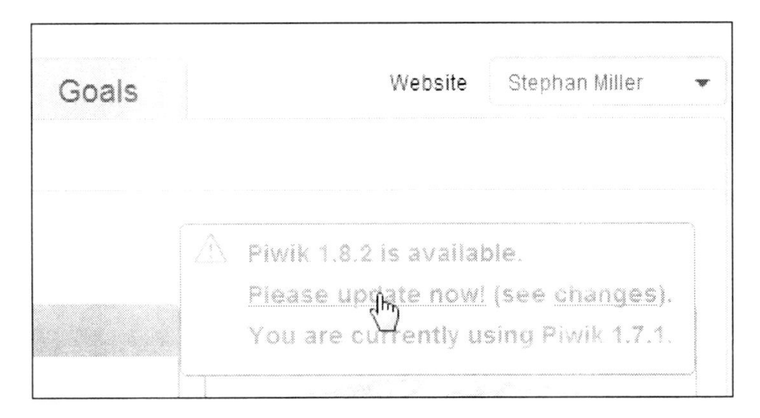

If the permissions on the directories in your Piwik installation are not correct, you will see a notification that your only option is to download Piwik and manually install the update.

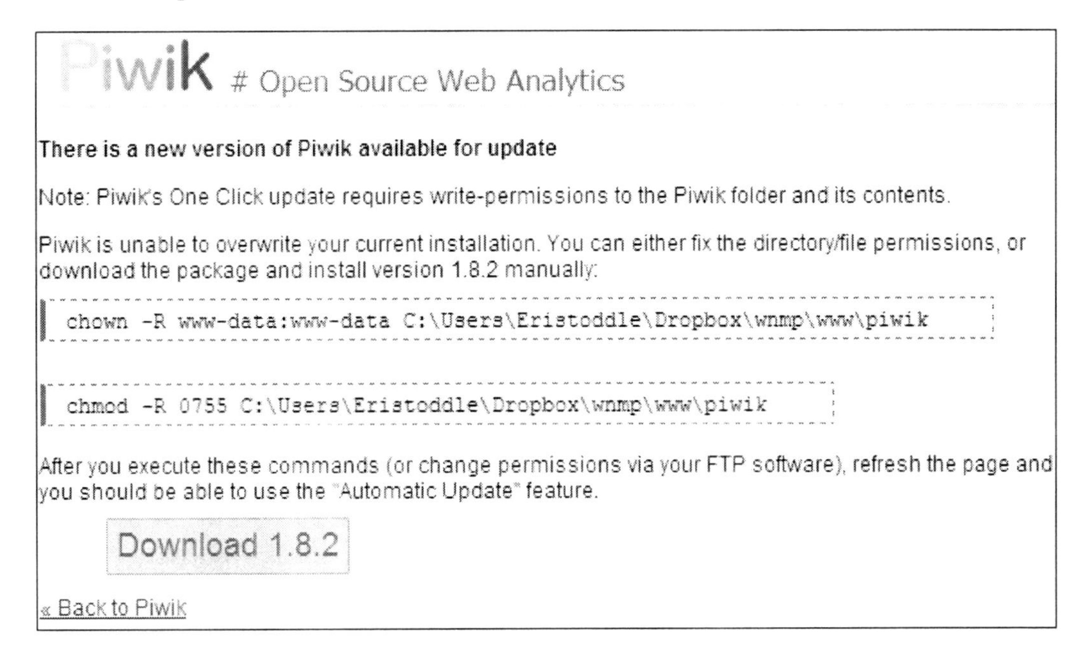

To fix this issue, you need to correct the file permission errors in your Piwik installation folder. Setting permissions for your Piwik installation was covered in the install process a few pages back. Follow those instructions; restart the update in your browser and you should now see a page like this:

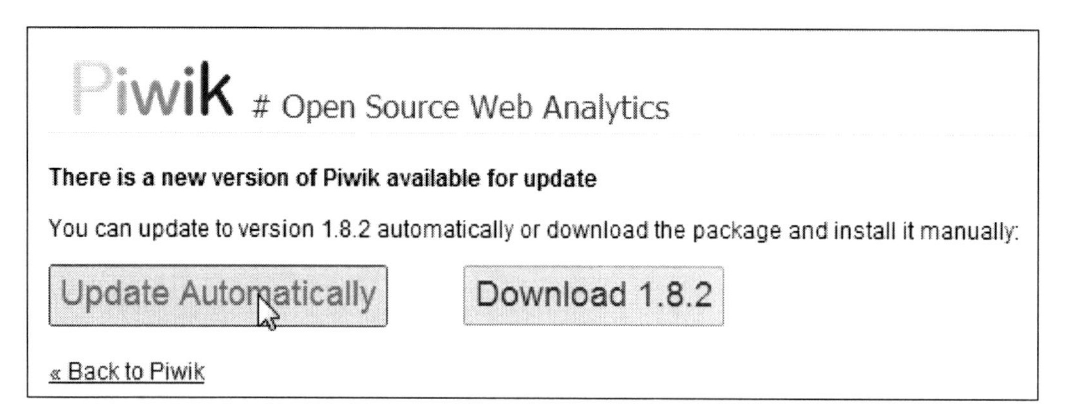

Click on the **Update Automatically** button. That should take you to a page similar to this:

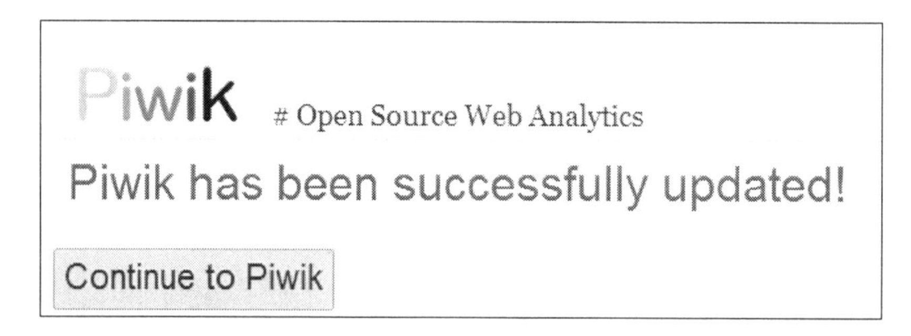

It may seem like the update is done now, but that is not necessarily so. Continuing to Piwik may involve a detour to a page that looks a lot like the following page:

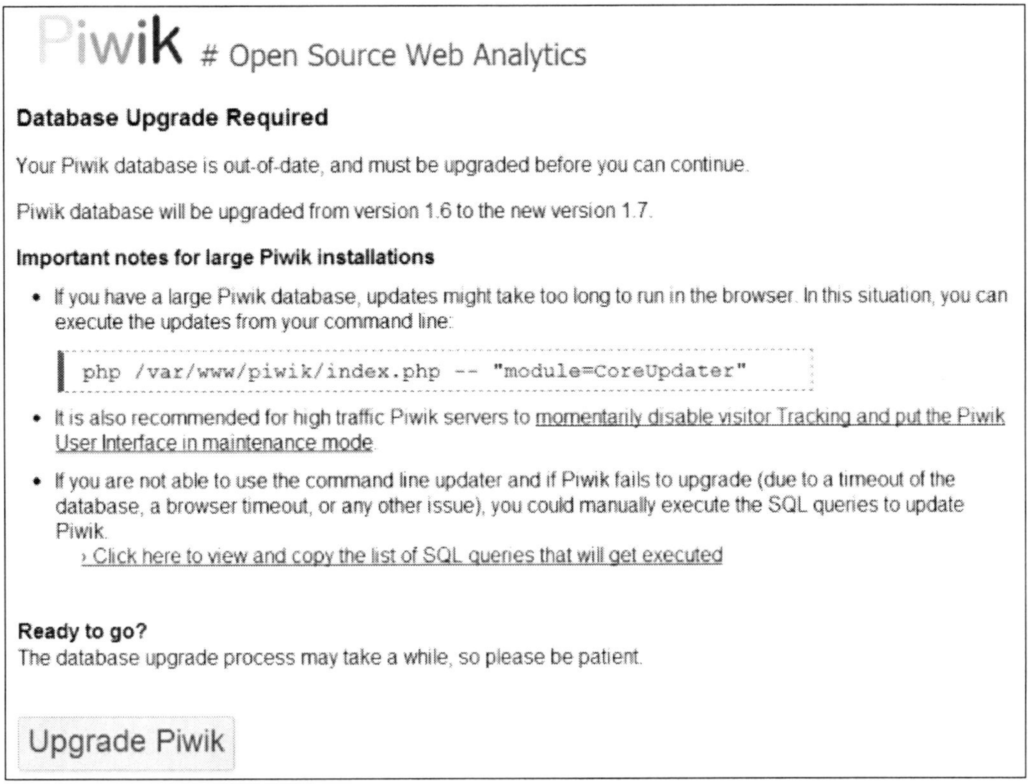

Piwik # Open Source Web Analytics

Database Upgrade Required

Your Piwik database is out-of-date, and must be upgraded before you can continue.

Piwik database will be upgraded from version 1.6 to the new version 1.7.

Important notes for large Piwik installations

- If you have a large Piwik database, updates might take too long to run in the browser. In this situation, you can execute the updates from your command line:

```
php /var/www/piwik/index.php -- "module=CoreUpdater"
```

- It is also recommended for high traffic Piwik servers to momentarily disable visitor Tracking and put the Piwik User Interface in maintenance mode.
- If you are not able to use the command line updater and if Piwik fails to upgrade (due to a timeout of the database, a browser timeout, or any other issue), you could manually execute the SQL queries to update Piwik.
  › Click here to view and copy the list of SQL queries that will get executed

Ready to go?
The database upgrade process may take a while, so please be patient.

Upgrade Piwik

This means that the files are currently up-to-date, but the database needs to be upgraded to support those new features that Piwik is bringing you. Click on the **Upgrade Piwik** button and you should be done and ready to check out any new Piwik goodies.

If you are running Piwik on a high traffic website, it can take a lot longer for a database upgrade to finish. It is recommended to update these types of installations through SSH or the command line prompt using this command:

```
$ php /path/to/piwik/index.php -- "module=CoreUpdater"
```

Here, `/path/to/Piwik/index.php` is the path to the `index.php` file in your Piwik installation.

Using Piwik for high traffic websites

It is every webmaster's dream to have a website that receives a million page views a month. But, if you do have a site that has this much traffic, can Piwik keep up? Or, what if you have to provide analytics data to thousands of clients? Or, if you own a multitude of sites that you would like to track with one Piwik installation. Will Piwik stand up to a beating like this? The answer is "Yes"—if you set up your installation correctly.

Using Piwik out of the box will be fine when you are tracking several hundred visits a day, but when that traffic moves up into the thousands, you are going to have to tweak a few things to help Piwik handle the stress. But that is the case with any software. It is just not going to perform the same under ten times the load, unless you prepare for it. Fortunately, there are a few quick and easy ways to help you on your way to scaling Piwik up to that million-page-views-a-month goal.

Dedicated server

One of the quickest fixes to execute in a traffic "problem" is to move your Piwik installation to a better server. If you are on a shared host, then move your installation to a Virtual Private Server. If you are already on a VPS, move Piwik to a dedicated host. There is really no such thing as unlimited in the server world. The only thing that counts here is real numbers. If you are maxing out a one core dedicated server, you might want to upgrade to a server with a four core processor. But don't just brute force your performance problem by throwing bigger servers at it. Make sure you use some of the other optimizations below, before you start waiting for the 64 core processor to come out.

Adding RAM

Every server benefits from more RAM, and every server enters critical territory when its RAM is maxed out. It is recommended that you have at least 4 GB of memory on a server running Piwik if you are tracking multiple websites or one website with a lot of visits. Piwik can use a lot of memory to archive data and process reports. Every extra bit of memory can help. Modern VPS hosts and cloud services like Amazon will even allow you to adjust your memory on the fly if you need more or less.

PHP caching

It could be necessary to run a PHP cache like APC or XCache to get better performance out of your high traffic Piwik installation. A PHP cache will optimize and cache intermediate PHP code. What this means to you is better performance out of your Piwik code.

Nginx or lighttpd

As I previously mentioned in the *Meeting system requirements* section of this chapter, once you start tracking sites with a lot of traffic, your standard Apache server may not be able to handle the load as well as a lighter web server like Nginx or lighttpd can.

If you plan on running Piwik on Nginx, you can find the configuration for it at `https://github.com/perusio/piwik-nginx` or at `http://wiki.nginx.org/Piwik`. Nginx does not use `.htaccess` files, and all of the data in these must be applied to the Nginx configuration file instead. It is not that hard to do once you become familiar with the Nginx configuration file syntax, but it does help to have step-by-step instructions or a prebuilt configuration file.

Nginx can be installed on a Linux server using the `apt-get` or `yum` commands. You can find download links for a Windows version of Nginx at `http://nginx.org`.

Cron your archiving

By default, Piwik triggers its report archiving process when the reports are viewed from the browser. You can disable this in the **Settings** | **General Settings** menu of Piwik and set up a cron job to automatically run the archiving process for you.

The cron shell script is located at `/misc/cron/archive.php`, in the Piwik folder. This is a Linux shell file. It is just a text file that contains a shell script, which will use a background process to archive your reports instead of your Piwik installation. It can be executed with this command: `/usr/bin/php5 /path/to/piwik/misc/cron/archive.php`. Make sure its permissions are set to `755`, and set up a cron job that points at the file. Setting it to run every hour or half hour is a good choice for medium and high traffic websites.

Reports will load instantly when you log into your Piwik installation, because the reports will have already been archived by the cron job instead of by your page load. This will provide a better user experience.

Disabling real-time reports

With its default configuration, a Piwik installation works in real-time. This is not really real time, but every 10 seconds. Processing the reports for a high-traffic website six times a minute can put a lot of extra stress on a server. And if you do not need your analytics data to update this frequently, you will see a performance increase by setting the report processing interval to something higher, like 3600 seconds. This can be done in the **Settings** | **General Settings** menu of Piwik.

Deleting old logs

If you don't need your old analytics data, you shouldn't keep it around. Deleting your old logs will free up a lot of space in your database and give you a slight increase in performance. You can configure Piwik to automatically delete old logs. Just log in to Piwik as the Super User, browse to **Settings** | **Privacy**, and click on the **Delete old visitor logs from database** link. You will be asked to enter the duration, in days, that you want to keep logs around. You can set the deletion process to run every day, every week, or every month, as well as specify the maximum number of rows to delete on each run.

Load balancers and multiple servers

Piwik can be used behind a load balancer. A load balancer distributes the workload of one application across multiple servers. Here are the steps you need to follow:

1. Synchronize the `config/config.ini.php` on all servers. You can use rsync to do this.
2. Delete the contents of the `tmp/*` folder every time you upgrade Piwik or one of its plugins.
3. Enable database session storage by setting the `session_save_handler` variable, in the `config/config.ini.php` file, to `dbtable`. If the variable is not currently in the file, you can add it under the `[General]` section, using this command: `session_save_handler = dbtable`.
4. Enabling SSL is recommended, but not required. This can be done in the `config/config.ini.php` file too. Add `force_ssl=1` under the `[General]` section.

Limiting tracked URLs

By excluding URL query parameters from the URLs being tracked, you increase Piwik's performance. The fewer URLs tracked, the better. If the website you are tracking with Piwik uses session ID parameters in its URLs, then these can be ignored and not tracked as new, separate pages. The Super User can edit the global list of query parameters that are being excluded from tracking, by navigating to **Settings** | **Manage Websites**. Every Piwik admin user can edit their own list of query parameters excluded from tracking by navigating to **Settings** | **Websites**.

Summary

In this chapter, you learned how to install Piwik and get it running on an Apache web server. You also learned that there is more than one way to install Piwik, depending on your preferences or server features. Later, you learned how to insert Piwik's JavaScript tracking code into your web pages, so that you could start analysing your traffic. You should now know how to make your Piwik installation as secure as possible, and have an idea of how you can set up Piwik to handle high traffic websites or many websites simultaneously. If an update for Piwik is required, you will have enough knowledge to run the update and fix any permission issues.

In the next chapter, you will learn the ins and outs of using the Piwik interface and generating reports with Piwik.

2

Using Piwik's Interface and Reports

Every website owner wants to increase and improve the traffic to their website. The first step in doing this is understanding and interpreting the data that our visitors provide for us. Fortunately, Piwik takes care of a lot of this with easy to understand reports, tables, and charts giving us more time to take actions to improve our traffic based on the data. In order to accomplish this, we need to get to know the user interface of Piwik. Most of the pages in Piwik are composed of widgets that we can add, remove, and customize to our specific needs once we get to know more about Piwik in this chapter.

In later chapters, we will be adding more features to the interface of Piwik by tracking goals and setting up e-commerce tracking that will only be available after setup. In this chapter, we will cover only the details of the interface available right after installation.

In this chapter, we will learn to:

- Use Piwik's menus to navigate to the report you need
- Customize the dashboard layout
- Add, move, and remove widgets on the dashboard
- Use Piwik's widgets to retrieve the data you need
- Customize Piwik reports
- Set custom metrics in graphs
- Manage e-mail reports

Navigating the Piwik interface

Now that you have a running Piwik installation, it's time to browse to your website and look around. So do that now. If you have not logged in, you will see a page much like the one pictured in the following screenshot:

Just enter the username of the super user that you created during the installation in the **Username** field and the super user password in the **Password** field and click the **Sign in** button. If you are on a computer that only you use, you can check the **Remember Me** box and Piwik will set a cookie in your browser so you will not have to log in again next time you visit.

If you have forgotten your password between the time you read the last chapter and this one, you can click on the **Lost your password?** link and you will see a form as shown in the following screenshot. Okay, I doubt you forgot your password that quickly, but knowing how to reset a password will be good information to pass on to any other users you may add to your installation.

Using Piwik's Menus

One way or another, you should be logged in now. Piwik's interface is clean and clutter-free, but holds a lot of valuable information. Your Piwik dashboard should look something like the following screenshot:

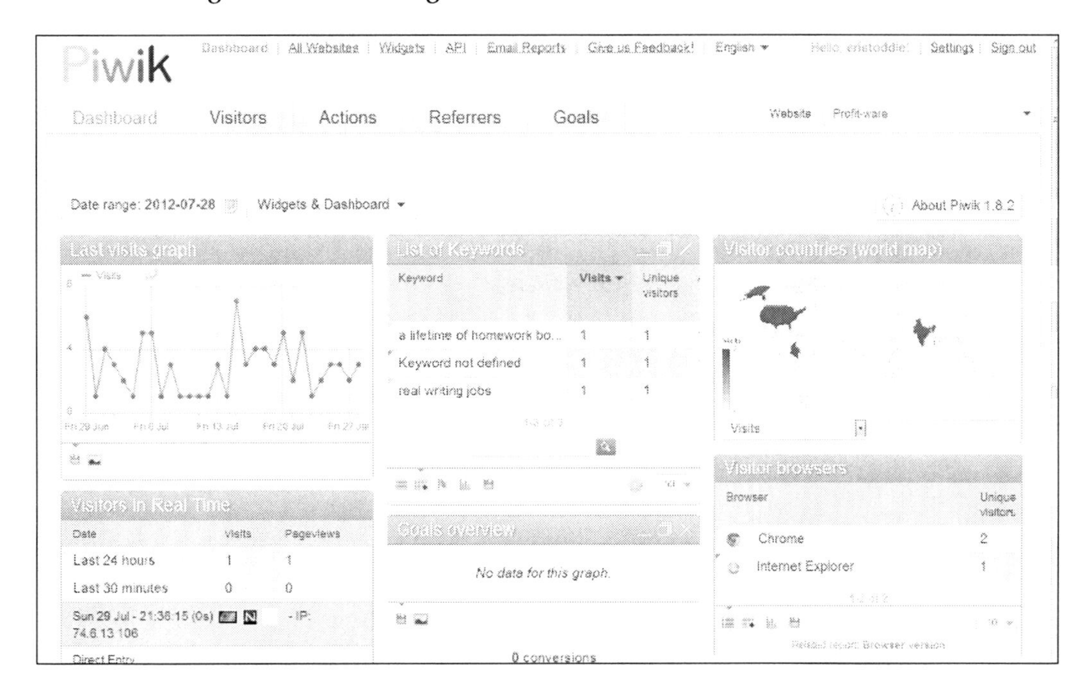

This is your Piwik dashboard. As the installation process involves setting up only one site and this is the first time you have visited the dashboard, what you see is the default set of widgets serving stats from your default website. Both the widgets and the default site can be changed, but first let's take a look at the navigation menus.

The Sign In menu

In the top-right corner of the screen is the Sign In menu. By default, any user that is not logged in will be sent to the login screen. If the default screen for anonymous users is set to the dashboard, the Sign In menu will read **Hello, anonymous | Sign In**. You can see an anonymous Piwik dashboard in action at `http://demo.piwik.org/`. When you are logged in, it will look similar to the previous screenshot with a **Sign Out** link and the **Settings** link. The **Sign Out** link signs you back out and the **Settings** link takes you to the **Settings** page where you can add users, add websites, activate plugins, and change the default global settings of your Piwik installation.

The top bar

At the top of the screen to the left of the Sign In menu is the top bar.

Dashboard | All Websites | Widgets | API | Email Reports | Give us Feedback! | English

Let's take a look at what we have available in this bar:

- In this menu is the link to the **Dashboard** which is unclickable, since that is where you are located currently in the site.
- Next to that is the **All Websites** link which takes you to a listing of the websites Piwik is currently tracking for you.
- Next to that is the **Widgets** link which takes you to a page where you can create widgets based on your stats to embed on other websites.
- Then there is the **API** link. This link will bring you to a page that lists your API token. You will need this token to access Piwik stats from remote applications such as the Piwik WordPress plugin. On the same page there are quick access links to the documentation of all the API calls available to you in Piwik.
- There is also an **Email Reports** link where you can create custom scheduled e-mail reports.
- If you have anything that you would like to say about Piwik, need help with issues or would like to contribute to Piwik, the **Give us Feedback!** link will take you there.
- And last but not least, we have the languages dropdown. You can choose from 46 languages to view the Piwik interface in.

The main menu

Below the Piwik logo, in the middle of the page, you will find the main menu with **Dashboard**, **Visitors**, **Actions**, **Referrers**, and **Goals**.

Next to that on the right-hand side of the page, you should see the name of the website you just added in a drop-down box. This drop-down box is the site selector. Once you have more than one website set up in Piwik, this dropdown will allow you to switch between the sites.

You will see the following tabs in the main menu:

- The **Dashboard** tab will give you an overview of the website chosen in the site selector. When you start adding more websites to your installation, you can set up the dashboard to show stats from any one of the websites you are tracking or show the **All Websites** view by default.
- **Visitors** will provide you with details of visitors to the chosen website.
- **Actions** will give you a breakdown of the actions those visitors performed at the website.
- The **Referrers** tab will show you where these visitors came from whether a search engine, a link on another website, or by direct entry.
- And, the **Goals** tab is the place to set up your conversion tracking.

Now that we have an idea where everything is located, let's look at each part in detail and customize the dashboard and widgets for our use.

Customizing the dashboard

Just about anything you can think of with Piwik is customizable in Piwik, from how you track your site, to the widgets in the dashboard. Now it's time to start customizing your Piwik installation to your liking. Let's start with the dashboard layout.

Changing the dashboard layout

When you browse to a default installation of Piwik, the widgets are laid out in three equal columns. But you don't have to keep the dashboard this way if you don't want to. To the left side of the widget area, right next to the **Date range** block, you will see a button that says **Widgets & Dashboard**. Clicking that button will bring up a menu as shown in the following screenshot:

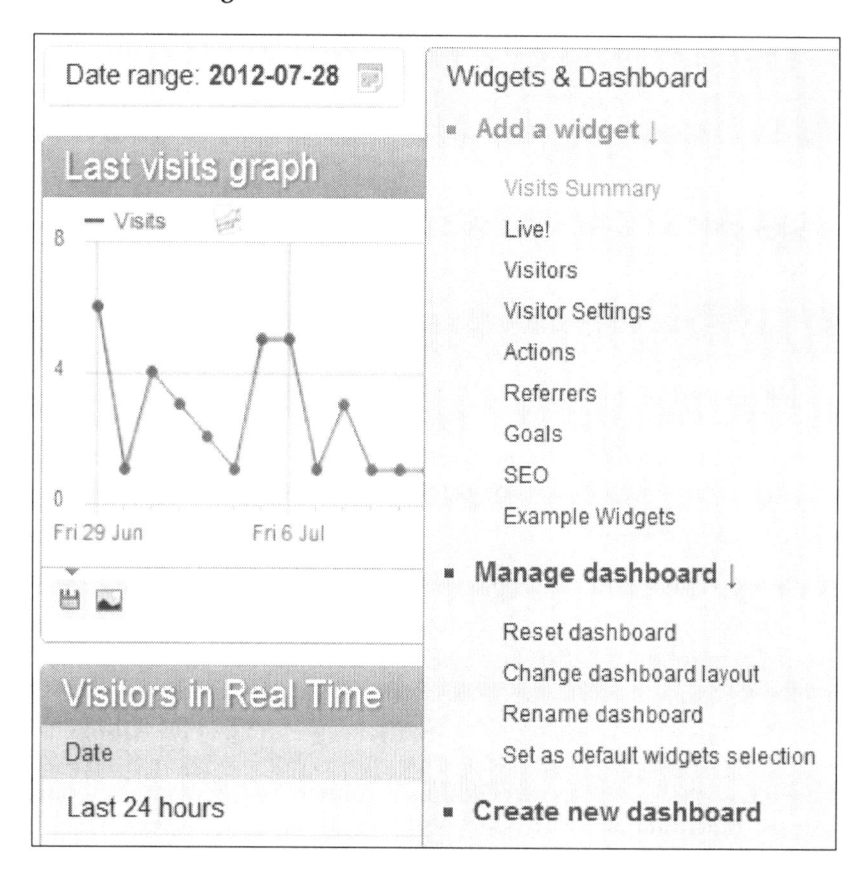

Under the **Manage dashboard** sub-heading, click that link if you want to make changes to the layout. When you do, the following lightbox pop-up will appear:

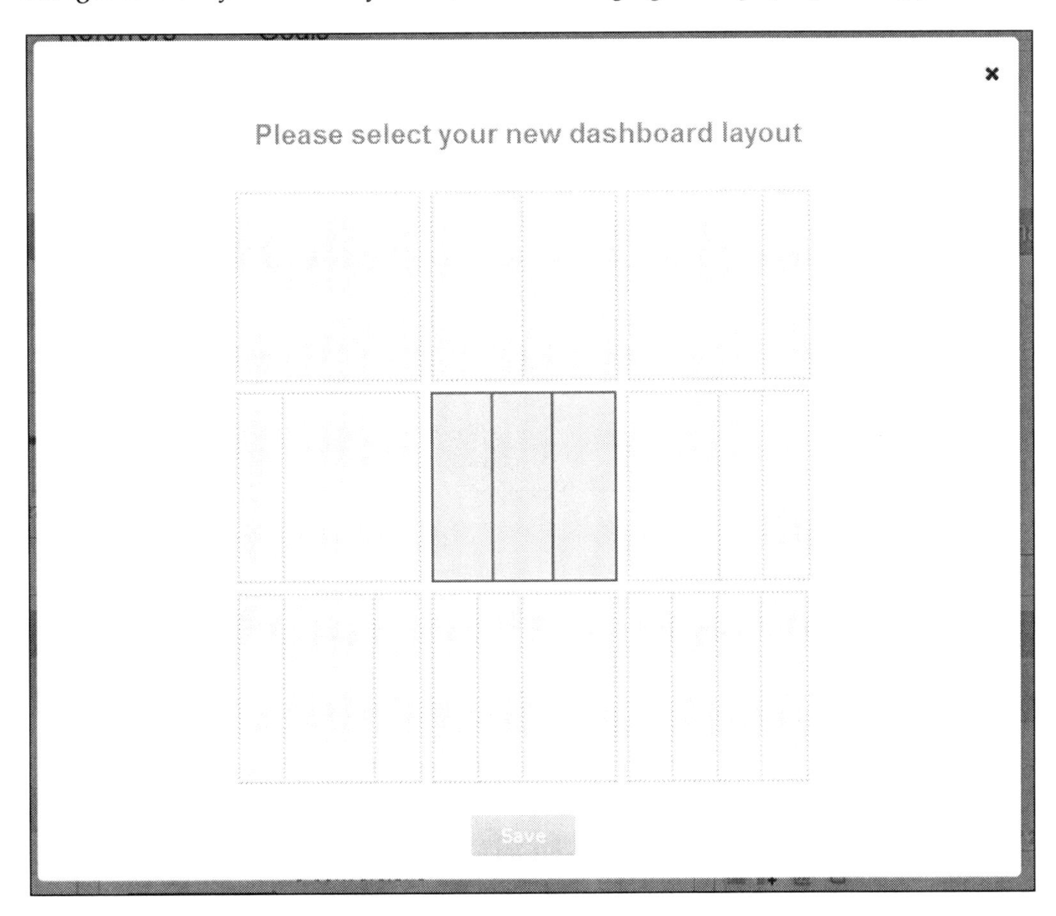

As you see, you can set up the widget layout in just about any configuration you want with one to four columns and with equal or unequal column widths. Just choose a layout you would like to try and click on **Save** at the bottom. As you get more familiar with the widgets and the data they present, you will be able to decide which layout works best for the statistics most important to you.

Setting a date range

When the Piwik dashboard first loads, the default date range that the dashboard widgets are presenting is for the previous date. You can change this default date range by clicking on the **Date range** block on the left side of the Piwik dashboard.

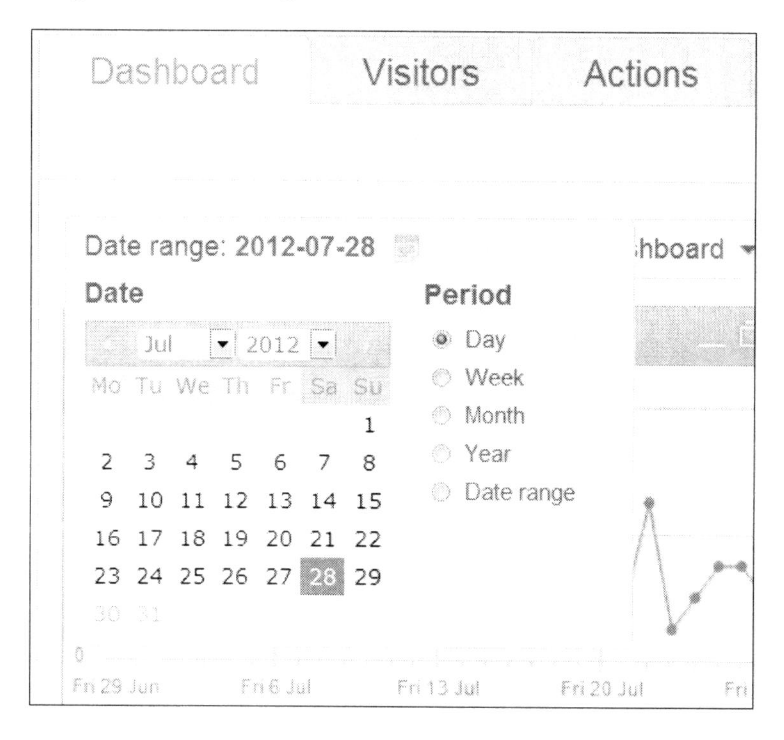

In the calendar, select the date you want to view. With the radio buttons under the **Period** heading, you can select a period of **Day**, **Week**, **Month**, **Year**, or **Date range**. This period will set the points on any graphed data to your choice. For example, the default is **Day** and the **Last visits** graph will display points on the graphs for every day. If you change this to **Week**, than each point on the graph will represent a week of visits.

Selecting **Date range** will allow you to change the range on the charts to anything you want. This feature is handy if you want to take a quick view of how traffic has increased on your site over the last three years, or even how visitors respond to new posts. In the following screenshot, you can see an example of setting a custom date range. Clicking **Apply Date Range** will put your new settings into effect. Sometimes, depending on the performance of your web server, it may take a second or two for Piwik to reload the data for your new report.

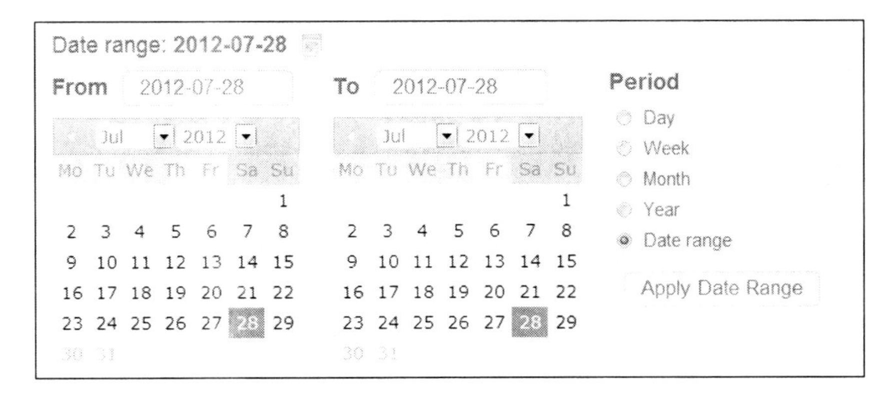

Adding widgets to the dashboard

Now that you have your layout chosen, let's take a look at the widgets. In the same **Widgets & Dashboard** menu where you found the link to change the dashboard layout, you will also find another menu marked **Add a widget**. In that menu, you will see a list of categories of Piwik widgets. By hovering over these categories, you will find a list of widgets each category holds, and by hovering over one of the widget names, you can preview the widget before you choose it.

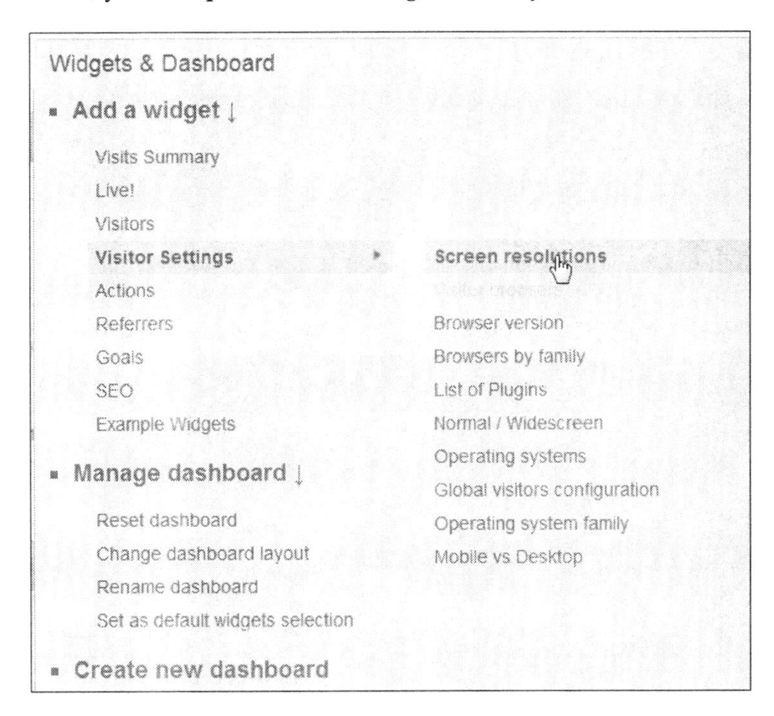

There are dozens of widgets available in the current version of Piwik.

Moving and removing widgets

There are a lot of widgets to choose from. If a widget link is unclickable, that is because that widget is already on the dashboard. To add a widget to the dashboard, click on the widget name. The default location for a new widget to appear will be in the top left of the dashboard, but it doesn't have to stay there.

If you don't like where a widget is positioned on the dashboard, no problem, you can move it. Just guide your mouse pointer over the gray title bar of the widget you want to move and your one arrow mouse pointer will turn into a drag-and-drop mouse pointer with four arrows. Just click on the title bar at this point and drag the widget to where you want it to go. As you drag the widget across the dashboard, blocks with dashed line borders will open up in the dashboard layout to guide you to places you can drop the widget.

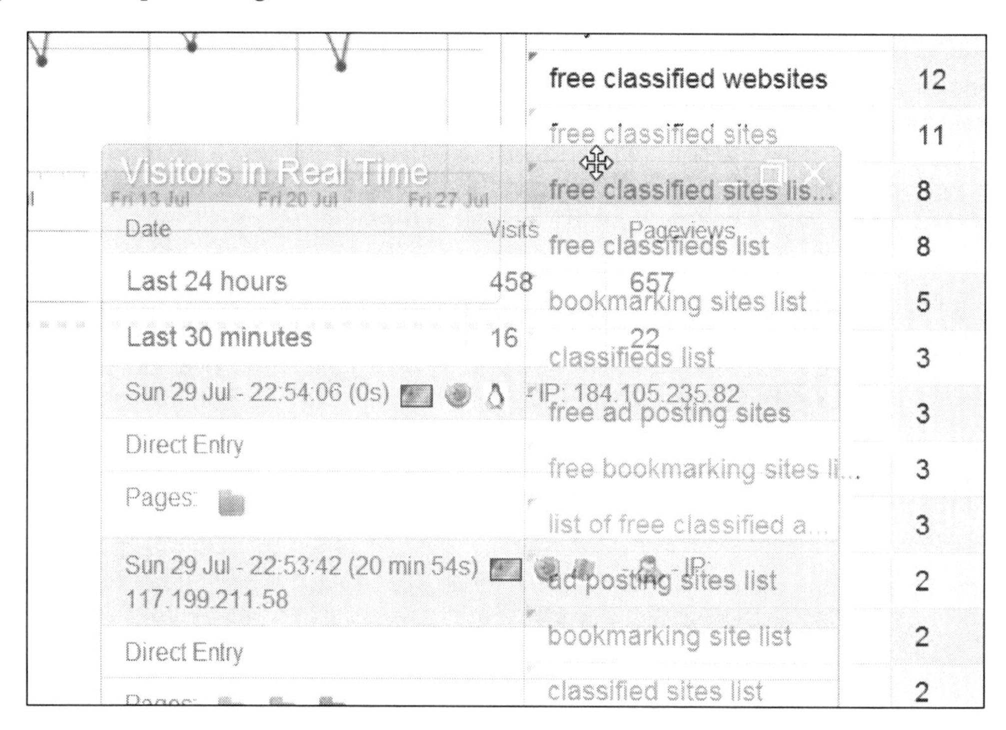

Once the title bar of the widget is hovered over, an **X** appears on the right end of the title bar. Removing a widget from the dashboard is as simple as clicking this **X**.

Finding the right report widget for the job

Most of the widgets you can add to the dashboard can already be found in the other panels of the Piwik installation, but adding them to the dashboard can give you a convenient overview of the data you want to see without having to click through all the panels. Click through the list of widgets and you will find widgets that contain feed readers, flash, text, graphs, tables, and images. In the **Example Widgets** section, you will see how the default Piwik widget set can be extended with custom widgets. We will learn more about creating your own widgets in *Chapter 9, Advanced Tracking and Development*.

You will notice that all widgets come with a default presentation setting, whether that is a table, a graph, a tag cloud, or one of the many ways Piwik can present data. But each widget can present the same data in a multitude of ways. First, let's get familiar with the widgets and what kind of information you can get from them and then we will learn how to customize them.

Visitors

Examples of the visitors' widgets can be found in the **Visitors** panel of your Piwik installation. You can also preview a widget by hovering over its name in the **Add a widget** list as mentioned previously. There are many visitor metrics including unique visitors, actions, actions per visit, or average time on site that can tell you a lot about the people who visit your site. One metric, bounce rate, deserves special attention. It is the percentage of visits that only had one page view. On most websites, a high bounce rate is a bad thing, meaning that visitors exit your site quickly without browsing. But on a rare occasion that you want visitors to hit your page and exit, it is not so bad.

Let's look at the widgets we have available:

- **Visitor countries** (world map): This is one of the default widgets on the dashboard. It is the picture of the world map with darker-colored countries indicating more visitors from that country. By default, the metric it shows is **Visits**, but you can have it show **Unique Visitors**, **Actions**, **Actions Per Visit**, **Average Time on Site**, or **Bounce rate**. You can also click on the full screen icon to view the map on your whole screen.
- **Visitor continents**: By default, this shows a bar graph of which continents visitors to your site came from.
- **Visitor countries**: This widget will show a table of countries your visitors most commonly come from.

- **Frequency overview**: This report widget presents data and mini-line graphs related to returning visitors. It will tell you how many returning visitors you have had, how many actions they have made, the average actions per returning visitor, the average visit duration, and the bounce rate.
- **Graph returning visits**: This widget is similar to the **Visits** graph on the dashboard but presents returning visitor numbers instead of a count of all visitors.
- **Length of visits**: By default, this widget is included on the dashboard and will give you data on the length of time visitors spent at your website.
- **Pages per visit**: This widget can give you information on how active visitors are at your site and how sticky your site is. By default, this widget has a tag cloud which is a visual, weighted list of the keywords used to reach your website.
- **Visits by visit number**: This widget will give you a table with the count of just how many (one, two, three, and so on) time visitors you have had along with the percentage each adds to your total visits. Visitors that come back multiple times are valuable assets.
- **Visits by days since last visit**: This widget also has a table by default and will tell you how long it takes a returning visitor to return.
- **Providers**: This widget presents a table with a count of the Internet service providers your visitors use.
- **Custom variables**: This widget will be useful after setting up custom variables, which we will get to in *Chapter 6, Tracking Events*.

Actions

The **Actions** panel of the Piwik dashboard houses report widgets that track the activity of visitors on your website. Generally, you want activity because that means people are sticking around your website. By default, all of these widgets are tables. Adding them to your dashboard can give you more insight on the popular pages and downloads on your site.

Here are the widgets that will display actions data:

- **Entry pages**: This is a table of the pages that visitors have landed on when coming to your website. It will tell you the entrance count and bounce rate of visitors to your most trafficked pages.
- **Exit pages**: This table will give you a count of exits, unique pageviews, and exit rate of the most commonly exited pages on your website.

- **Pages**: This is a table of the pages that visitors have visited on your website. It will tell you the pageviews, unique pageviews, bounce rate, average time on page, and exit rate of visitors to your most trafficked pages.
- **Page titles**: This presents data similar to the Pages widget but lists popular pages on your site by their page title rather than their URL.
- **Outlinks**: This report will list the URLs visitors clicked to exit your site. Piwik uses JavaScript to detect links on the page and the anchor URLs, and will report a click on a link that doesn't match your URL as an outlink. We will learn more about how this works in the next chapter.
- **Downloads**: This table will give you a count of downloads for any downloadable file on your site.

Referrers

The **Referrers** panel in Piwik holds reports that detail the sites that referred your visitors to your website. By analyzing the data in these reports, you will learn what keywords are working for you, what ad campaigns are effective, which search engines favor your site, and who is linking to you.

Here are the **Referrers** widgets available to you:

- **List of keywords**: This table will list the keywords visitors entered in search engines to find your site along with how many times each keyword was used, how many actions visitors who used that keyword performed on the website, and how long visitors who used the keyword stayed at your site on average.
- **List of campaigns**: This report will list data about campaigns you are tracking. We will cover marketing campaigns in *Chapter 5, Tracking Marketing Campaigns*.
- **List of external websites**: This table lists a count of visits that you got from external websites, not counting search engines.
- **Best search engines**: This table ranks the visitors to your site that came from search engines.
- **Overview**: This report compares visitors from search engines, visitors who came from a link on another website, and those that came directly to your site.

SEO

SEO stands for **Search Engine Optimization**. Much of the visitor data you will be receiving from Piwik can be used for SEO purposes. This category is for widgets that don't fit well in the other categories.

There are two SEO widgets available:

- **Top keywords for page URL**: This is not a widget for your dashboard but actually one to put on the web site you are tracking. It presents a list of top keywords based on the page it is added to. It uses the Piwik API which we will cover later.
- **SEO rankings**: This widget will give the Google PageRank, Alexa Rank, and Domain Age of the website you are tracking or actually any website by entering the URL of the site in its form and clicking the **Rank** button.

Visitor settings

This set of widgets will give you details on the computers and software that the visitors to your website are using.

Here are the **Visitor** widgets available:

- **Screen resolutions**: Knowing the screen resolution of your visitors can give important information when it comes to design changes to your website. This widget will give you a list of the size of computer screens your visitors are using.
- **Visitor browsers**: This widget will list the browsers your visitors use, so you know if an average visitor to your site will even notice that cutting edge effect you are thinking of adding to your site.
- **Browsers by family**: There are many browsers but there are only a few browser engines. This widget will tell you the breakdown of Gecko (Firefox), Webkit (Safari/Chrome), Trident (Internet Explorer), and Presto (Opera) users in your visitors.
- **List of Plugins**: This report will tell you the percentage of visitors to your site who have cookies enabled, flash installed, PDF installed, and so on. The detection of plugins works in every major browser except Internet Explorer where it can trigger Windows security warnings and other user experience issues. For IE, this functionality is currently deactivated in Piwik since version 0.4.2.

- **Normal/Widescreen**: This widget simplifies the screen resolution report by breaking down resolutions into **Wide**, **Normal**, and **Mobile** screen sizes.
- **Operating systems**: This report will give you data on the operating systems your visitors are using.
- **Global visitors configuration**: This table groups your visitors settings together rather than separately. For example, you may learn that a common combination for your visitors is Windows XP with Firefox and a 1024 x 768 screen resolution.

Goals

Goals are specific actions or sets of action you want visitors to perform on your site. They are an important part of improving the traffic to your website and the experience for visitors at your website.

- **Goals overview**: This widget will give you an overview of how many goals have been completed on your website and the conversion rate for the goals.

Visits Summary

Visitors are what Piwik tracks so it makes sense that there is another set of widgets that apply to visitors. This set of widgets will give you a broader, big picture view of the traffic on your website.

- **Last visits graph**: The default line graph shows how many visitors you have had over your selected date range.
- **Visits overview**: This report gives you a text summary and small line graphs on important visitor data.
- **Overview with graph**: This report combines the last two reports into one.
- **Visits by local time**: By default, this report is a bar graph charting the times visitors are on your site, using your local time zone.
- **Visits by server time**: This report is the same as the last report but uses your web server's time zone.

Live!

The **Live!** widget is displayed by default on the Piwik dashboard. It refreshes every 10 seconds automatically and displays data about your visitors in real time. Real time actually depends on the processing time which you can set in **Setting | General Settings**. By default, this time is set to 10 seconds which is close enough to real time for most people.

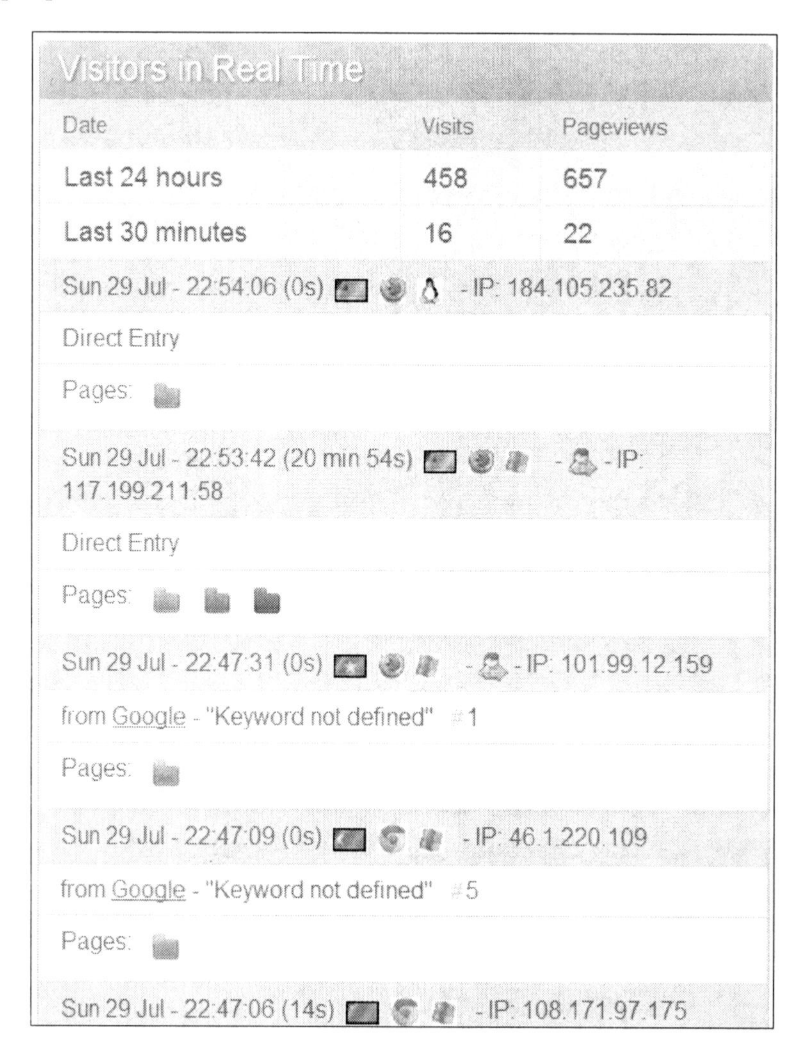

As you can tell from the previous screenshot, this report contains a lot of data.

It gives you a count of visits and pageviews for the **Last 24 hours** and **Last 30 minutes** at the top. And below that, it lists recent visitors and data on their visit. First you will see the date and time they first landed on your website and after that in parentheses is the time they have been on your site, followed by icons which indicate the country they are from, the browser they use, and their operating system. Hovering over these icons with your mouse will bring up more details such as screen resolution and browser plugins. On the same line you will notice the IP they are located at.

And below that is the referrer row, which will display **Direct Entry**, list the referring website or list the keyword, search engine, and possibly the rank of the keyword in the search engine the visitor used to find your site. The data for keyword rank is extracted from a search engine's referring URL.

Underneath that row, you will see **Pages:** and a list of colored folder icons. These represent the pages that visitors to your site have visited while there. Hovering your mouse pointer over them will bring up the page name and clicking the icon will open the page listed in another tab of your browser.

The **Visitor Log** report in the **Visitors** panel is similar to the **Live!** widget and has all of the same data, but since it is allowed a full page in the **Visitor** panel, the folder icons are replaced with an **Actions** column which list pages visited by name and time on the page. The **Visitor Log** can also track custom variables once you have set some up.

Reading a Piwik report

As you check out your Piwik dashboard, you may notice a few icons along the bottom of the report widgets. By clicking these icons, you can change the way a report displays in the widget. You can also hover over them and view their tooltips to get a description of what each does.

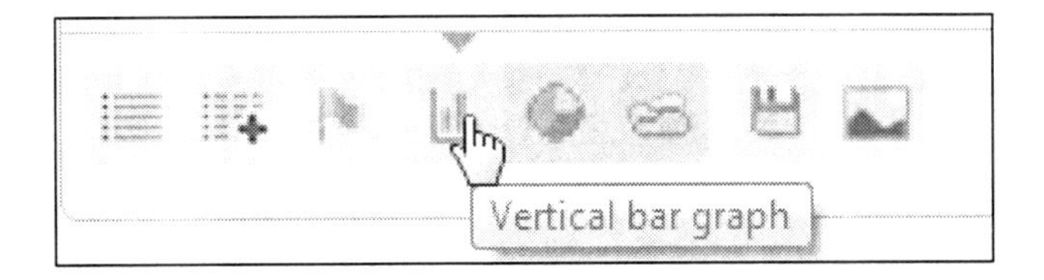

Here is what each of the icons does:

- The first icon from the left will display a table of only the metric the widget features. The previous screenshot is an example of that choice.
- The second icon will display a table with more metrics. When you click it, a lightbox will pop up displaying a larger table with the expanded set of metrics. Once you close the lightbox, the widget will then also display the new set of metrics. What type of metrics is added depends on the widget. The **Best search engines** widget, when displaying the expanded set of metrics, will have columns for unique visitors, actions, actions per visit, average time on website, and bounce rate.
- The third icon with the flag will display goal information once you have set up goals.
- The fourth icon will display a bar graph of the data presented and hovering over it opens up two other options.
- The fifth icon displays the data in the report as a pie chart.
- The sixth icon displays the data as a tag cloud where the size of text is used as an indicator of magnitude.
- The seventh icon of the floppy disk will export the data in CSV, TSV of Excel, XML, JSON, RSS, or as a PHP serialized array.
- You may also see an image icon which will save graph reports as images.

Customizing graph metrics

For any Piwik report, there may be many metrics that apply. One example of these reports is in the **Last visits graph** in the next screenshot. The standard report will show you a count of visits plotted across time. But many other details about the visits can be plotted simultaneously, so you can compare visits and pageviews or visits and people who left the site via a link.

You can graph as many metrics as you want on the same graph by hovering over the little graph icon in the top-left corner of the widget and choosing the metrics that you want to plot from the menu that drops down. You may not want to graph too many though, as the graph can easily become cluttered with lines and end up being unreadable if you go overboard.

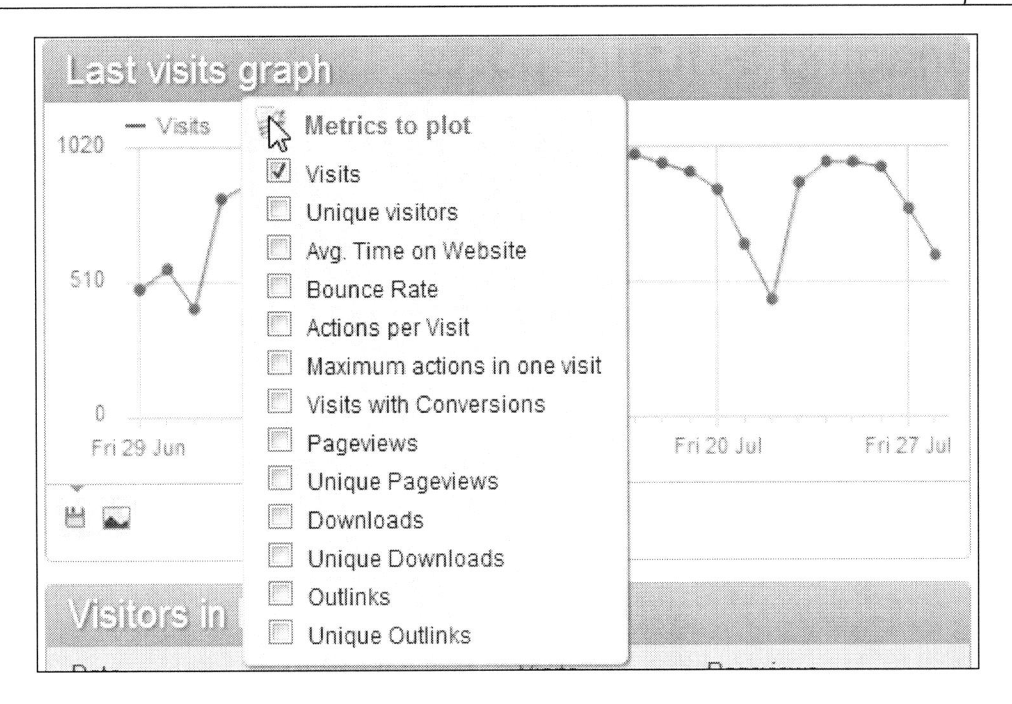

Once you make the choice of your metrics, each metric will be given its own color of line. The guide to which color stands for which metric is in the upper-left corner of the widget. In the following screenshot, **Visits**, **Pageviews**, and **Outlinks** are graphed:

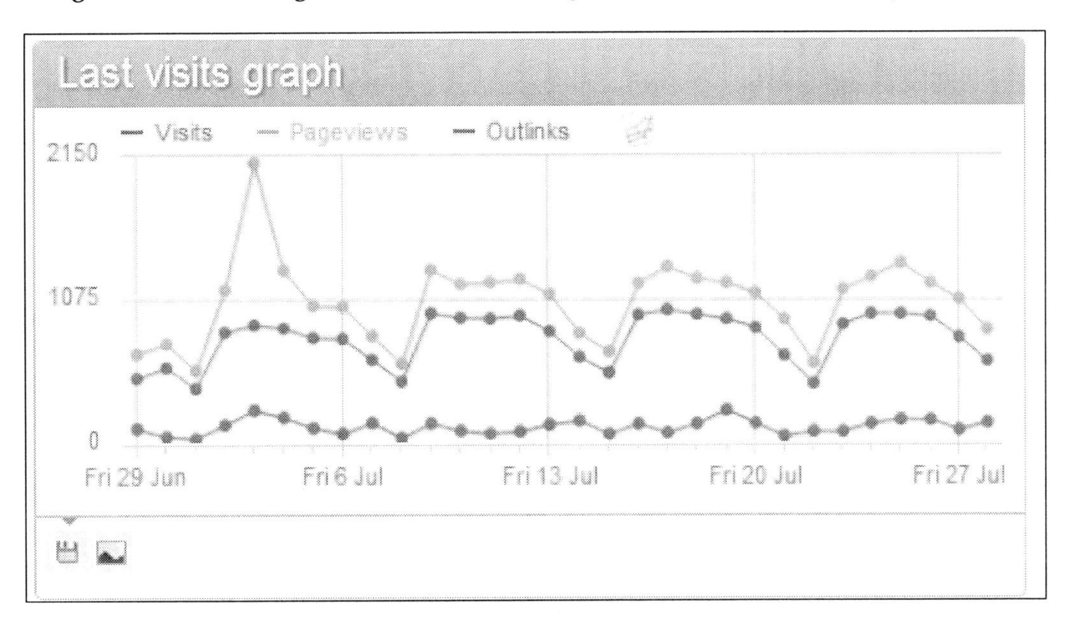

Managing e-mail reports

Creating e-mail reports is a great way to get specific data about a website you are tracking, without visiting your Piwik installation and setting the data range and metrics each time. If you are a webmaster in charge of providing analytics data to the marketing division of your company or to clients, setting up custom e-mail reports can be the perfect way to make sure the right people get the data they need when they need it. If this is the only feedback they receive about their traffic, setting up scheduled e-mail reports can be one of the most important parts of your job. You can even choose to send the report in HTML or as a PDF file suitable for printing depending on your preferences or those of your clients.

Once you have chosen the website you are creating the report for in the **Website** dropdown, click the **Email Reports** link and we will get started with creating a report:

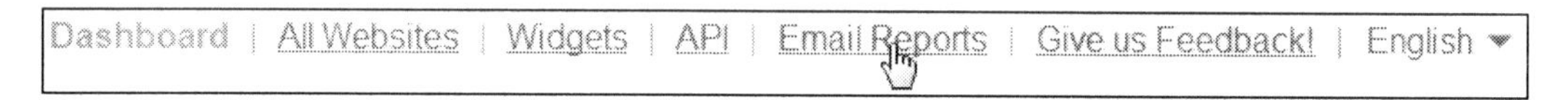

You will land on a pretty empty page stating that you haven't yet created any reports. Click on the **Create and Schedule a report** link:

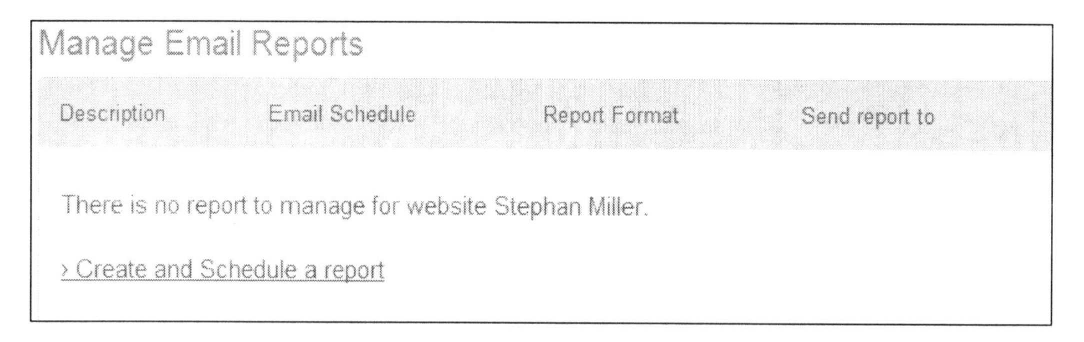

You will now be on the page where you can start creating a report for your site. In the first half of the form, you will have to set up the basics of the report.

Let's say that you want a basic report of your visitors and the sites and keywords that referred them.

In the **Description** field, enter a description of the report that will help you to identify it. This description will be on the first page of the generated report and will also be listed on the **Email Reports** page.

Next, choose how often you would like the report you are creating to be generated by selecting either **Never**, **Daily**, **Weekly**, or **Monthly** in the **Email Schedule** field. Choosing **Never** will save your report to your report list so that you can download it or e-mail it as needed. Weekly reports will be sent out every Monday and monthly reports will be sent out on the first of each month.

In the **Send report to** row, you should see the checkbox by the e-mail you signed up with checked by default. If this is a report only for others, you can uncheck your e-mail address so as not to receive the report. Below that is a text area where you can add multiple report recipients. Just make sure to separate each e-mail address with a line break.

All that is left is to choose either PDF or HTML from the **Report Format** row and we'll be ready to start setting up the details for what will be in the report.

Create and Schedule a report

Website	Stephan Miller
Description	The report description will be displayed on the first page of the report.
Email Schedule	Weekly Weekly schedule: report will be sent on Monday of each week Monthly schedule: report will be sent the first day of each month
Send report to	☑ Send to me (*stephanmil@gmail.com*) Also send the report to these emails (one email per line):
Report Format	PDF

You have a lot of options, as far as the details you can send in the report. You can choose any or all of the report tables shown in the following screenshot:

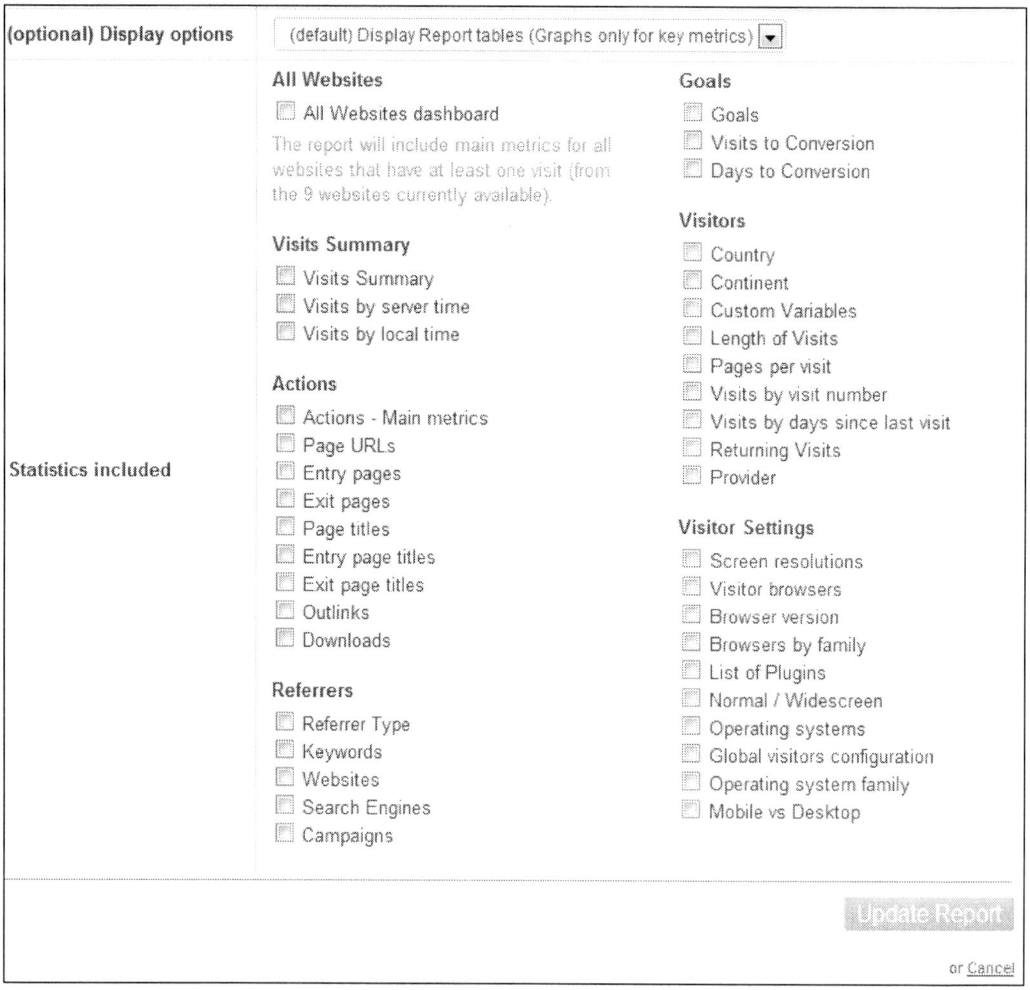

(optional) Display options — (default) Display Report tables (Graphs only for key metrics)

Statistics included

All Websites
- All Websites dashboard

The report will include main metrics for all websites that have at least one visit (from the 9 websites currently available).

Visits Summary
- Visits Summary
- Visits by server time
- Visits by local time

Actions
- Actions - Main metrics
- Page URLs
- Entry pages
- Exit pages
- Page titles
- Entry page titles
- Exit page titles
- Outlinks
- Downloads

Referrers
- Referrer Type
- Keywords
- Websites
- Search Engines
- Campaigns

Goals
- Goals
- Visits to Conversion
- Days to Conversion

Visitors
- Country
- Continent
- Custom Variables
- Length of Visits
- Pages per visit
- Visits by visit number
- Visits by days since last visit
- Returning Visits
- Provider

Visitor Settings
- Screen resolutions
- Visitor browsers
- Browser version
- Browsers by family
- List of Plugins
- Normal / Widescreen
- Operating systems
- Global visitors configuration
- Operating system family
- Mobile vs Desktop

Update Report

or Cancel

You can then click on **Send Report now** to send out the report to the e-mail addresses listed. You can also download the report directly by clicking on the **Download** link. If you made any mistakes or want to change some details in your report, you can click on the **Edit** link to change it. And when you no longer need the report, you can click on **Delete** to delete it permanently.

Manage Email Reports

Description	Email Schedule	Report Format	Send report to	Download	Edit	Delete
My Report	Weekly	PDF	stephanmil@gmail.com myother@email.com Send Report now	Download	Edit	Delete

› Create and Schedule a report

When you receive the report by e-mail or download it, you will notice that the report looks just about the same as the reports in Piwik's dashboard, except that they are not dynamic.

Piwik

Website Stephan Miller

My Report - Date range: Sunday 29 July 2012

Report list

- All Websites dashboard
- Visits Summary
- Referrer Type
- Keywords
- Websites
- Search Engines

All Websites dashboard

Website	Visits	Actions	Revenue
Stephan Miller	603	988	$ 0
FootPrint Finder Google Scraper	9	17	$ 0
Profit-ware	3	3	$ 0
24-7 Phoenix Locksmith	1	1	$ 0
Eristoddle	1	1	$ 0

Back to top

Visits Summary

Name	Value
Unique visitors	537
Visits	603
Actions	988

At the top of the report will be the Piwik logo and below that the name of the website the report was created for, and the description you entered when creating the report.

Next, there is **Report list**, which is clickable and will take you directly to the part of the report named.

The report in the previous screenshot has the default report format with graphs only for key metrics and you will notice that the **Visits Summary** has both a graph and a table. Visitors and goals are two examples of metrics that will include a graph of the data over time when this default setting is chosen.

Summary

After reading this chapter, you should know your way around your Piwik installation pretty well. You also learned how to lay out Piwik's dashboard with your custom set of widgets. You have added and moved widgets on the dashboard and you have a good idea of what kind of widgets are available, so you can find the right report for the job. This knowledge of Piwik's widgets was useful when you learned how to set up e-mail reports for people who don't want to log in to Piwik all the time, or just as a reminder that you need to keep an eye on your stats.

In the next chapter, we will go in depth on tracking visitors and move beyond pasting the default Piwik tracking code in your footer.

3

Tracking Visitors with Piwik

Now that we have a working Piwik installation and know how to customize our Piwik dashboard, we are going to go a little deeper into how our visitors are being tracked and how to modify the JavaScript tracking code to our needs. The default tracking code that Piwik provides us with will do a lot, but sometimes we may need to tweak it for special cases.

In this chapter, we will cover the following topics:

- Using the Piwik JavaScript tracking code
- Functioning of default JavaScript
- Triggering page views manually
- Customizing page names
- Customizing page URLs, referrer URLs, and domain names
- Configuring Piwik's tracking cookies
- Setting up download and outlink tracking
- Using other Piwik JavaScript API methods
- Using multiple trackers
- Using asynchronous tracking

Using the Piwik JavaScript tracking code

In the past, the most frequently used method of tracking visitors on a website was the server log files. Raw log files are text files that your web server uses to record events and visitors on your website. Log files are readable in their raw form, but must be parsed by other software in order to make any sense of the data they contain. Usually, the free analytics software that comes preinstalled on your web server, like Webalizer or AWStats, is of this type.

But log file analysis limits what you can do with your analytics, in the following ways:

- It can only help you track those actions that can be logged by your web server
- It cannot track events in JavaScript, Flash, or Ajax
- It will not count pages cached by a user's browser or proxy as a visit
- Robots and spiders may get counted and artificially inflate visitor counts and page views in logfile-based analytics, if they are not filtered out effectively

The technology that Piwik uses to track visitors actually started with web counters, which were popular in the nineties. By requesting the web counter image from a web counter vendor's server, a webmaster could get a rudimentary visitor count that required no software to be installed on his own server. Eventually, more advanced web bug or page tag web analytics, which used JavaScript, came along.

Piwik's JavaScript allows webmasters to track many more details about their visitors than server log parsing does. The collection of data begins when a visitor first visits your website. A visitor's action of opening a page of your website in their browser generates a request to your web server. When the page loads in their browser, every JavaScript code on the page will execute, including the tracking code from Piwik. Let's take a look at the tracking code and examine how it works step-by-step, so that the changes we make to it make more sense:

1. First, log in to your Piwik installation. Then click on the **Settings** link on the top right corner of the interface:

2. Then, click on the **Websites** tab in the **Settings** menu. This will take you to the **Websites Management** page, and you will see a list of the websites you are tracking, in a table:

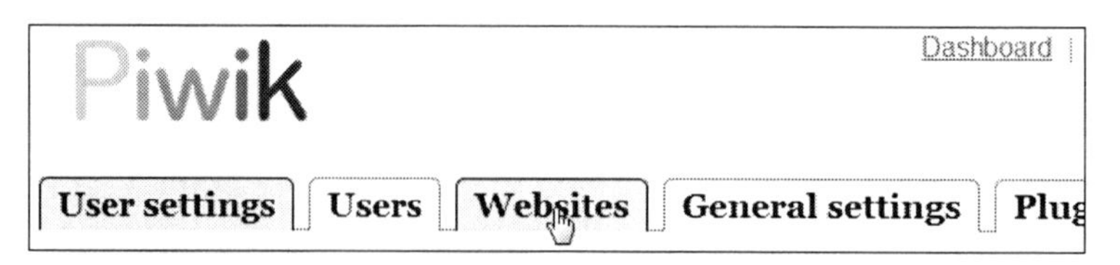

3. Click on the **View Tracking code** link at the end of the table, for the website you want to track:

Time zone	Currency	Ecommerce			JavaScript Tracking Code
America/Chicago	USD	-	Edit	Delete	View Tracking code
America/Chicago	USD	-	Edit	Delete	View Tracking code

This will take you to the tracking code page for the chosen website:

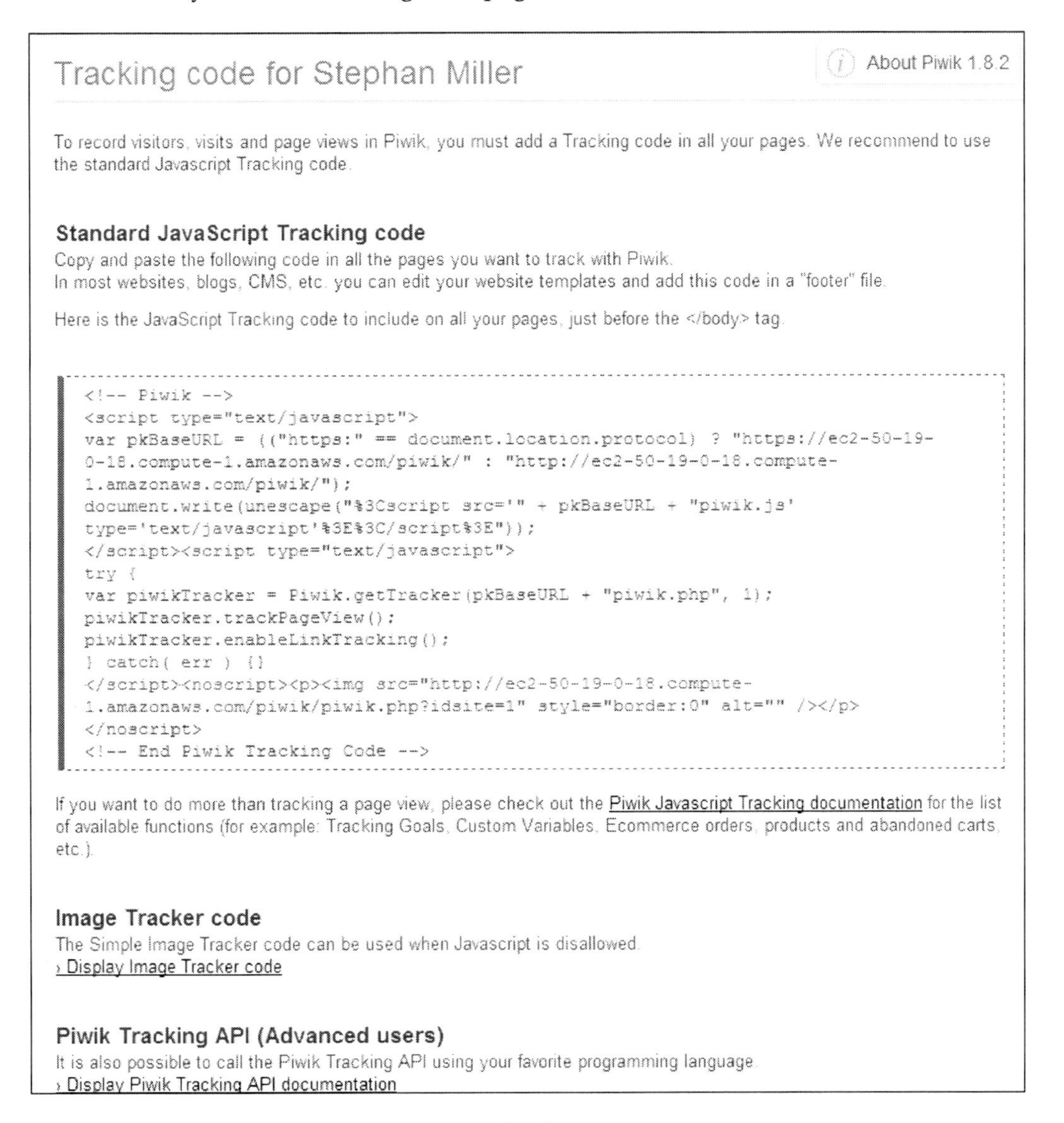

Tracking code for Stephan Miller

About Piwik 1.8.2

To record visitors, visits and page views in Piwik, you must add a Tracking code in all your pages. We recommend to use the standard Javascript Tracking code.

Standard JavaScript Tracking code

Copy and paste the following code in all the pages you want to track with Piwik.
In most websites, blogs, CMS, etc. you can edit your website templates and add this code in a "footer" file.

Here is the JavaScript Tracking code to include on all your pages, just before the </body> tag.

```
<!-- Piwik -->
<script type="text/javascript">
var pkBaseURL = (("https:" == document.location.protocol) ? "https://ec2-50-19-
0-18.compute-1.amazonaws.com/piwik/" : "http://ec2-50-19-0-18.compute-
1.amazonaws.com/piwik/");
document.write(unescape("%3Cscript src='" + pkBaseURL + "piwik.js'
type='text/javascript'%3E%3C/script%3E"));
</script><script type="text/javascript">
try {
var piwikTracker = Piwik.getTracker(pkBaseURL + "piwik.php", 1);
piwikTracker.trackPageView();
piwikTracker.enableLinkTracking();
} catch( err ) {}
</script><noscript><p><img src="http://ec2-50-19-0-18.compute-
1.amazonaws.com/piwik/piwik.php?idsite=1" style="border:0" alt="" /></p>
</noscript>
<!-- End Piwik Tracking Code -->
```

If you want to do more than tracking a page view, please check out the Piwik Javascript Tracking documentation for the list of available functions (for example: Tracking Goals, Custom Variables, Ecommerce orders, products and abandoned carts, etc.).

Image Tracker code

The Simple Image Tracker code can be used when Javascript is disallowed.
› Display Image Tracker code

Piwik Tracking API (Advanced users)

It is also possible to call the Piwik Tracking API using your favorite programming language.
› Display Piwik Tracking API documentation

This page has three headings: **Standard JavaScript Tracking code**, **Image Tracker code**, and **Piwik Tracking API**. We want to take a look at the code in the blue box under the **Standard JavaScript Tracking code** header. The code should be easy to copy and paste from the blue box to a text editor, that is, without any formatting issues. Here is an example of the code Piwik will give you:

```
<!-- Piwik -->
<script type="text/javascript">
var pkBaseURL = (("https:" == document.location.protocol) ?
"https://$PIWIK_URL" : "http://$PIWIK_URL");
document.write(unescape("%3Cscript src='" + pkBaseURL + "piwik.js'
type='text/javascript'%3E%3C/script%3E"));
</script><script type="text/javascript">
try {
var piwikTracker = Piwik.getTracker(pkBaseURL + "piwik.php", $SITE_
ID);
piwikTracker.trackPageView();
piwikTracker.enableLinkTracking();
} catch( err ) {}
</script><noscript><p><img src="$PIWIK_URL/piwik.php?idsite=1"
style="border:0" alt="" /></p></noscript>
<!-- End Piwik Tracking Code -->
```

Here, `$PIWIK_URL` is the URL of your Piwik installation and `$SITE_ID` is the ID that Piwik has assigned to the website you are tracking.

Functioning of default JavaScript

The code seen previously executes when a page or a frame being tracked loads in a browser. It contains all the logic that Piwik needs to track a visitor.

The first executable line in this code occurs when the variable `pkBaseURL` is set. The tracking code determines whether the URL currently loaded is SSL or Non-SSL, and creates `pkBaseURL`—the URL for your Piwik installation—with either a leading `http://` or `https://`. Once the URL to Piwik has been generated, the JavaScript code includes the `piwik.js` file from your Piwik installation in the loaded page.

After the `piwik.js` file has been delivered to the visitor's browser, a tracker object is created with the variable name of `piwikTracker`. This object will be used to track all the actions that this visitor will perform on the site. The Piwik JavaScript function was loaded with the `piwik.js` file and holds the `getTracker` function, which creates the tracker object.

`Piwik.getTracker(trackerUrl, siteId)`: This function gets a new instance of the tracker, where `trackerUrl` is the location of the `piwik.php` file on your Piwik installation, and `siteId` is the ID of the site you are tracking in Piwik.

This `getTracker` function is the same type of function as `_getTracker(account)` in Google Analytics or `getTracker(account)` in Yahoo! Analytics.

As soon as the Piwik tracker object is created, a page view is triggered with `trackPageView`.

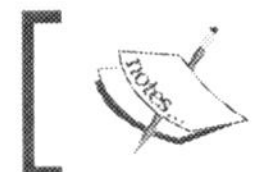

`trackPageView([customTitle])`: This function logs a visit to the page, with an optional custom title for the page.

This function is the same as `_trackPageview(opt_pageURL)` in Google Analytics or `submit()` in Yahoo! Analytics.

The final bit of executable code in the JavaScript is the function call `enableLinkTracking`. This allows Piwik to track clicks on links that leave your website and file downloads.

`enableLinkTracking(enable)`: This function will add link tracking on link elements. By setting the enable parameter to `true`, Piwik will use a pseudo-click handler to track browsers which don't generate click events for the middle mouse button.

Click tracking with JavaScript is a rather complex process, because a link can be clicked with the right, middle, or left mouse buttons, and the manner in which browsers handle these mouse events is not consistent. Piwik's `enableLinkTracking` hides this issue and gives you a simple interface to use.

After the last script tag is the `noscript` section that loads Piwik's simple image tracker code. This code includes the `piwik.php` file as an image in the page you are tracking. This fake image will allow you to track visits from people who have JavaScript blocked.

There may be times you have to use an image tracker alone, such as on a site like eBay or MySpace that won't allow you to include JavaScript in your content, but will allow an HTML image tag. The image tracker code is also available by itself on the tracking code page of a website in the Piwik interface, right under the standard JavaScript code. The disadvantage of using the image tracker is that some user information like keywords, screen resolutions, referrers, and page titles will not be tracked. But *some* tracking is better than none.

This tracking code will work fine out-of-the-box for many sites. But, sometimes, there may be reasons when you need to customize this code. You may need to track each part of a page as if it were a page itself. You may want to simplify page names, so that you can recognize them more easily in reports. Once you catch the tracking bug, default settings are usually not enough. So let's get to customizing this tracking code.

Triggering page views manually

There was a time when—on the Internet—a page view was a page view. New content meant a new page. But with JavaScript and Flash, the definition of a page view can be a little bit different. If you have a slide show in Flash, isn't each slide a page? What about AJAX applications that load content in the browser without a reload? A visitor could land on an AJAX enabled site, be there for an hour browsing through content and register only one traditional page view. If you had server-based tracking, you could track each of these AJAX hits to the server. But there are still more advantages to using JavaScript to track visitors. You will get data on screen resolution, browser plugins, and other details not available in server logs. Luckily, you can manually trigger page views with Piwik, but it is up to you to determine what a page view is.

You may even have to trigger a page view when it has nothing to do with Flash or JavaScript. A good SEO practice, to concentrate Google PageRank on more important pages, is to move pages like About Us, Shipping Information, Privacy Policy, and Return Policy into one page. These pages are really unimportant when it comes to search engine optimization purposes, but very important to visitors. You still keep the menu linking to each section in the sidebar, but change the links from links to separate pages, to links to anchors in one page.

Even though all of these links point to the same page, visitors clicking on the links are going to completely separate sections of the page. One visitor may be visiting the About Us page to check what shipping costs were, while another may be more interested in the return policy. While these page sections are unimportant for any search engine optimization purposes, they are still important pages to track separately. So let's take a look at the menu code in its original form before we add the JavaScript code.

```
<ul>
    <li><a href="#About">About Us</a></li>
    <li><a href="#Shipping">Shipping Info</a></li>
    <li><a href="#Privacy">Privacy Policy</a></li>
    <li><a href="#Returns">Return Policy</a></li>
<ul>
```

So what you want to do is count each click to one of these links as a page view. So, all we do is add an `onclick` event to each link that triggers Piwik to count another page view.

```
<ul>
    <li><a href="#About" onclick="javascript:piwikTrack.
trackPageView('Menu/About');">About Us</a></li>
    <li><a href="#Shipping" onclick="javascript:piwikTrack.
trackPageView('Menu/Shipping');">Shipping Info</a></li>
    <li><a href="#Privacy" onclick="javascript:piwikTrack.
trackPageView('Menu/Privacy');">Privacy Policy</a></li>
    <li><a href="#Returns" onclick="javascript:piwikTrack.
trackPageView('Menu/Returns');">Return Policy</a></li>
<ul>
```

You will notice our old friend, `trackPageView`, in the code above. This is the same `trackPageView` function we saw in the tracking code we inserted in our web page, except this time a new page view is tracked with each click.

You may also notice that each `trackPageView` has an argument, like `trackPageView('Menu/About')`. The `Menu/About` in this case is the optional custom title argument. Since these are not really pages, we have to come up with page titles for the links ourselves. They can be just about anything that makes it easy for you to identify them. But this is not the only way you can set custom page names in Piwik.

Another way to track clicks is to add a listener to a DOM element or a group of DOM elements on the web page.

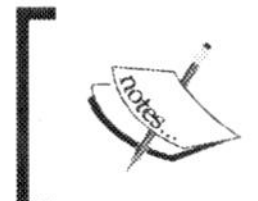

`addListener(element)`: This function adds a click listener object to the specific DOM element, which is its argument. When the element is clicked, Piwik will log the click automatically.

This method is added to the Piwik JavaScript tracking code before `trackPageView` is called. Let's say you have a shoutbox in the sidebar of your site and want to track button clicks. This is what you would do:

```
...
var shoutboxButton = document.getElementById( "myShoutboxButton" );
piwikTracker.addListener(shoutboxButton);
piwikTracker.trackPageView('ShoutBoxClick');
...
```

First, we call `document.getElementById` to grab the `shoutbox` button element and put this in the `shoutboxButton` variable. Then we use that variable as the argument in the `addListener` method. For the sake of brevity, the rest of the Piwik tracking code has been removed and replaced with ellipses. We will be doing this through the rest of this chapter.

You may instead want to trigger a page view to be counted using jQuery. jQuery is a JavaScript library that makes JavaScript a bit easier to use. When we use jQuery, we don't have to worry about modifying any of the default code. Instead of adding a listener from within our Piwik tracking code, we will be triggering the execution of the `trackPageview` function when a click event occurs on our `shoutbox` button.

```
$(document).ready(function(){
    $('#myShoutBoxButton').click(function() {
       piwiTracker.trackPageView('ShoutBoxClick');
    });
});
```

This code works on any page that you have included in the jQuery library. First, we check if our document is ready. When the document is finally loaded, we add a jQuery click handler to the element of our page that has the `myShoutBoxButton` ID. The function we assign to this click event is an anonymous JavaScript function that instantly executes the Piwik tracker `trackPageView` function. The same result is obtained, either way we choose to do it.

Customizing page names

By default, the **Pages** widget in the Piwik interface uses the URL of the tracked page as the page name. This works out fine for something like a Wordpress site that uses readable URLs. But you may not want to stick to this default setting because your URLs are unreadable or you want to add identifying tags to the page names. A screenshot of the **Pages** widget is as follows:

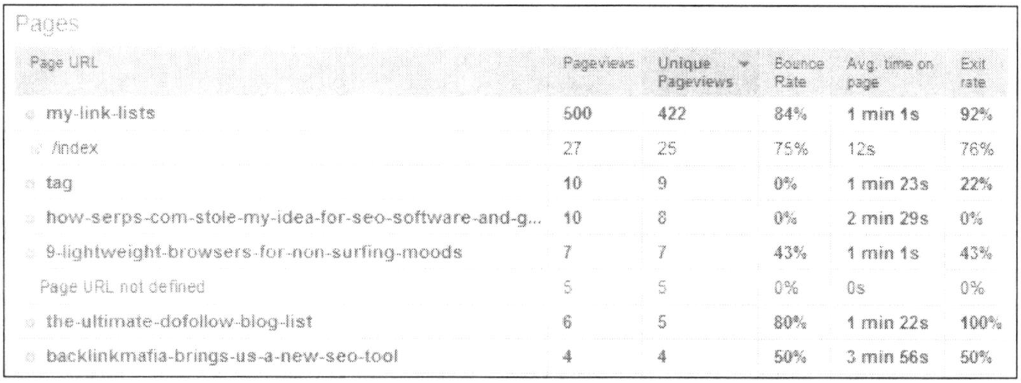

Pages

Page URL	Pageviews	Unique Pageviews	Bounce Rate	Avg. time on page	Exit rate
my-link-lists	500	422	84%	1 min 1s	92%
/index	27	25	75%	12s	76%
tag	10	9	0%	1 min 23s	22%
how-serps-com-stole-my-idea-for-seo-software-and-g...	10	8	0%	2 min 29s	0%
9-lightweight-browsers-for-non-surfing-moods	7	7	43%	1 min 1s	43%
Page URL not defined	5	5	0%	0s	0%
the-ultimate-dofollow-blog-list	6	5	80%	1 min 22s	100%
backlinkmafia-brings-us-a-new-seo-tool	4	4	50%	3 min 56s	50%

If the URL you are tracking looks like a string of letters, numbers, and ampersands, a good option is to set the page name that Piwik will use to `document.title`, available to JavaScript. This only involves inserting one line of code in the standard Piwik tracking code.

```
...
var piwikTracker = Piwik.getTracker(pkBaseURL + "piwik.php", $SITE_
ID);
piwikTracker.setDocumentTitle(document.title);
piwikTracker.trackPageView();
...
```

You may want to add a special tag to the page name if you are tracking a site with many subdomains. This way, you can easily identify which pages are on which subdomain. In this case, you can just use the `document.domain` variable.

```
...
var piwikTracker = Piwik.getTracker(pkBaseURL + "piwik.php", $SITE_
ID);
piwikTracker.setDocumentTitle(document.domain + "/" + document.title);
piwikTracker.trackPageView();
...
```

If the page you are tracking is generated by code such as PHP, you can use that code to dynamically generate the page name for the JavaScript code.

```
...
var piwikTracker = Piwik.getTracker(pkBaseURL + "piwik.php", $SITE_
ID);
piwikTracker.setDocumentTitle("<?php echo $MyCustomPageName; ?>");
piwikTracker.trackPageView();
...
```

But the page name is not the only data you can manually set in Piwik's tracking code.

Customizing tracking URLs

One of the things that make a modern web analytics tool handy is the fact that it does just about everything for you, without much intervention. But there are times you may need to set data manually, just like we did for the page name.

If you want, you can override a tracked page's reported URL. Maybe the URL you present to the world has been made pretty with a mod rewrite for SEO's purpose, and the actual query string version of the URL and its parameters is more useful information. Sometimes, the dirty version of a URL will have category information and similar data. If this is necessary, you can do this using:

```
...
piwikTracker.setCustomUrl('http://mydomain/customurl.php');
piwikTracker.trackPageView();
...
```

`setCustomUrl(string)`: This function overrides the tracked page's reported URL with the value in the parameter `string`.

You can override the referrer URL with a similar method.

`setReferrerUrl(string)`: This function overrides the tracked page's reported referrer URL with the value in the parameter `string`.

Configuring Piwik's tracking cookies

It is impossible for a page tag-based web analytics solution to be useful without cookies. Cookies are key-value pairs stored in text format by your browser. They are set by a web server so that you can be identified across pages or time. Session cookies only last for the duration of your visit to a website, and persistent cookies are stored for a longer period of time—set by the `Max-Age` value. Piwik must use both session and persistent cookies to accurately track visitors.

Cookies can also be first-party or third-party. This difference has to do with the domain the cookie is set with. First-party cookies use the domain or subdomain of the website in the browser address bar, and third-party cookies are set with a domain other than the actual domain the visitor is at. There is no intrinsic difference between first-party cookies and third-party cookies. The difference lies in the fact that another site, which you didn't even visit, will be tracking your actions. Third-party cookies are usually used by businesses like advertising companies, who need to track visitors across a multitude of websites. An example would be an official Twitter button added to a site. This Twitter button will actually set a cookie in your browser and send data back to Twitter about your actions. This brings up a privacy issue with a lot of Internet users and as a result most browsers block third-party cookies by default. Piwik has used first-party cookies since version 1.2.

Although using a first-party cookie prevents a browser from instantly deleting your Piwik cookies, that does not mean the visitor himself could have his browser configured to delete or to block them. This brings up an important point: using cookies to track visitors is relatively accurate, but it's not perfect. There are many ways in which tracking data can be skewed due to the limitations of browser cookies. Some of these are:

- Visitors rejecting or deleting cookies: A visitor rejecting a cookie has obvious implications. Piwik will have to fall back to image tracking and the limitations that come with it. When a cookie gets deleted, Piwik will record a returning visitor as a new visitor. This is because Piwik depends on persistent cookies to tag returning visitors.
- Multiple users using the same computer and browser: In this case, Piwik will record the visits of all these users as one.
- One user using multiple browsers or multiple computers: Here, returning visitors will be counted as new visitors and unique visits will be over counted.

With current technology, there is not much you can really do about this, except know that this happens, and that your data will never be 100 percent perfect.

Piwik sets three cookies in the visitor's browser:

Cookie Name	Max Age	Contents
_pk_id	2 years after the latest page view	This contains a 64-byte int `UUID` that is generated when the cookie is created. It contains a timestamp of the cookie creation date in UTC, which is used to process the days it took for goal conversion. It contains a visits count that is updated when a _pk_ses cookie is created and this is used to calculate Visits to conversion. It contains a timestamp of the last page view of the last visit before this visit, which is used to process Days since last visit and Days to purchase.
_pk_ses	30 minutes after the latest page view	This contains no data. Every time a new _pk_ses is created, 1 is added to the visits counter in the _pk_id cookie.
_pk_ref	6 months from the date of creation	This contains the referrer URL, which is truncated at 1024 bytes. It also contains the time the referrer URL was set.

Piwik creates these cookies for each domain and subdomain. If you are tracking a website with a few subdomains and you want these subdomains to share the same cookie, then you will have to modify the Piwik tracking code that directly affects these cookies. This involves using the `setCookieDomain` method in Piwik.

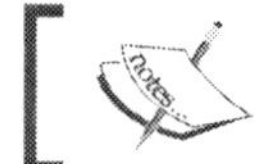

setCookieDomain(domain): This function sets the domain of Piwik's cookie. By default, it is the domain of the document.

One example of a site you would want to use this on is a blog farm. Let's say you installed Wordpress in multisite mode and want to start four or five blogs on different subdomains of the installation. Now, these blogs are going to be closely related in subject matter, and for the most part you can consider them parts of one site. You are only separating the subject matter into five blogs for search engine optimization purposes, or siloing, to be exact. So, you should probably have Piwik set the same cookies across the domain and all subdomains of the site. Here is code similar to what you will use:

```
...
tracker = Piwik.getTracker(pkBaseUrl + "piwik.php", 1);
tracker.setCookieDomain('*.example.com'); tracker.setDomains('*.
example.com');
tracker.trackPageView();
...
```

In this section of code, we set the cookie domain to `*.example.com`, where `example.com` is the domain of our Wordpress multisite. The asterisk is a wildcard character that can be replaced with any character, which allows this string to work for `www.example.com`, `blog1.example.com`, and any other subdomain of `example.com`.

You will notice that below `setCookieDomain` is another method call.

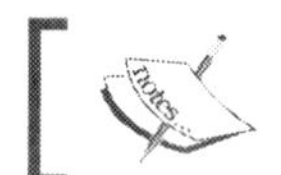

setDomains(array): This function sets the array of hostnames or domains that will be treated as local by your Piwik tracker.

The cookie domain has already been set and now it is time to tell Piwik's tracker that any links with this same domain should be counted as local and not as outlinks. We use `setDomains` to do that. You can use the asterisk as a wildcard with this call too.

Let's look at another case where we might have to customize cookies. A perfect example would be a social network where the user's pages are in subdirectories of the site, and we want to offer every user his own private analytics for those pages he controls. Instead of adding subdomains to a domain we are tracking, we are going to split a domain into multiple websites.

In the example site, you will be using one tracker for the analytics of the main part of the social website. These would be pages like the home page, sign up page, login pages, and about pages.

```
...
tracker = Piwik.getTracker(pkBaseURL + "piwik.php", $SITE_ID);
tracker.trackPageView();
...
```

We are assuming that the website ID of the main part of this website is 1.

Now, for each specific user of the site, or a new website, we create a new ID in Piwik.

```
...
tracker2 = Piwik.getTracker(pkBaseUrl + "piwik.php", 2);
tracker2.setCookiePath('/users/username/*');
tracker2.trackPageView();
...
```

But you see, this is not all we do. In order for the cookies to work separately for each user, we set a cookie path. We set its parameter to the path on the domain where all of this user's pages reside, and we use a wildcard asterisk to include any directories under that path.

> `setCookiePath(path)`: This function gives you the chance to specify a directory where the cookie is active. The default is "/".

You can also change the prefix of Piwik's cookie names, if needed.

> `setCookieNamePrefix(prefix)`: The default prefix is `'_pk_'` (that is, `_pk_id`, `_pk_ses`, `_pk_ref`).

If you want, you can change the default timeout of each one of Piwik's cookies.

> `setVisitorCookieTimeout(seconds)`: The default is 2 years.
>
> `setSessionCookieTimeout(seconds)`: The default is 30 minutes.
>
> `setReferralCookieTimeout(seconds)`: The default is 6 months.

Setting up download and outlink tracking

In the default tracking code given to you by Piwik, download and outlink tracking is enabled by default. This line of the tracking code does it:

```
...
piwikTracker.enableLinkTracking();
...
```

The easiest way to disable all download and outlink tracking is to comment out this line of code; like so:

```
...
//piwikTracker.enableLinkTracking();
...
```

Disabling link tracking

If you still need to track some links but not all, an easy way to do it is by using CSS classes. Piwik lets you specify which classes of links will not be tracked.

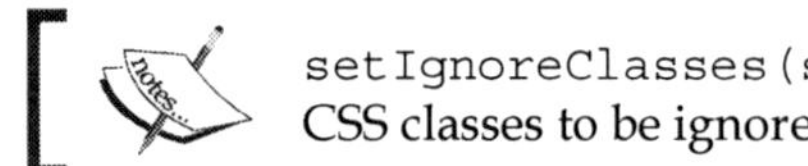

`setIgnoreClasses(string|array)`: This function sets CSS classes to be ignored, if present in the link.

So, if you have a set of links to other sites on a specific page on your site that you want Piwik to ignore, you just have to give them a common CSS class that can be used to tag them. If they have the same CSS class already, and are the only items on the page that do, the current CSS class can be used.

Let's say we created a class called `notrack`, and then, to this class, we added a link that we don't want to track.

```
<a href='http://site.com' class='notrack'>The Link</a>
```

Now that the link has a class, all we have to do is tell Piwik to ignore this class of links. We do this by calling `setIgnoreClasses` with the name of the class as `notrack`. This method also accepts an array of class names if you are ignoring more than one class.

```
...
piwikTracker.setIgnoreClasses("notrack");
piwikTracker.trackPageView();
...
```

You don't have to go this far if you don't want to. By adding the `piwik_ignore` class to any link in a tracked page, Piwik will ignore it.

```
<a href='http://site.com' class='piwik_ignore'>The Link</a>
```

Triggering link tracking

On the other hand, you may want to add link tracking to a link that Piwik does not recognize. Some sites don't link directly to a download file, but instead use a PHP file link to launch the download. To track a download link like this, you will need to tag the link manually. An easy way is to use a CSS class that Piwik already understands, like `piwik_download`.

```
<a href='download.php?id=1' class='piwik_download'>
The File</a>
```

Another way is to set your own classes that contain download links in the Piwik tracking code.

```
...
piwikTracker.setDownloadClasses("download");
piwikTracker.trackPageView();
...
```

Then mark all the download links with that class. The `setDownloadClasses` method will also accept an array of class names if you need to use more than one.

Some websites are configured to send outlinks through a PHP file first, to track external clicks within the CMS itself. Since these links appear to be on the same domain but actually redirect to other websites, the clickthroughs will not be counted as outlinks by Piwik. To manually tell Piwik to record a click on a link as an outlink, you have the same two options as you did with the download links: a special CSS class, or a function to set your own CSS classes.

You can mark links that you want to consider as outlinks in the `piwik_link` class.

```
<a href='http://site.com/myredirect.php?id=2'
class='piwik_link'>My Outlink</a>
```

Or you can set your own classes that will contain outlinks, using `setLinkClasses`.

```
...
piwikTracker.setLinkClasses("outlander");
piwikTracker.trackPageView();
...
```

This will make Piwik see all links with the `outlander` class as outlinks. There is yet another way to set outlinks—using JavaScript to trigger a click on an outlink (and this will work for other Piwik functions link page views or file downloads).

```
<a href="mailto:gmail@gmail.com" target="_blank" onClick="javascript:p
iwikTracker.trackLink('http://www.gmail.com
', 'link');">gmail@gmail.com</a>
```

This uses the Piwik function `trackLink`.

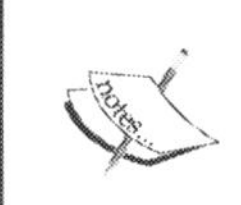

`trackLink(url, linkType)`: This function manually logs a click from your own code. `url` is the full URL that is to be tracked as a click. `linkType` can either be `link` for an outlink, or `download` for a download.

Downloading file extensions

By default, files with the following extensions are counted as downloads to Piwik:

```
7z | aac | arc | arj | asf | asx | avi | bin | bz| b z2 | csv | deb
| dmg | doc | exe | flv | gif | gz | gzip | hqx | jar | jpg | jpeg |
js | mp2 | mp3 | mp4 | mpg | mpeg | mov | movie | msi | msp | odb |
odf | odg | odp | ods | odt | ogg | ogv | pdf | phps | png | ppt | qt
| qtm | ra | ram | rar | rpm | sea | sit | tar | tbz | tbz2 | tgz |
torrent | txt | wav | wma | wmv|wpd | xls | xml | z | zip
```

You can replace this whole list by using the Piwik method `setDownloadExtensions`.

```
...
piwikTracker.setDownloadExtensions( "zip|rar|7z" );
piwikTracker.trackPageView();
...
```

Now, only files with `.zip`, `.rar`, and `.7zip` extensions will be tracked by this tracking code. Notice that this function accepts a string of extension names separated by the pipe character.

If all we want to do is add extensions to track to the default list, we can use `addDownloadExtensions`.

```
...
piwikTracker.addDownloadExtensions( "mp52|mp69" );
piwikTracker.trackPageView();
...
```

And now, our magical new advanced `mp52` and `mp69` files will be counted as downloads. This function uses the same pipe-delimited-string format for the extensions parameter.

The download/outlink pause timer

In order for Piwik to record a file download or a click on an outbound link, it must add a delay before the user is redirected to the file he wants or the link he is going to. This gives your Piwik installation time to record the action before the user is sent to his/her destination. The default value for this delay in Piwik is 500 milliseconds, but it can be manually set in the API code if you desire a shorter duration of delay time. If the delay time is too short though, you risk not tracking the data at all. Here is how you set the pause timer to 300 milliseconds, in our example in the tracking code:

```
piwikTracker.setLinkTrackingTimer(300);
piwikTracker.trackPageView();
```

Using other Piwik JavaScript API methods

Here are even more ways you can customize your Piwik JavaScript tracking code.

setRequestMethod(method)

This function will set the request method that Piwik uses to either the `GET` or `POST` methods. By default, this is set to `GET`. In order to set Piwik's request method to `POST`, your Piwik installation must be on the same server as the tracked website. Just add this function call above the `trackPageView` call in your tracking code, like so:

```
...
piwikTracker.setRequestMethod('POST');
piwikTracker.trackPageView();
...
```

Some hosting providers use `mod_security`, which blocks requests that contain URLs. In this case, Piwik will not be able to track URLs. If your hosting provider won't relax the settings for your account, one way around this `mod_security` issue is to set Piwik's request method to `POST`.

discardHashTag(bool)

By setting this method's Boolean value to `true`, you can have Piwik disregard hash tags in URLs. Add it before the call to `trackPageview`, like so:

```
...
piwikTracker.discardHashTag(true);
piwikTracker.trackPageView();
...
```

setCountPreRendered(bool)

WebKit-based browsers like Chrome can download your page resources in the background and cache them to improve the page load time of any linked resources. This is called prerendering. These days, even Google search results trigger prerendering of top search results, since there is a high chance of users clicking on top links. It is possible that prerendering may inflate page views.

Setting `setCountPreRendered` to true will track when pages get prerendered:

```
...
piwikTracker.setCountPreRendered(true);
piwikTracker.trackPageView();
...
```

setDoNotTrack(bool)

The "Do not track" setting, that allows users to notify the websites they are visiting that they do not wish to be tracked, is a feature offered by browsers. This is in the form of a a field in the HTTP header that the browser sends when it requests content from a website.

Although websites are currently not legally required to comply with the "Do not track" setting, the FTC called for a "Do not track" system as early as 2010. Mozilla browsers (Firefox), Internet Explorer, Safari, and Opera currently support this setting and Chrome will be supporting it by the end of 2012.

Very few websites recognize or respect this signal, because they are not required to, but Piwik has the `setDoNotTrack` method, which disables tracking for visitors who have set this setting in their browser. Just set its argument to true and add it before the `trackPageView` call in your Piwik tracking code.

```
...
piwikTracker.setDoNotTrack(true);
piwikTracker.trackPageView();
...
```

killFrame()

There may be many reasons why another website may frame your site. The social network StumbleUpon allows users to browse through, comment on, and pass along websites through the use of frames. Google translate uses frames to translate a web page from one language to another. So, the fact that another website is framing yours may actually benefit you. But another site could be using frames to steal traffic. So, there are trade-offs to using Piwik's `killFrame` method, which prevents websites from framing your site. This method will be called after `trackPageView`, unlike the Piwik methods we have examined so far. This will allow the page view of the framed version of your site to be counted.

```
...
piwikTracker.trackPageView();
piwikTracker.killFrame();
...
```

redirectFile(url)

This Piwik method forces the browser to load the live URL of a tracked website, if this page is loaded from a local file, for example, if someone saved it to their desktop. This "file buster" can be added before `trackPageView`. The URL parameter is optional. By default, this method redirects back to the URL of the saved page.

```
...
piwikTracker.redirectFile();
piwikTracker.trackPageView();
...
```

setHeartBeatTimer(minumumVisitLength,heartBeatDelay)

This Piwik JavaScript API method will help you tweak the way Piwik reports a visitor's time on a page, which also affects bounce rate. It is added before the `trackPageView` call.

```
...
piwikTracker.setHeartBeatTimer(2,5);
piwikTracker.trackPageView();
...
```

You will notice that this method has two parameters. The first is `minimumVisitLength`, which is the minimum time in seconds that you will count as a visit. The second parameter, `heartBeatDelay`, is the time in seconds between pings back to the Piwik server.

getVisitorId()

You can use this method if you ever need the 16-digit ID that Piwik creates for each visitor.

getVisitorInfo()

This Piwik method returns the contents of the visitor's Piwik cookie in an array.

Using multiple trackers

If you ever need to add more than one Piwik tracker per page, that is not a problem. You can do it and load `piwik.js` one time as it helps speed up page loading time. This works because each call to `Piwik.getTracker` will return a unique tracker object. It works even if each Piwik tracker is pointing at a different server. Here is an example of this in action:

```
<script type="text/javascript">
var protoCol = ('https:' == document.location.protocol ? 'https://' :
'http://');
document.write(unescape("%3Cscript src='" + protoCol + "URL_1/piwik.
js' type='text/javascript'%3E%3C/script%3E"));
</script><script type="text/javascript">
try {
var piwikTracker1 = Piwik.getTracker(protoCol + URL_1/piwik.php", 1);
piwikTracker1.trackPageView();
var piwikTracker2 = Piwik.getTracker(protoCol + URL_2/piwik.php", 4);
piwikTracker2.trackPageView();
} catch( err ) {}
</script>
```

This time the first part of the script only creates a `protoCol` variable instead of a complete base URL, so that `http://` or `https://` can be appended appropriately to either URL that we will be getting a Piwik tracker from.

Since we only need to use one instance of piwik.js, we just grabbed this from the first Piwik URL where URL_1 represents this URL. We could just as easily have included piwik.js from URL_2. An even smarter option when it comes to saving load time is to download piwik.js from one of the Piwik installations and upload it to the site we are tracking, so that it can be included in the pages from a local file.

Then we created two instances of Piwik.getTracker, calling one piwikTracker1 and the other piwikTracker2. We set the Piwik tracker URL and website ID for each when we create the trackers. Then call trackPageView with each tracker to register a page view with each Piwik installation.

You can also set the Piwik tracker URL and website ID of a Piwik tracker instance after it has been created instead of at its instantiation, due to the flexibility of the Piwik API.

```
var piwikTracker = Piwik.getTracker();
piwikTracker.setSiteId(2);
piwikTracker.setTrackerUrl("http://mysite.com/piwik/");
piwikTracker.trackPageView();
```

Here, we replaced Piwik.getTracker("http://mysite.com/piwik/", 2); with four lines of code. It is more code, but it may help with readability while learning how Piwik works.

We mentioned downloading the piwik.js file from your Piwik installation and uploading it to your tracked sites for local inclusion. This eliminates one more DNS lookup a visitor's browser has to do and can speed up load time. Another thing that can speed up load time when using Piwik's tracking code is asynchronous tracking.

Using asynchronous tracking

Traditionally, the JavaScript in an HTML page loads when a web page does, and if the code only has to execute to do its job and isn't designed to be triggered by a mouse click or some other user interaction, it executes right away. In fact, it must be executed before the browser can begin to render the page. And this can be a problem. Anything below the script or the location where the script is included in the page will be blocked until the browser executes that code.

But JavaScript code can be used to trigger the loading of other JavaScript code after the page itself has fully loaded. Loading JavaScript in this lazy fashion can visually speed up a site with heavy JavaScript a great deal. In truth, the total payload a browser has to download is the same, but the visual, readable elements load faster. Piwik supports asynchronous tracking for those sites that need it.

The asynchronous version of Piwik's tracking code has a few benefits. They are as follows:

- Because this code can execute in the background, without blocking other scripts and content in your site, your web pages will appear to load faster and visitor experience will be improved.
- Because this code is added to the head of the page, you will get a more accurate count of visits. The visit can be counted even if the complete web page does not load.

Piwik's asynchronous tracking code is a little different than the standard tracking code, but not by much. You can take a look at an example below:

```
<!-- Piwik --> <script type="text/javascript">
var _paq = _paq || [];
(function(){ var u=(("https:" == document.location.protocol) ?
"https://{$PIWIK_URL}/" : "http://{$PIWIK_URL}/");
_paq.push(['setSiteId', {$IDSITE}]);
_paq.push(['setTrackerUrl', u+'piwik.php']);
_paq.push(['trackPageView']);
_paq.push(['enableLinkTracking']);
var d=document, g=d.createElement('script'), s=d.
getElementsByTagName('script')[0];
g.type='text/javascript';
g.defer=true;
g.async=true;
g.src=u+'piwik.js';
s.parentNode.insertBefore(g,s); })();
 </script>
<!-- End Piwik Code -->
```

Here, `$PIWIK_URL` is the URL of your Piwik installation and `$IDSITE` is the ID of the site being tracked.

This code works by creating the `_paq` variable, which is a JavaScript array (a queue in which tracking events will be added). This variable will then be used to execute the code. The code first checks if `_paq` exists; it uses the existing `_paq` if it does. If not, it creates a new empty array. This prevents the removal of any events that may have been queued before our code executed.

```
var _paq = _paq || [];
```

Next, the HTTP or HTTPS version of Piwik's location is generated and placed in the variable `u`.

```
(function(){ var u=(("https:" == document.location.protocol) ?
"https://{$PIWIK_URL}/" : "http://{$PIWIK_URL}/");
```

After that, all the default functions in the standard Piwik tracker are pushed onto the end of the `_paq` array using the following syntax:

```
_paq.push([$Method_Name, $arg1,$arg2]);
```

Where `$Method_Name` is the Piwik API method and `$arg1` and `$arg2` are two example optional arguments (use them only if the method you are using requires them). You will notice in the tracking code above that `setSiteID` is pushed onto the `_paq` array with the ID of the site as the argument and when `trackPageView` is pushed onto the `_paq` array, it has no arguments.

Any function in Piwik's JavaScript API can be executed in the same way. For example, if you want to set the page name manually, you would just push the function onto the end of the `_paq` array, like so:

```
_paq.push(["setDocumentTitle",document.domain + "/" +
document.title]);
```

We've gone over the nuts and bolts of how to modify the asynchronous code. The magic happens in the final bit of code:

```
var d=document, g=d.createElement('script'), s=d.
getElementsByTagName('script')[0]; g.type='text/javascript';
g.defer=true;
g.async=true;
g.src=u+'piwik.js';
s.parentNode.insertBefore(g,s); })();
```

This JavaScript actually writes a line to include `piwik.js`. `piwik.js` is given the `defer` and `async` script attributes. Both of these attributes tell the browser that the code being included can be executed after everything on the page is done loading. Once the page is loaded, the `_paq` array is parsed and the functions executed.

Downloading the example code

You can download the example code files for all Packt books you have purchased from your account at `http://www.PacktPub.com`. If you purchased this book elsewhere, you can visit `http://www.PacktPub.com/support` and register to have the files e-mailed directly to you.

Summary

We covered a lot of ground in this chapter. We dug into Piwik's JavaScript tracking code and discovered how it does its job. We learned that it may be worthwhile for you to tweak the way you use Piwik, because not every website is the same. Then we examined what changes we could make to our tracking configuration. We dug into cookies and found out how we can change the cookies that Piwik sets. We learned how to customize the data Piwik receives, such as page names, page URLs, and referrer URLs, from a tracked website. We also set up some download and outlink tracking. And this is not even all you can do with the JavaScript API. We will be examining methods specific to campaigns, goals, e-commerce, and setting custom tracking variables in future chapters that are devoted to those topics.

In fact, the next chapter will be about setting up and tracking goals in Piwik, where we will learn how to use Piwik to measure and reach business objectives with website analytics.

4
Setting Up and Tracking Goals

If you don't have goals for your website to reach, you may be missing out on some of the features that Piwik provides for you. You would be tracking traffic for no real reason. If you have a website without analytics, you have no clue what is driving business to your site. A decade ago, anyone with a niche idea or product could, if he knew what he was doing, launch a website, start selling a product or products, and had a good chance of becoming relatively successful. Now, for any product you are selling at your online store, you can find 20 other stores selling the same thing. Having a dream and a little technical knowledge is not enough anymore. You have to build traffic. And you have to build traffic that converts. In order to even know that traffic is converting, you need an analytics system, such as Piwik, and you need goals for your website to reach. These goals can be as simple as having twice as many visitors next month to your blog, or as complex as increasing your average shopping cart's total by 25 percent.

This chapter will teach users how to measure and reach their business objectives using goal conversion tracking. The following is a list of the topics we will be covering:

- Defining goals
- Conversions and conversion rate
- Setting up goals in Piwik
- Using revenue tracking with goals
- Triggering conversions manually
- Using and reviewing goal reports

Defining goals

So what goals are you going to track with Piwik? What do you want your website or business as a whole to do? Identifying your goals helps you define what success is in your business. In fact, the process of defining concrete goals may help you redefine or tweak what you thought were your business goals because it forces you to quantify those goals.

Piwik or any web analytics software cannot track anything that is not quantifiable. If you can't put a number on it, there is no way for a software to analyse it. Having happier customers next month sounds like a great goal in your mind, and may work as a mantra you repeat to yourself every morning, but to be a goal in Piwik, you need numbers. A customer's happiness factor cannot really be measured. But you can count how many orders are completed at your website, so finalized orders are a perfect goal. But this may not be your only goal. If you have a newsletter on your e-commerce site, another goal of yours could be newsletter signups, as these can also be counted.

But a newsletter signup doesn't bring in any money. How can it be a goal? It is a goal because not every goal instantly adds revenue. **Transaction goals** do add to your revenue. Transactional goals are any goals that have a monetary value. The second type of goal is **engagement goals** which don't initially have a cash value but build brand equity and future conversions. Newsletter signups, product demo downloads, and comments are examples of engagement goals. Although transactional goals affect your business as it stands, it is possible that those customers who complete engagement goals could be more valuable in the long run in future transactions. One newsletter signup can result in many future completed transaction goals.

With engagement goals in the picture, anything seems like it could be a goal, even a page view. But adding too many goals can clutter your data and defeat the purpose of making goals in the first place. Goals should simplify viewing your data. The amount of data Piwik can present in over thirty widgets can be overwhelming and unnecessary. By setting a goal, you narrow down this data to the exact metric you need. So a goal should be something more than a page view even though a page view might be the end result that triggers the goal to be counted.

A website goal should be aligned with business objectives. Goals are not new. They have been around since before the Internet. A website just makes everything easier to track. A goal could be something that:

- Increases revenue
- Cuts cost
- Drives interest
- Generates leads
- Builds subscribers
- Increases usage
- Raises awareness
- Raises engagement

Some questions you may ask yourself when defining goals for your website are:

- What is the main purpose of your website?
- What type of marketing do you use to drive visitors to your site?
- What percentage of business comes from your website?
- How do you define online success?

Desired actions

Once you have a list of your goals, it is time to map these goals to a **desired action**, and then find a method of measuring that action. We are going to turn the vagueness of a goal like raising awareness into downloading an informational PDF, and then find a way to measure that action in a way that Piwik can track.

Having a visitor complete an order is an obvious goal on an e-commerce site because it increases revenue. To measure this action, you will use page views on the Payment success page of your software. Each time a visitor loads this page, we know a sale has been made, and we can add a one to our Completed sale goal.

But what about visits to your FAQ page, chat usage, or contact form submission? For larger businesses with a lot of phone calls, these types of visitor actions can cut costs and could be considered a transaction goal because as the old saying goes, "a penny saved is a penny earned". So, in this case we would find the chat links and measure the actions by tracking the clicks on it.

In the case of paid advertising links, a goal could be to have a visitor click on a link that takes them away from your site. If advertisers are paying for a banner or a link because they want traffic, sending more traffic through a link rather than less could be a transactional goal that allows you to charge more for your advertising slots. In this case, you would make sure a goal is triggered when a visitor clicks on the link to this external website. Some other desired actions might be:

- Signing up for a newsletter
- Viewing or requesting product demo
- Download Viewing software, whitepapers, or videos
- Giving feedback on a product or service
- Leaving a comment on a blog
- Completing a registration form
- Personalizing a profile
- Watching a video
- Viewing a certain amount of pages
- Staying on the site for a specific amount of time
- Interacting with Flash elements

Conversions and conversion rate

When a visitor reaches a goal, we say that the visitor has converted or a **conversion** has happened. In order to evaluate how well our website converts visitors over time, we use the **conversion rate**, which is the percentage of your traffic that takes a desired action, or ratio of conversion to unique visits.

Once you have chosen your goals and desired actions, the conversion rate of each desired action will become your main focus. It is this metric that you will improve over time by tuning and tweaking your website. It also helps determine how well your search engine marketing efforts are working out. When you set up campaigns in Piwik as well as goals, you can see just how well specific marketing efforts are converting. We will learn more about marketing campaigns in the next chapter.

One example of a goal would be increasing revenue to $1 per 100 page views. Let's say it is currently at $0.75 per 100 page views. You now have a goal you can measure. As you tune your site, you obviously want this revenue to increase, and any decrease in revenue per page view would be a wrong turn. This goal will be your gauge to measure any changes.

Now that we have a good idea of what we want our website to do and what actions visitors must take in order to achieve our business goals, it is time to learn how we can track and analyse these actions with Piwik.

Setting up goals in Piwik

The goals functionality of Piwik is actually a plugin that can be enabled or disabled in the **Settings | Plugins** page. By default, it is enabled. In fact, most of Piwik's features come through the use of plugins. **Plugins** are bundles of code files and supporting media that will add functionality to Piwik. By making even some of the core functionality of Piwik available as plugins, Piwik developers have made their software highly configurable and modifiable.

To create a goal, first make sure that the website that you wish to create a goal for is chosen in the **Website** drop-down menu. Then, click on the **Goals** link in the main Piwik menu:

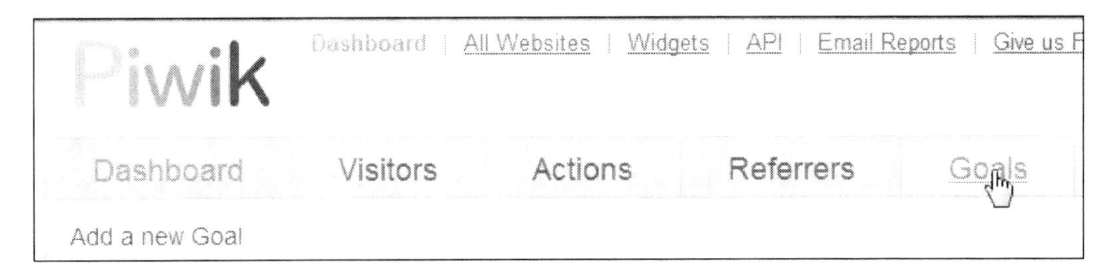

This will take you to the **Goals** dashboard, or when you have yet to create any goals, to the **Goal creation** page:

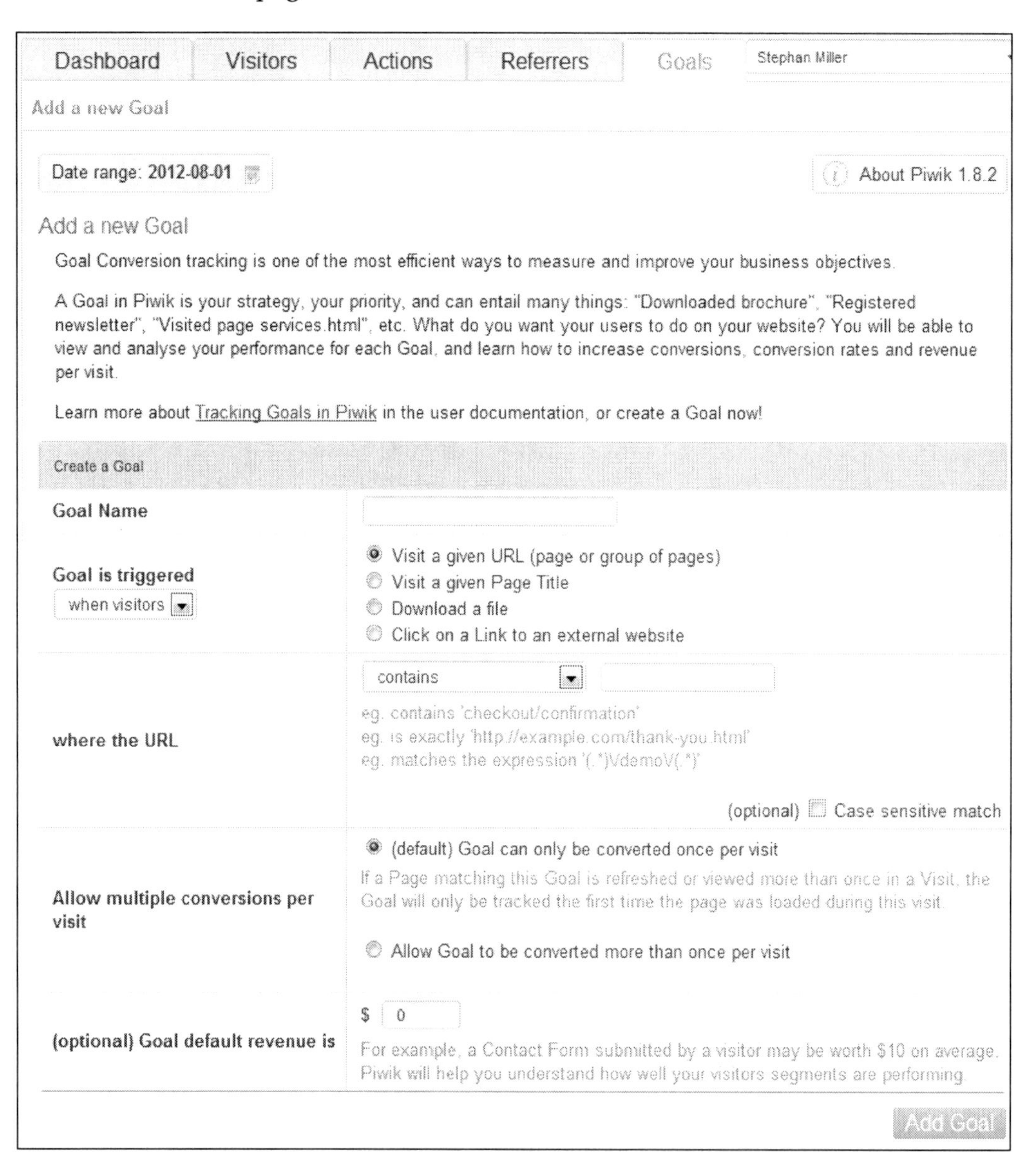

The first field on the page you will see is **Goal Name** where you add the name of the goal you are going to be tracking or more likely, the name of the desired action you want your visitor to complete. As we read earlier in this chapter, a goal is more of a business objective, such as increasing revenue or getting more paid newsletter subscribers. If there is more than one avenue on your site that visitors can travel to complete these goals, then it is likely you will need to create a goal in Piwik for each of these avenues, although the goal may be the same.

But let's not get bogged down in semantics. Just name your goal something that you can easily identify, and leave room for future goals that may fit in the same basket. Make it short enough to read quickly, and long enough to understand alongside similarly named goals. If you have only a few goals, names like "Newletter Subscription" and "PDF Download" will work. If you have similar goals, you may want to try "Newsletter Subscription - Taxes and Newsletter Subscription - Real Estate".

The next row in the form is where you will be setting how the goal is triggered. You can choose to trigger the goal based on a visitor's action, or manually trigger the goal. When you use a visitor's action to trigger the goal, you have four choices of actions to choose from. They are as follows:

- Visiting a given URL
- Visiting a given page title
- Downloading a file
- Clicking on a link to an external website

Each one of these values is a string of characters that Piwik can filter in a few ways. Only those URLs or page title strings that match the filter get tracked as a goal. The next row in the table will allow you to set this filter:

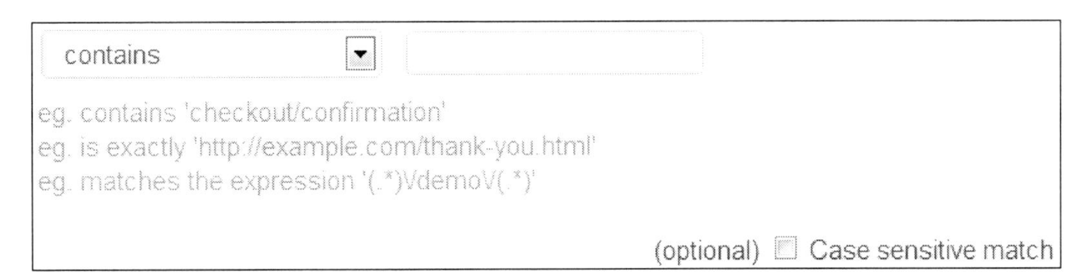

The default filter is **contains**. It will trigger a conversion if the URL or page title contains the string you enter in the field beside it. Entering the string `checkout/confirmation` in the field will cause a goal to be triggered for any one of the following pages:

- `http://mysite.com/checkout/confirmation?ses=5d4g6s54`
- `http://mysite.com/checkout/confirmation/ses/df2s44f55`
- `http://mysite.com/checkout/confirmation/dl2d45f65`

Another option you can also choose is **exactly**, which only does an exact match, although by default it is not case sensitive. If you want to make any match case sensitive, you can check the box labeled **Case sensitive match**. You will have to enter complete URLs and complete page titles in order to trigger the conversion correctly.

The last option **matches the expression** involves using **regular expressions** which is a specialized syntax for matching a particular pattern of characters. It is much more advanced than using the **contains** option. A discussion of regular expressions is beyond the scope of this book, but if you know them, this might be the option to choose for really complicated URLs and page names.

In the next row, we can choose whether or not we are going to allow multiple conversions per visit. A shopping-cart site is a good example of where you would want multiple goals per visit. If you set a goal of adding a product to a shopping cart, this can happen more than once per visit. But if your goal is something like downloading a PDF file, you would want to leave this set at default. If a visitor downloads the same PDF multiple times, it will still only be one conversion.

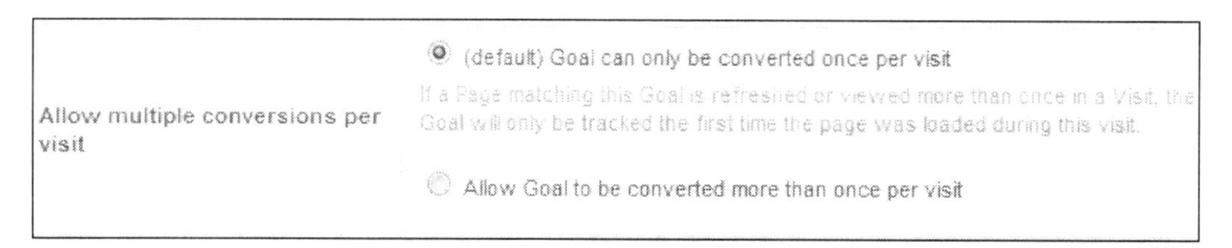

Next we have revenue tracking, which we will cover in the next section.

Setting up revenue tracking

You may want to set up revenue tracking even if your website is not of the e-commerce variety. Unless you are just blogging to blog, your interest in reading this book probably has to do with the fact that your website in one way or another makes you some money.

Now you may have a website that is not much more than an online business card with two or three pages giving visitors the basics of what your business does. The fact is you are still making money with it just like you do with a Yellow Pages ad, actually more. This is the 21st century. The Internet makes it so much easier to track revenue that is hard to track in the paper and phone line world. A contact form or free estimate form is the perfect candidate for revenue tracking. All you need to know is how much each filled form is worth to you.

The good news is that you don't have to worry about setting up e-commerce tracking if your website makes you money. It would probably be overkill in some cases. But there may be times when the opposite is true. You may want to set up e-commerce tracking for a website that does not take credit cards. We will get to that in *Chapter 7, E-commerce Tracking*. E-commerce tracking deserves its own chapter. But if you only have a few goals on your website that you can attach revenue to, then tracking revenue along with a goal will be the best choice. If you charge for ad space on your site and charge your advertisers $1 per 100 views, then you would want to create a goal for each view of your ad. Then you would add a revenue value of $0.01 to this goal.

You will be using the last field in the **Goal** form to enter this revenue:

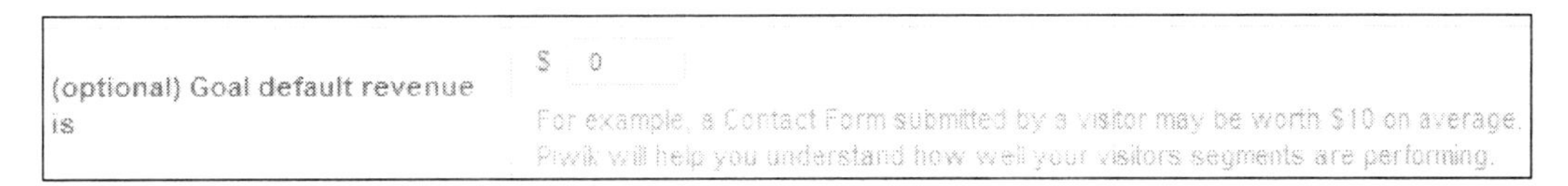

Now, if for some reason, the currency shown in the form is not the currency of your country, there is an easy fix. First, click on the **Settings** link in the top-left corner of Piwik's interface:

Then click on the **Websites** tab as shown in the next screenshot:

Currency is set on a site-by-site basis in Piwik. This is handy for Piwik installations that track websites for owners who are around the world. Click on the **Edit** link next to the website whose currency you want to change as shown in the next screenshot:

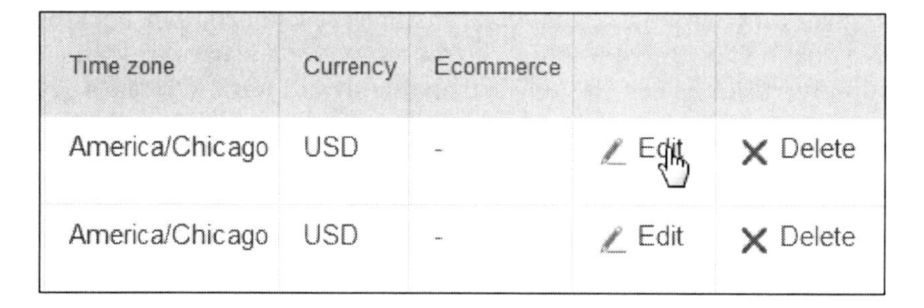

After clicking on the link, you may have to scroll horizontally in order to reach the **Currency** field:

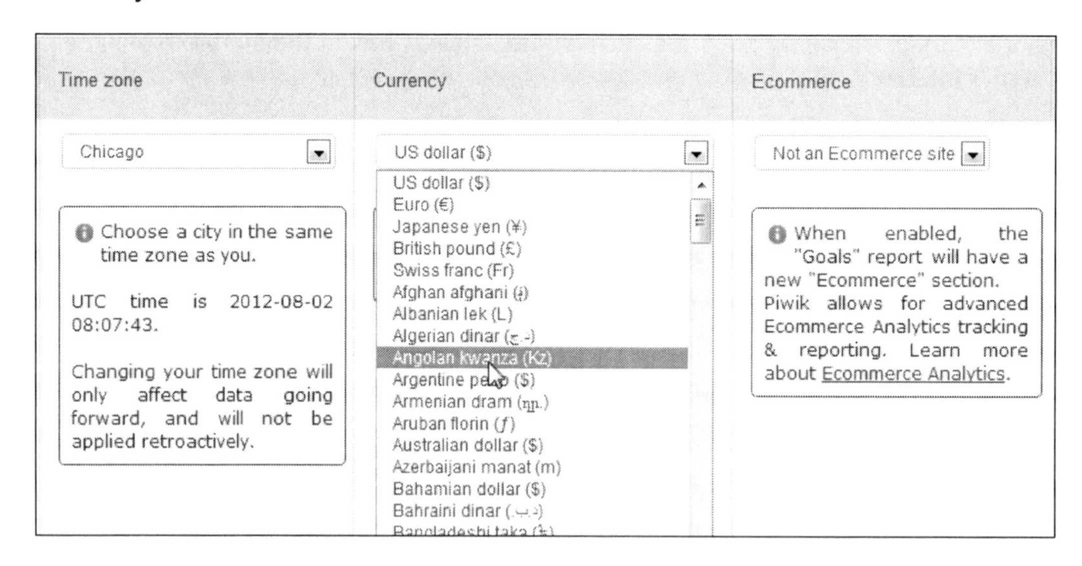

From the drop-down field in the form, choose your desired currency, whether peso, yen or franc, or one of the other dozens of currencies available. Where you once clicked **Edit**, there should now be a **Save** button to save your changes.

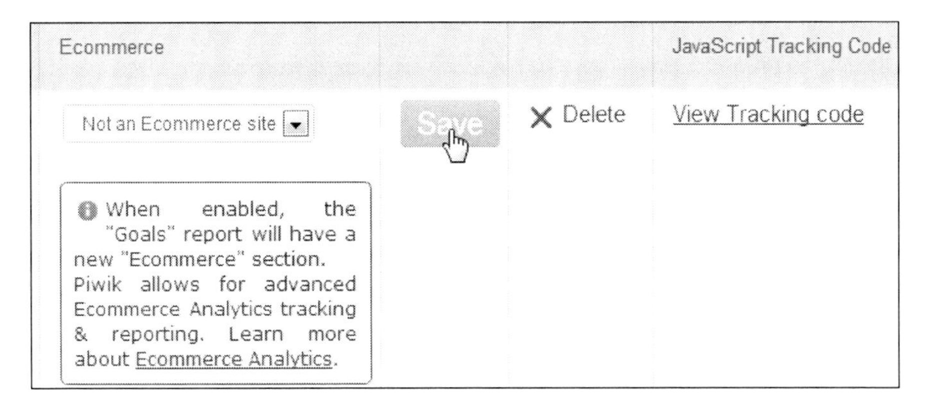

You will notice the **Ecommerce** drop down. If we have more than a few goals that we add revenue to, setting our site up with e-commerce tracking would be the best choice. But we will get to that in *Chapter 7, E-commerce Tracking*. Now that we have the correct currency set up, we can add revenue tracking to our goal. But we have yet to figure out what our goal is worth.

Over time, you will begin to pick up sales off your free estimate or contact form, and if your Internet staff is doing their job, they will be logging where these sales come from. From that, you can build an average revenue per contact or estimate form submission. When you have that average, you can edit the goal's default revenue to reflect that average value. It is good to revisit this average periodically and update the goal's revenue, because the value may change over time.

Triggering conversions manually

In the last chapter, we learned about changes we could make to Piwik's JavaScript code or the HTML of our web pages to manually trigger page views, link clicks, or download actions. There may be times that you have to do this with your conversions. In fact, many types of goals may have to be manually triggered, because there is just no other way to do it. Some of these cases are:

- When a visitor submits a contact form
- When a visitor comments on a blog
- When a visitor plays an embedded movie
- When a visitor plays a game
- When a visitor has stayed on site for a given period of time

In each of these cases, a conversion will never be logged by using any of the standard rules that we set up to trigger a goal. There is no page title to match, no file to download, and no outbound link to click. We will have to trigger the conversion ourselves.

We are going to create a goal now that will be triggered manually, so go back to the **Goals** tab on Piwik's main menu and we will get started. Let's create a **Newsletter Subscription** goal.

We will assume that the newsletter subscription form is a standard HTML form. If a form posts to a page other than the page it is located on, and you have added Piwik's JavaScript tracking code to that page, there is no need to manually trigger a conversion. Piwik will automatically handle it. But in this case, we are going to send the form posts back to its page.

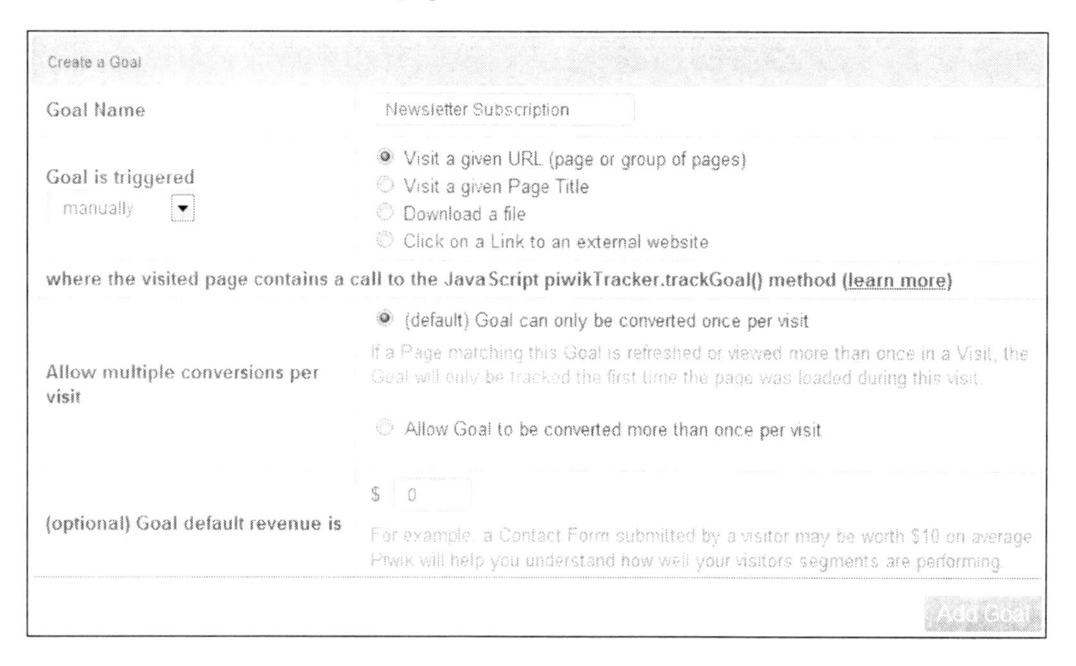

Name your goal and chose **manually** from the **Goal is triggered** field. We will be allowing the goal to be triggered once per visit, the default setting, since a visitor can subscribe to a newsletter only once per visit anyway. We will assume we were smart enough to set up tracking at the same time we started our newsletter, so we know we might make some money but have not made any yet, so we can leave the **Goal default revenue is** field with its default of **0**. Later, when the money comes rolling in, we can edit the goal and add revenue tracking.

Click on the **Add Goal** button. You will see the new **Newsletter Subscription** link in your **Goals** menu:

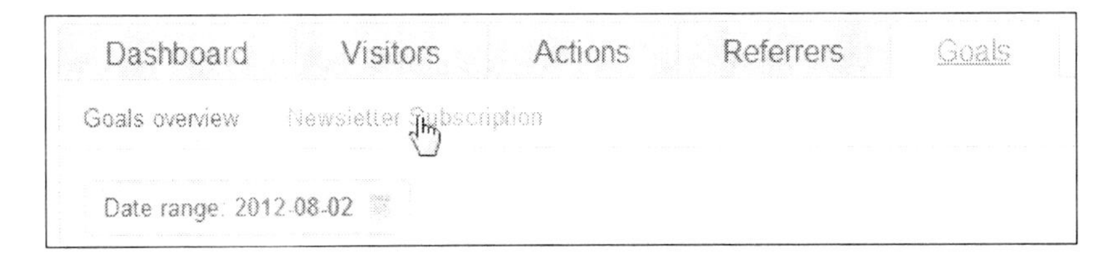

Now in order to trigger a conversion, we will need to know the ID that Piwik gave this goal. So click on either the **Goals overview** link or on the **Goals** link in the main menu. Either link will take you to the **Goals overview** dashboard:

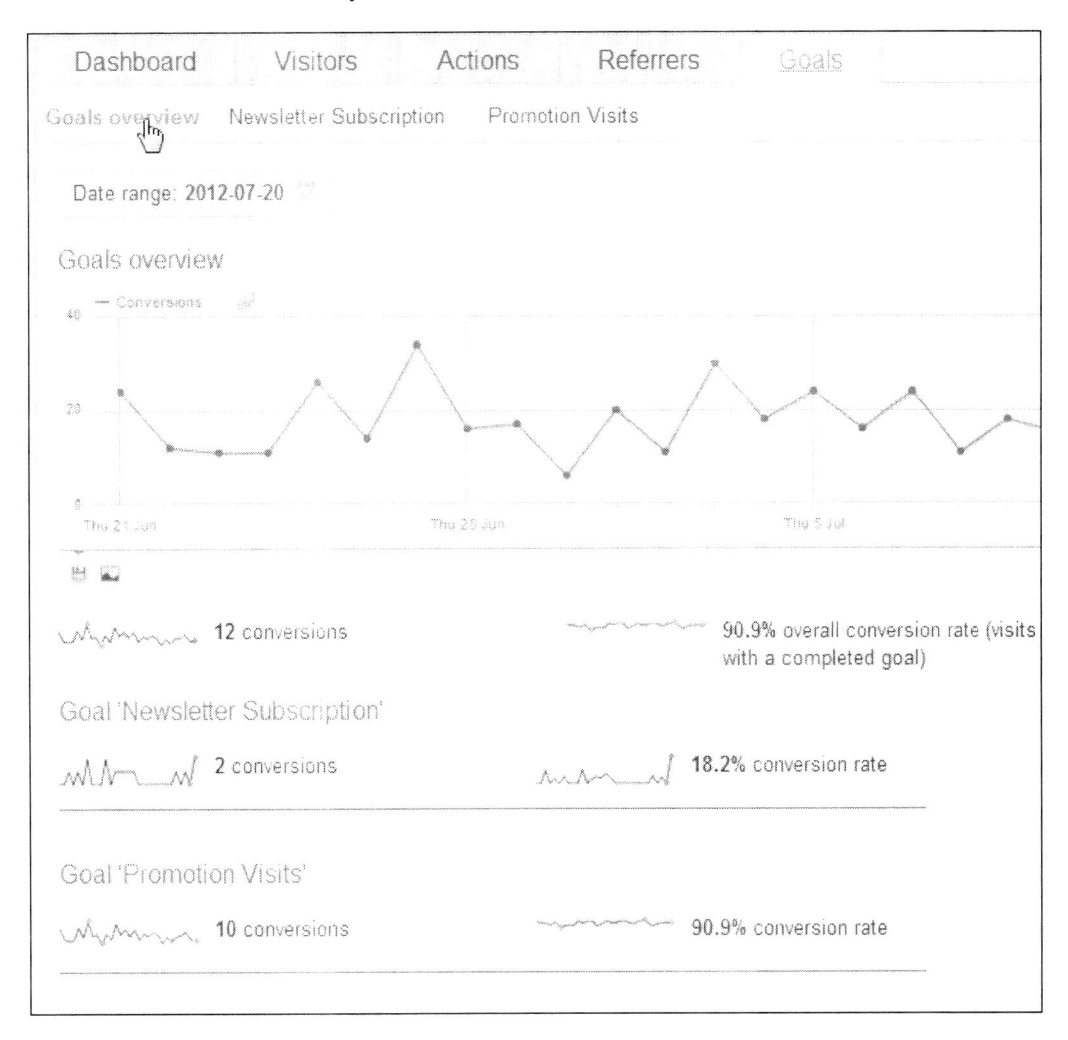

Scroll to the bottom of the page and click on the **View and Edit Goals** link. When you do, a table containing the list of your goals will open at the bottom of the page:

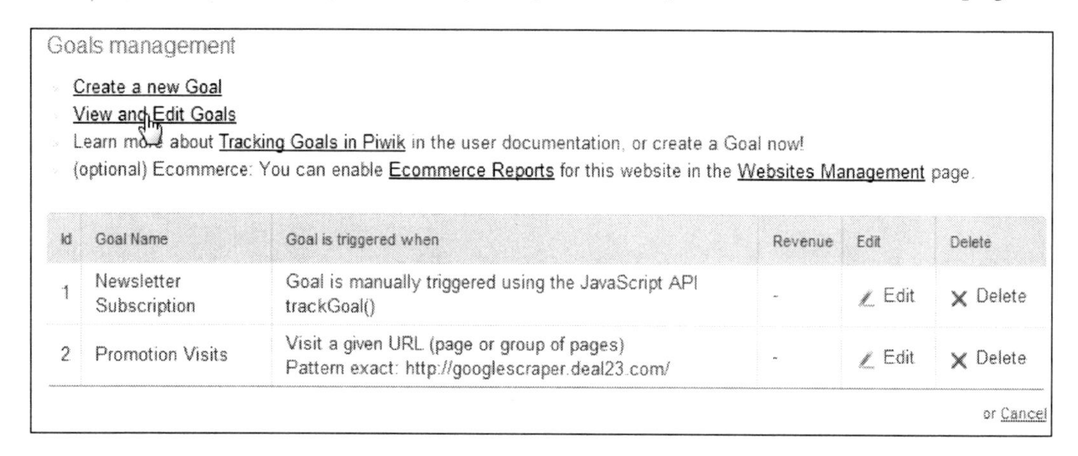

From this menu you can edit or delete goals. Once we have some money coming in, we will have to come back and add revenue to this goal. But for now all we need is the **Id** in the left-hand side of the table.

Triggering a goal manually involves calling your Piwik tracker's `trackGoal` function with the ID of the goal you are tracking.

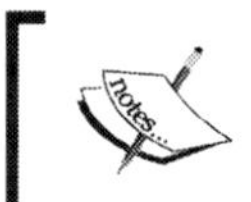

`trackGoal(idGoal, [customRevenue])`: Manually logs a conversion for the goal `idGoal`, passing in the custom revenue `customRevenue`, if specified.

You will notice that you can also add custom revenue as a parameter. This is good if you have to set the revenue for any goal dynamically. Let's say you had a website that charged for video by the minute. You might have to go back to the 1990s first in order to make this business profitable, but stick with me. If you set a simple goal of having a visitor just watch a movie, you could find out what amount of money the average visitor spent over time, edit your goal, and put this average in. But you could track revenue down to the penny by passing in a custom revenue number based on the length of time the visitor watched the movie.

But for now, let's get back to our newsletter. Here is what I have in the newsletter subscription page:

```
<!DOCTYPE html PUBLIC "-//W3C//DTD XHTML 1.0 Strict//EN"
    "http://www.w3.org/TR/xhtml1/DTD/xhtml1-strict.dtd">
<html xmlns="http://www.w3.org/1999/xhtml">
<head>
```

```
  <title>My Subscription Page</title>
</head>
<body>
  <form method="post">
    <table class="mySubscriptionForm" border="0" cellpadding="2">
      <tbody>
        <tr>
          <td>First Name:</td>

          <td><input id="firstname" name="firstname" size="50"
type="text" /></td>
        </tr>

        <tr>
          <td>Last Name:</td>

          <td><input id="lastname" name="lastname" size="50"
type="text" /></td>
        </tr>

        <tr>
          <td>Your email address:</td>

          <td><input name="email" type="text" /></td>
        </tr>

        <tr>
          <td><input type="submit" value="Subscribe" /></td>
        </tr>
      </tbody>
    </table>
  </form>
  <!-- Piwik -->
   <script type="text/javascript">
   var pkBaseURL = (("https:" == document.location.protocol) ?
"https:$MyPiwikUrl" : "http://$MyPiwikUrl");
   document.write(unescape("%3Cscript src='" + pkBaseURL + "js/'
type='text/javascript'%3E%3C/script%3E"));
   </script><script type="text/javascript">
   try {
     var piwikTracker = Piwik.getTracker(pkBaseURL + "piwik.php", 5);
     piwikTracker.trackPageView();
     piwikTracker.enableLinkTracking();
   } catch( err ) {}
```

```
    </script><noscript><p><img src="http://ec2-50-19-0-18.compute-1.
amazonaws.com/piwik/piwik.php?idsite=5" style="border:0" alt="" /></
p></noscript>
    <!-- End Piwik Tracking Code -->
</body>
</html>
```

You can see our Piwik tracking code at the bottom of the web page. A page on an actual website would have much more content, and most likely some PHP code to capture the form's data once it is submitted back to the page, but we will work with this.

There are a few ways we can call `trackGoal`. Since visitors will have to click the **Submit** button on our page to subscribe, we will use JavaScript's `onclick` to tell Piwik to track the goal. First we need to locate the submit button in the HTML.

```
<tr>
          <td><input type="submit" value="Subscribe" /></td>
        </tr>
      </tbody>
    </table>
  </form>
```

It is near the bottom of the form right before the Piwik tracker. Since the `id` of the newsletter subscriber goal was 1, we just modify the page, as shown in the following code:

```
<tr>
          <td><input type="submit" value="Subscribe"
onclick="piwikTracker.trackGoal(1);"/></td>
        </tr>
      </tbody>
    </table>
  </form>
```

Now when a visitor clicks on the button to subscribe, Piwik will add one goal conversion to the **Newsletter Subscription** goal. This method of triggering a goal conversion will work even if you use a newsletter subscription service offsite to handle your subscribers, because all it depends on is a click.

But let's say that we are getting paid $1 for each of these newsletter subscriptions. We could edit the goal and set a default revenue. The other option is to set it when we track the goal.

```
        <tr>
          <td><input type="submit" value="Subscribe"
onclick="piwikTracker.trackGoal(1,1);"/></td>
        </tr>
      </tbody>
    </table>
  </form>
```

In this code snippet, the first `1` in the call to `trackGoal` is the goal's ID and the second `1` is the dollar we are getting paid for each subscription.

There is more than one way that you can trigger a goal manually. All you have to do is call `trackGoal`. But sometimes you may have to get creative in order to trigger this function. Let's say we are using a link cloaker, which is an intermediate page on your site that dynamically loads an offsite link, making the link on the page look like it is a local link. Clicking on the link will not trigger a page visit and the link itself is not pointing offsite. So a goal using these types of links would have to be triggered manually, but the question is how?

Further on in the book, we will learn about Piwik's analytics API, which would be a good solution to this problem. The analytics API allows you to trigger a goal with programming languages other than JavaScript, such as PHP. In this case, we could use a call to this API in the redirect page and have PHP add another conversion goal. But we can also do the trick with a little JavaScript.

We could create a page that redirects with a meta-refresh rather than programmatically through PHP. Here is the page source when downloaded by a browser. Keep in mind that the URL `http://myoutlink` was generated by PHP on the server side. But we aren't worried about that. Take a look at how the goal conversion gets triggered:

```
<!DOCTYPE html PUBLIC "-//W3C//DTD XHTML 1.0 Strict//EN"
    "http://www.w3.org/TR/xhtml1/DTD/xhtml1-strict.dtd">
<html xmlns="http://www.w3.org/1999/xhtml">
<head>
  <meta http-equiv="refresh" content="1;url=http://myoutlink" />
</head>
<body>
```

```
  <!-- Piwik --><script type="text/javascript">
//<![CDATA[
  var pkBaseURL = (("https:" == document.location.protocol) ?
"https://$PIWIK_URL" : "http://$PIWIK_URL");
  document.write(unescape("%3Cscript src='" + pkBaseURL + "piwik.js'
type='text/javascript'%3E%3C/script%3E"));
  //]]>
  </script><script type="text/javascript">
//<![CDATA[
  try {
  var piwikTracker = Piwik.getTracker(pkBaseURL + "piwik.php", $SITE_
ID);
  piwikTracker.trackGoal(1);
  //piwikTracker.trackPageView();
  //piwikTracker.enableLinkTracking();
  } catch( err ) {}
  //]]>
  </script><noscript>
  <p><img src="$PIWIK_URL/piwik.php?idsite=1" style="border:0" alt=""
/></p></noscript>
  <!-- End Piwik Tracking Code -->
</body>
</html>
```

When this page loads, the following line in the header of the page causes the page to stay loaded for one second and then redirect to `http://myoutlink`.

```
<meta http-equiv="refresh" content="1;url=http://myoutlink" />
```

The number `1` before the semicolon is the duration in seconds that the browser will wait before redirecting to our link. This gives the Piwik tracking code, which makes up most of the page, time to work. Notice that we have `piwikTracker.trackGoal(1)` in there. This time we track the goal the instant the code is done loading, because we know the user is about to get redirected to our link. I have also commented out `piwikTracker.trackPageView()` and `piwikTracker.enableLinkTracking()` because this is not really a page view, only a redirect, and we don't need link tracking because there are no links on the page.

Now let's look at some reports in the next section.

Viewing Goals overview reports

The **Goal overview** report will allow you to see the stats on all your goals for a chosen website. It combines the data for a broad overview of how your website is converting.

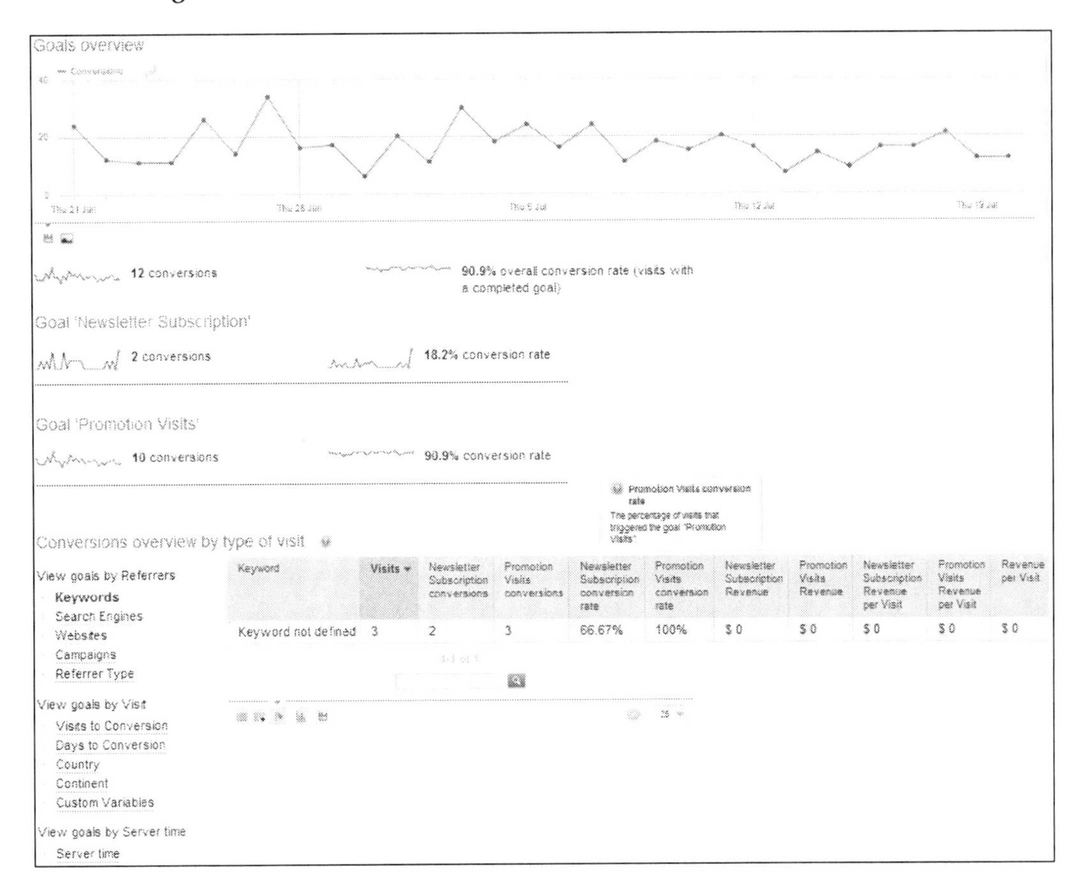

At the top of the page is a chart of your conversions across time. Using the **Date range** drop-down, you can set your date range as discussed in *Chapter 2, Using Piwik's Interface and Reports*. You can also add other metrics to the chart to see more data simultaneously.

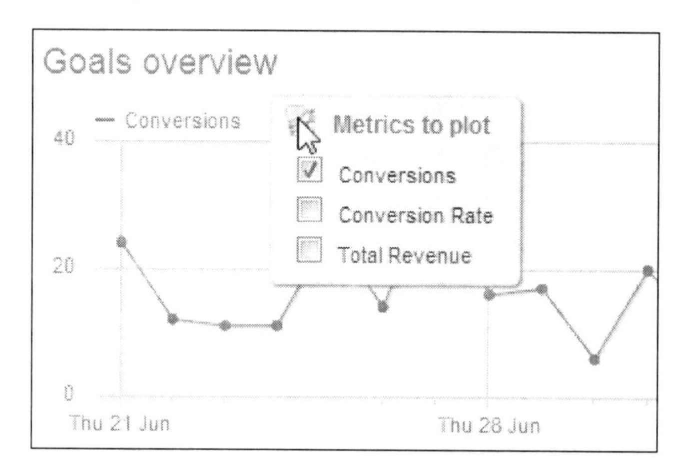

The metrics available are:

- **Conversions**
- **Conversion Rate**
- **Total Revenue**

The following is an example of the graph with the conversion rate added. Notice that conversion rate percentages of 8 percent and 4 percent also appeared on the left-hand side of the chart with the new line.

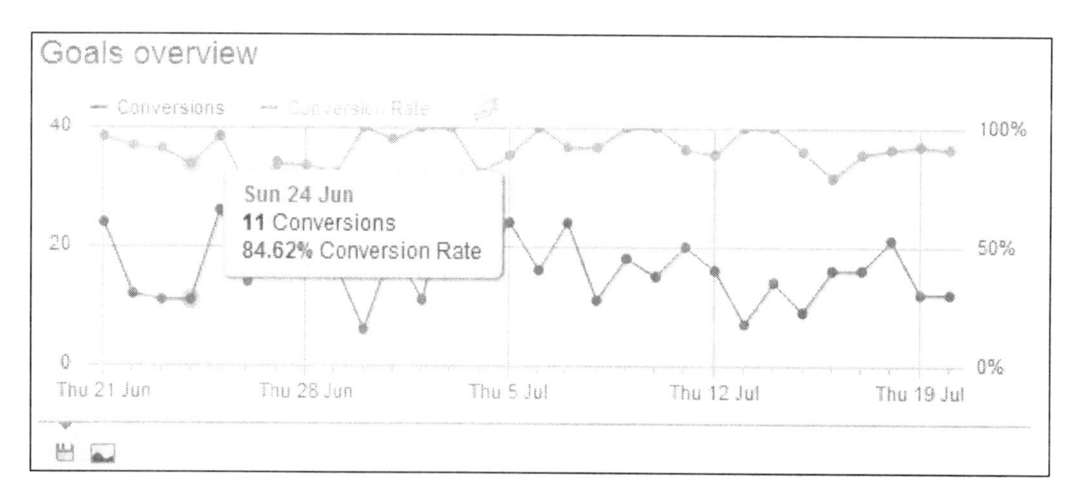

Below the chart, on the left-hand side, you will notice the familiar buttons for modifying and using your chart. The first button will change the chart style to a bar graph. The second button will allow you to export the data in **CSV**, **TSV (Excel)**, **XML**, **Json**, **Php** array, or RSS feed format.

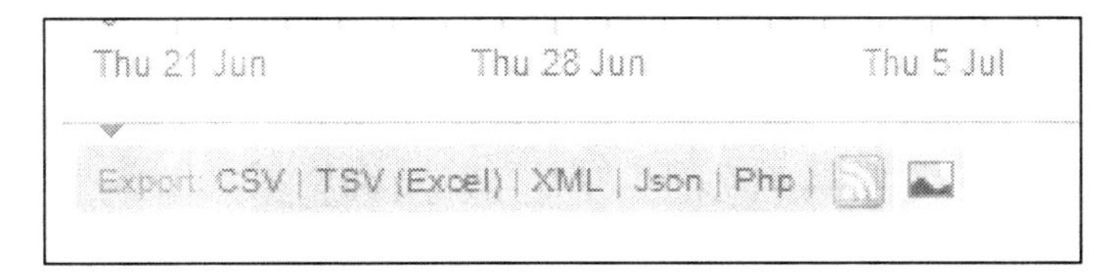

The third button will create a lightbox style popup of the chart that you can right-click and save to your desktop.

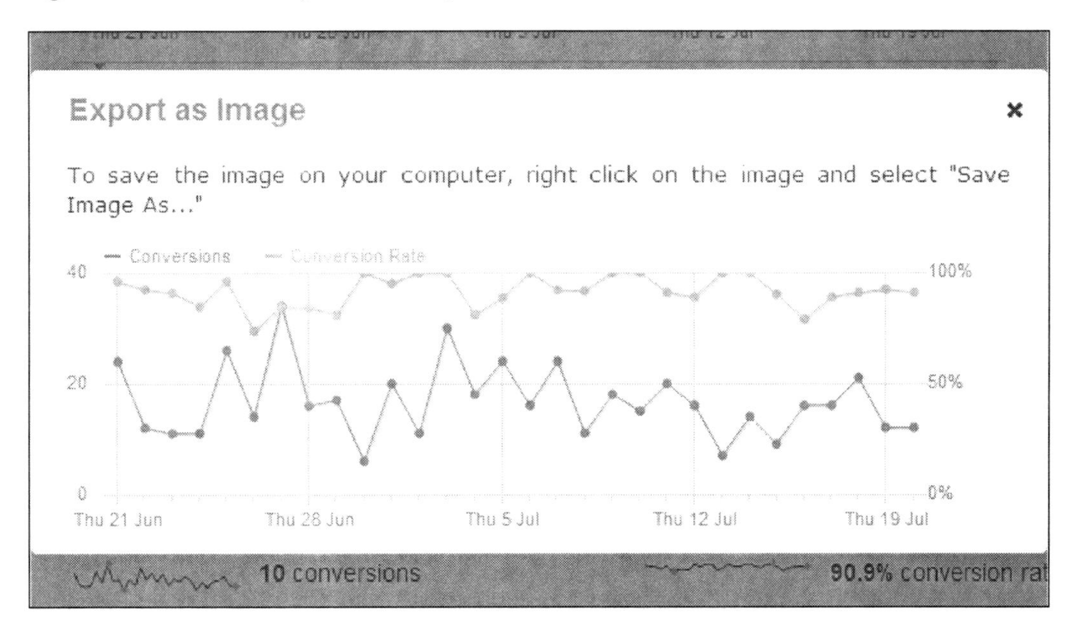

Below the chart is a simple breakdown of all of your goals, followed by each one of your goals. Each will show a miniature chart for your conversions, conversion rate, and revenue over your selected time period.

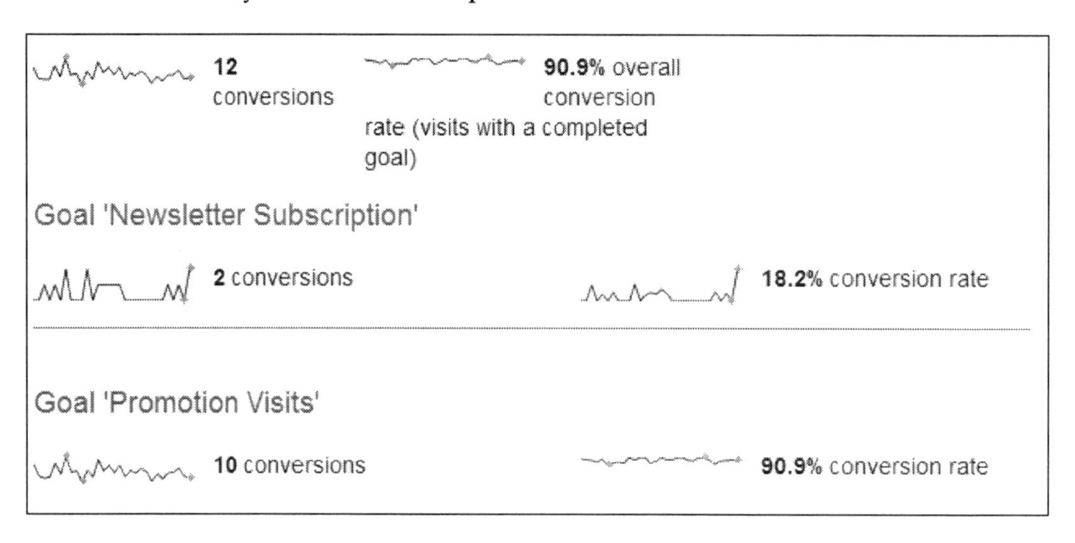

Underneath that section is **Conversions overview by type of visit:**

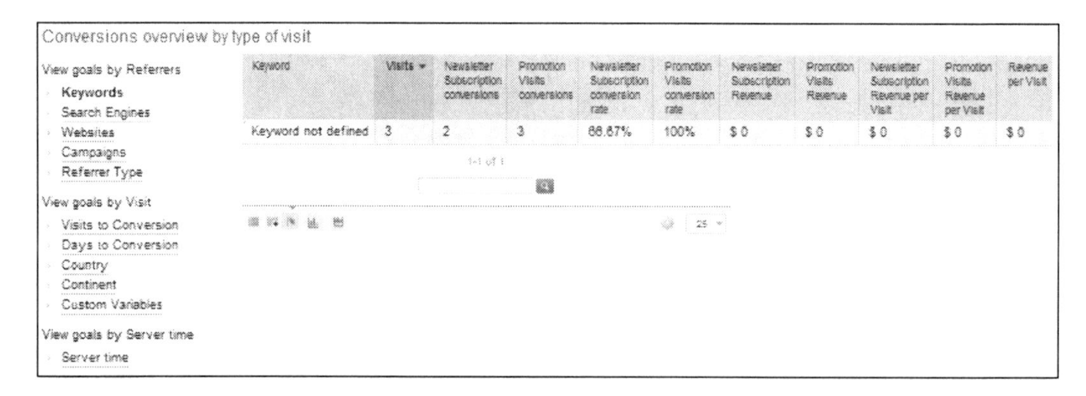

This overview presents the data from all the goals and conversions on your website as a whole. On the left-hand side of the page is your choice of reports. In the middle is the report currently selected. In the previous screenshot, the **Keywords** report is selected. Most of the reports, such as **Keyword**, **Search Engines**, **Websites**, **Campaigns,** and **Referrer Type** are available in this menu as tables:

Keyword	Visits	Newsletter Subscription conversions	Promotion Visits conversions	Newsletter Subscription conversion rate	Promotion Visits conversion rate	Newsletter Subscription Revenue	Promotion Visits Revenue	Newsletter Subscription Revenue per Visit	Promotion Visits Revenue per Visit	Revenue per Visit
Keyword not defined	3	2	3	66.67%	100%	$ 0	$ 0	$ 0	$ 0	$ 0

In the table, you'll see a list of the segments for each one of the visit types. In the previous **Keyword** table, we see a column of keywords, and for each of these keywords, the following data for each goal is shown as well as the data for all goals as a whole:

- Conversions
- Conversion Rate
- Revenue
- Revenue per Visit

The **Visits to Conversion** report displays a simple table of data:

Visits to Conversion	Conversions
1 visit	10
2 visits	1
3 visits	0
4 visits	0
5 visits	0
6 visits	0
7 visits	1
8 visits	0
9-14 visits	0
15-25 visits	0
26-50 visits	0
51-100 visits	0
101+ visits	0

Using goal detail reports

If you want to view the stats for only one goal, you would choose a **Goal details** report. Goal detail reports can be viewed by choosing the goal in the goal's sub-menu:

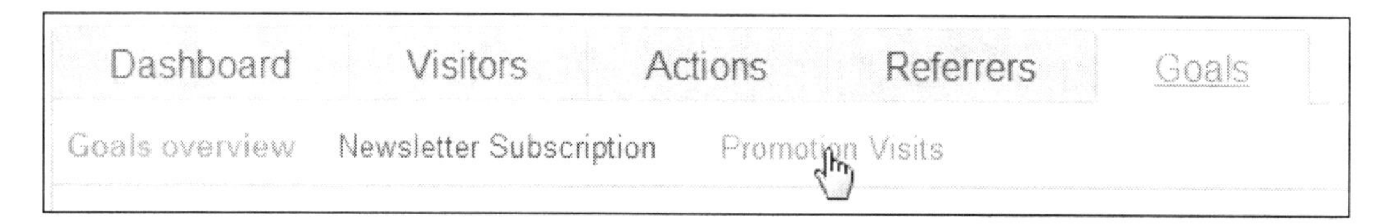

There are only a few differences in the goal detail report when compared to the goal overview report. These differences are:

- All data presented is for the specific goal rather than all goals as a whole
- Detail reports have a **Conversions Overview** section

The **Conversions Overview** report takes the data from the goal **Promotion Visits** by type of visit and gives you a summary of your best performing segments. It will tell you:

- Top converting countries
- Top converting keywords
- Best converting websites
- The conversion rate of returning visitors
- The conversion rate of new visitors

Conversions Overview

- Your best converting countries are: United States, Poland and Indonesia
- Returning visitors conversion rate is **100.0%**, New visitors conversion rate is **88.9%**

Analysing reports

Now that you have all these reports, you may be wondering what to do with them. The simple answer is make the conversions, conversion rate, and revenue go up. Most websites are losing out on revenue because they don't change anything to increase their conversion rate. With Piwik, you have a tool where you can test changes and see the results in a few days to a few weeks depending on your daily traffic. There is always room for improvement and always tests to do.

- Increase the visibility of your top performing product and see if revenue increases
- Change the prices on a product and see if there is a sales goal increase
- Reword a sales page and see if conversions pick up
- Try a special offer or coupon and see if revenue increases
- Add a bonus to a product and see if the conversion rate is better
- Move your newsletter subscription form above the fold of your page and see if you get more subscriptions
- Add a product guarantee and see if you sell more of that product
- Add testimonials and see if that affects your conversion rate
- Change the design of your web page to emphasize the video section of your website and see how much that increases viewing of videos

The list is endless. Website tuning, as it is called, is an art and science that is beyond the scope of this book. It takes a mix of web design, general design, psychology, and usability to fully explore website tuning, but some of the concepts are simple, like price changes and visibility.

So the process of tuning your website goes something like this:

1. Find the goals that apply to your website.
2. Brainstorm and research changes you can make to improve the conversion rate for the goals.
3. Study the results in Piwik to see how the changes affect the conversion rate or revenue.
4. Rinse and repeat consistently because the Internet is a changing place, and there is always room for improvement and new technologies to explore.

This can also get advanced as split testing, which runs two pages side by side, checks the results, keeps the winner, creates a new contender, and does it again. Split testing will keep your conversion rate going in the right direction. By constantly picking the winner and doing repeated cycles of testing, you'll be turning your website into a conversion machine.

Summary

Now that we have made it through this chapter, you know what a goal is, and you know that you use the conversion rate for that goal as a tool to track and improve how well your website is performing. You have created goals in Piwik and added revenue tracking to have a concrete idea of how much money you are making and what you can do to increase that revenue. You have even triggered goals programmatically when the standard triggers just won't do.

In the next chapter, we will learn how to track visitors, conversions and revenue from paid ads, display ads, e-mail campaigns, and other marketing channels.

5
Tracking Marketing Campaigns

A marketing campaign is anything you spend time or money on to increase the traffic and conversions at your website; and anything you spend time or money is worth targeting with your tracking to make sure you are getting a good return on your investment. Unless you are tracking the results of your various marketing campaigns, you could be throwing money away and not knowing it.

You can use Piwik to track all sorts of marketing campaigns including paid ads, display ads, e-mail campaigns, and affiliate marketing campaigns and use this data to increase **ROI** (**Return on investment**) from your website. It all depends on how your business defines marketing. If interaction with visitors via a help or contact link is part of your marketing effort, then Piwik will help you do that too.

In this chapter we will learn how to:

- Track campaigns with URL parameters
- Use campaign URLs to track Google Adwords and other paid advertising
- Track social media campaigns
- Use Piwik.org's URL Builder tool
- Customize campaign parameters
- Read campaign reports

Starting with this chapter, I will be using an example e-commerce website fictitiously located at `http://holyhandgrenadesareus.com`. This example is not meant to be offensive or promote anything. I am just a fan of Monty Python. I guess I could have used a "widget" example, but that is no fun. Anyway, it is meant to be an example just like any other used in the book.

Tracking campaigns using URL parameters

So let's say you have one landing page and it is designed to get people to buy your brand new one-of-a-kind holy hand grenade. Now this is not the original Holy Hand Grenade of Antioch, but a commemorative version, a replica. You have hired the best ad writers to write your copy and the best web designers to design your site and you are ready to rock and roll and sell some grenades.

But your domain, `holyhandgrenadesareus.com`, is new. You have yet to build links or promote it. But the new team of social media experts, search engine gurus, and advertising experts that you have hired are going to get you that traffic and get it fast.

So in other words, you spent a lot of money to get this business of Holy Hand Grenades going and you expect some results. You need to know who to fire and who to give a bonus to. You need to know where your marketing dollars are best spent. There are many marketing channels on the Internet. Some may work for your company and some may not. And you have one page to track all of these visitors with.

You don't necessarily have to do it this way. You could create a page for Google Adwords, a page for each one of the Banner Ads you placed at various forums where hand grenade aficionados hang out, the newsletter ad you placed in the Hand Grenade Weekly, and on and on.

But this is very inefficient and could easily become tedious. And you have grenades to sell and don't want to get bogged down in details. You just want to try everything you can to sell more, stop unprofitable marketing campaigns, and spend more time and money on those campaigns that are working well.

Standard tracking with Piwik will still tell you a lot about the visitors and actions that occur on this page as is. You could visit the **Referrers** tab and look at the overview of websites that referred visitors to you but this will only give you general information about your visitors.

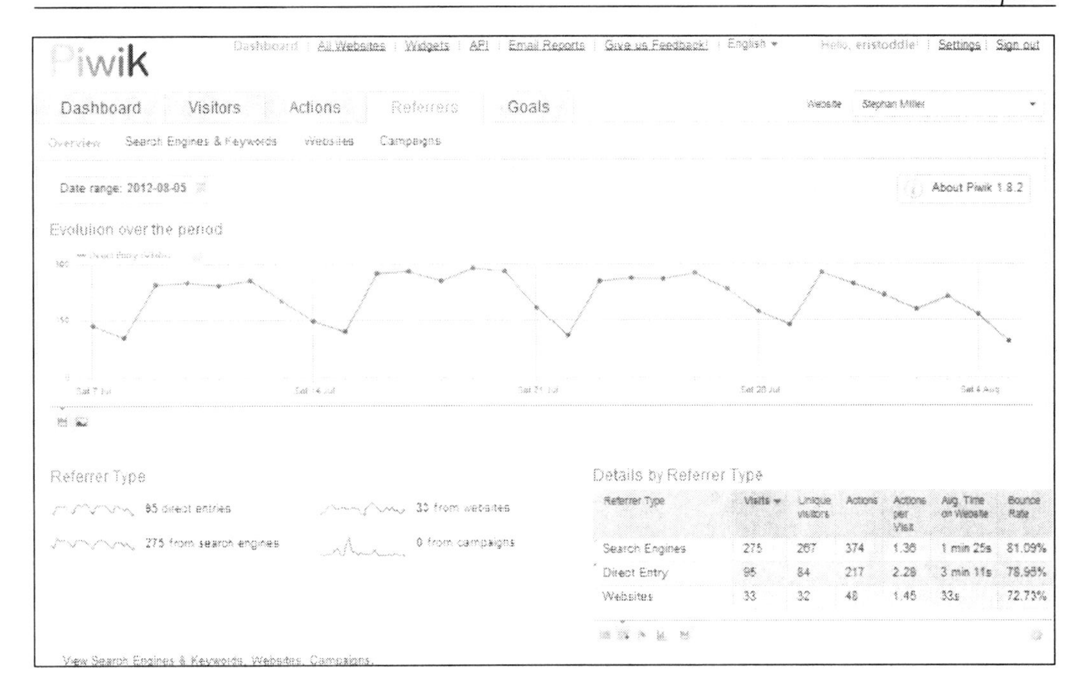

All of this information is useful when you are tracking the effects of search engine optimization, but for marketing campaigns there is just not enough data to track your ROI. The **Websites** tab may help a bit. It will tell you which domains are sending you traffic and which pages on your website are getting that traffic.

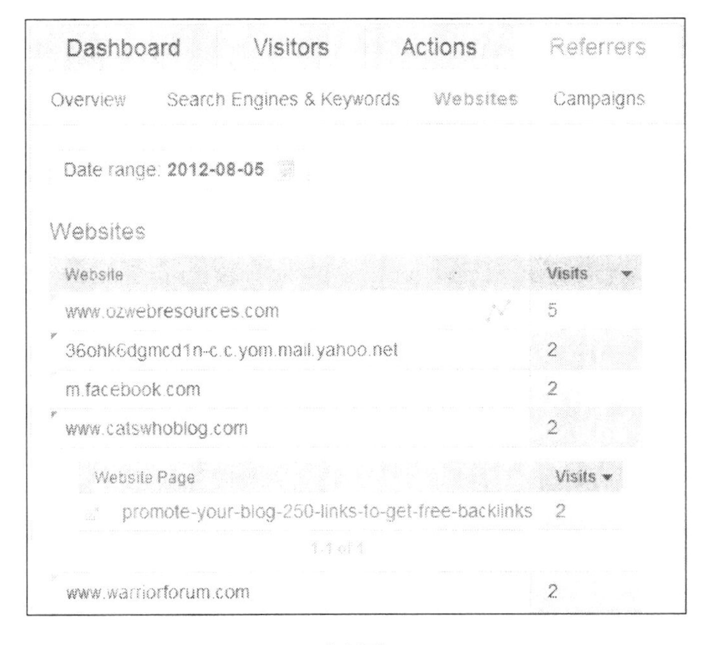

But this is still not enough data to accurately track your marketing campaigns. What if you need to track keywords? And what if you want to track your banner ads by location as well as domain? You need something more.

Tracking campaigns in Piwik requires no setup in Piwik. To track campaigns with Piwik, you add one or two parameters to your website URL. Parameters are stored in the query part of the URL, the part after the question mark. Piwik's tracking code picks up these parameters or tags and uses them to track campaigns. The existence of certain parameters in the URL you are tracking automatically makes it part of the campaign.

Here is the **Campaigns** tab in the **Referrers** menu before any campaigns are tracked. You will notice the absence of **Create Campaign** or any similar button. The campaign is created by the parameters.

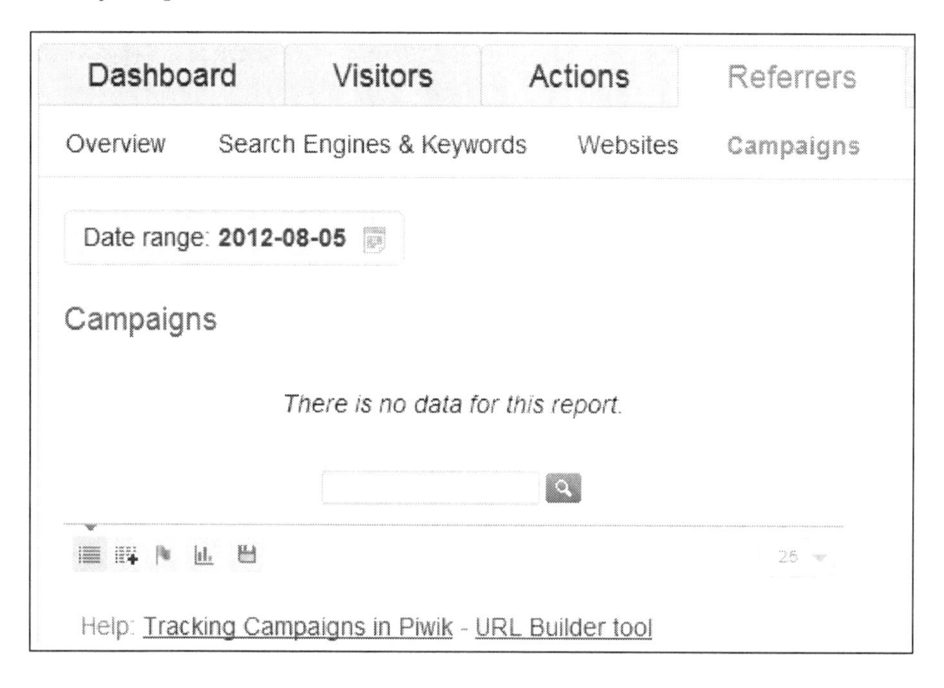

In order to track a campaign, we can use the `pk_campaign` URL parameter. First you take the landing page, which is `http://holyhandgrenadesareus.com/grenade_landing_page.html`.

The page already has the standard, custom, or asynchronous Piwik tracking code, whatever is the case, inserted in the HTML. In order to track a campaign, we do nothing to the code on the page. We just add `?pk_campaign=From-Email-Signature` to our URL so the URL we put under our name in each of our outgoing personal e-mails becomes `http://holyhandgrenadesareus.com/grenade_landing_page.html?pk_campaign=From-Email-Signature`.

This brings up a good point about tracking and e-mails. You will want to use campaign tracking in all e-mails. Chances are that some of the people you send e-mails or newsletters to use software to download their e-mail. If they click on the link in the e-mail software, it opens a new browser tab in your browser. As far as Piwik knows, they opened the browser tab themselves from a bookmark and so Piwik will count them as Direct Entry visits. Using campaign tracking in any links that may end up in software as this is good practice.

And as soon as you open that link in your browser, you will be able to back to the **Campaigns** tab in Piwik and see a visit resulting from that campaign link.

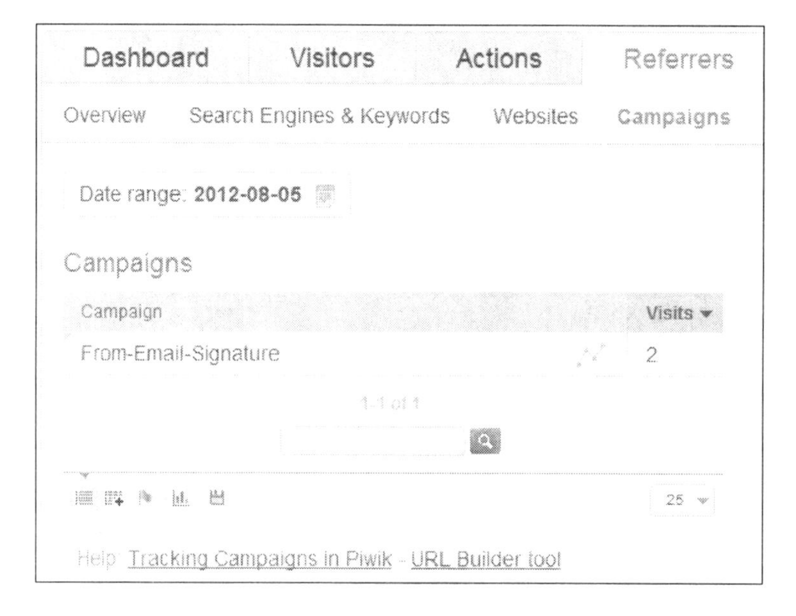

You can actually test it now on any web page that you have added Piwik tracking code to.

1. Open an Incognito Window, Private Browsing Window, or a window in your browser that does not track previous cookies. Another option is to use the standard browsing mode of your browser, but clear the cookies first. This will insure your browser has no previous cookies or history from tracking tests you have made in the past.
2. Navigate to the page you want to test campaign tracking on.
3. Figure out a name for your toy campaign.
4. Remove or replace the spaces in your campaign name.

5. Add `?pk_campaign=NameOfYourToyCampaign` to the end of the URL in the browser where `NameOfYourToyCampaign` is the name from step 3.
6. Hit *Enter* to load the new URL in the browser.
7. Navigate to the **Campaigns** menu in Piwik and check it out.

But newsletters are just the beginning. If you pay for banner ads on someone else's site, you will want to create custom campaign URLs for each location your ad will be placed at. If you have affiliates that sell your products, you can use campaign URLs to track each affiliate's performance. Any time you want to give a link special attention, use campaign tracking.

This type of campaign tracking with only one parameter, `pk_campaign` will work for many of your advertising campaigns. But there are times you may need more data, which is why Piwik also provides the `pk_kwd` parameter, which we will learn about next.

Tracking paid searches

If you aren't tracking your ROI in the search results that you are paying for, you could easily be throwing money down the drain. Paying for the number one slot in Google Adwords or another search engine is not always the best way to make a profit.

Pay per click search is highly competitive in the sense that a lot of the top bidders could be losing more than they are making. Sometimes businesses do this because they know they will gain some returning visitors if they can just get people to their site in the first place. But other advertisers may be driven to be first by whatever means they can or may just not be tracking their ROI and just throwing money at the search engines. You can never be sure that you are making any money from pay per click unless you are tracking your campaigns.

Fortunately, the big three search engines that you buy ads from allow you to add special tags to your ad's destination URL. These will add that ad's campaign data to the URL itself, which you can then turn into Piwik's URL parameters. The big three search engines I speak of are Google, Bing, and Yahoo!. Each will give you enough data to fine tune your campaigns.

Using Google ValueTrack

Using ValueTrack in Adwords can give you a lot of data about each specific click. Most of the time, you will only be using a fraction of the tags available. You add the tags to the destination URL when you are creating an Adwords ad.

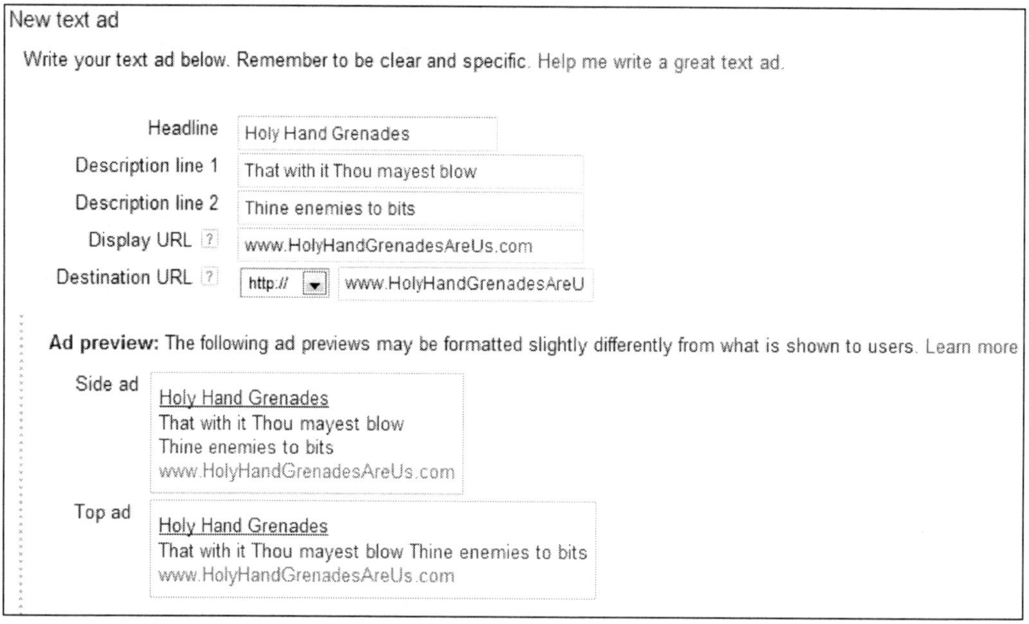

New text ad

Write your text ad below. Remember to be clear and specific. Help me write a great text ad.

Headline: Holy Hand Grenades
Description line 1: That with it Thou mayest blow
Description line 2: Thine enemies to bits
Display URL: www.HolyHandGrenadesAreUs.com
Destination URL: http:// www.HolyHandGrenadesAreU

Ad preview: The following ad previews may be formatted slightly differently from what is shown to users. Learn more

Side ad
Holy Hand Grenades
That with it Thou mayest blow
Thine enemies to bits
www.HolyHandGrenadesAreUs.com

Top ad
Holy Hand Grenades
That with it Thou mayest blow Thine enemies to bits
www.HolyHandGrenadesAreUs.com

Each of the tags must be surrounded with braces in your destination URL: `http://www.HolyHandGrenadesAreUs.com/grenade_landing_page.html?pk_campaign=Paid-Adwords-10PercentOff-{keyword}`.

The tag between the two braces, in this case `keyword`, will be replaced with the actual keyword the visitor entered in Google to reach your website. But as I said, Piwik also gives you the `pk_kwd` parameter, so a better URL would be: `http://www.HolyHandGrenadesAreUs.com/grenade_landing_page.html?pk_campaign=Paid-Adwords-TenPerCentOff&pk_kwd={keyword}`.

You will notice that in the URLs above, the `pk_campaign` value is `Paid-Adwords-TenPercentOff`. It is good to start out with a naming convention when it comes to setting the `pk_campaign` value to keep your data consistent. The one used here is actually three values separated by dashes. They must be separated by dashes or something similar, because we can't have spaces in our URL.

- The first value is `Paid` which will allow us to spot the paid ads campaigns in Piwik. We could have used PPC or something similar, as long as we stick to it throughout our ad URLs.

- The second value is `Adwords` which tells which type of paid advertising we are using.
- The third value is `TenPercentOff` which tells us the Adwords campaign that this ad is in.

This is just one of the many ways you can create campaign names in Piwik and it is probably the bare minimum to accurately track your ROI.

If you want to drill down things more, you can create a URL such as this: `http://www.HolyHandGrenadesAreUs.com/grenade_landing_page.html?pk_campaign=Paid-{ifsearch:AdWordsSearch}{ifcontent:AdWordsDisplay}{ifmobile:AdwordsMobile}-TenPerCentOff&pk_kwd={keyword}`.

This campaign URL will tell you where in the Google Adwords network your click came from. These `if` URL parameters will add the text after the colon if the click matches the `if` type. In the previous URL, if the click came from search, `AdwordsSearch` will be added to the URL; if the click came from a mobile device, `AdwordsMobile` will be added to the URL; and if the click can from an Adsense ad on someone's website, `AdwordsDisplay` will be added to the URL. A campaign URL such as this will tell you which part of the Adwords network is most profitable to you and which bids may have to be lowered in order to increase ROI.

The following are all the useful tags you can add to your destination URLs in Google Adwords:

Google Adwords Tags	
Parameter	**Value**
`{keyword}`	On search sites, this will be the keyword that triggered the ad and on content sites, the best matching keyword.
`{matchtype}`	The matching option of the keyword that cause your ad to be shown whether it is exact, phrase, or broad which is returned as "e", "p", and "b".
`{network}`	This value will be either "g" if the click came from Google search, "s" if the click came from a search partner, or "d" if it came from the display network.
`{ifmobile:[value]}`	If the click came from a mobile device, the text after the colon will be returned.
`{ifsearch:[value]}`	If the click came from the Google Search Network, the text after the colon will be returned.
`{ifcontent:[value]}`	If the click came from the Google Display Network, the text after the colon will be returned.
`{creative}`	This value will be the unique ID for the creative.

Google Adwords Tags	
Parameter	**Value**
`{placement}`	Domain name of the website where the ad was located.
`{target}`	The placement category.
`{aceid}`	The control ID or the experiment ID from Adwords Campaign Experiments, Ad Sitelinks, and Product Extensions.
`{adposition}`	This is an abbreviated value which represents the ad's position on the page, such as "1t2" which equals: page 1, top, position 2.

Using Microsoft Ad Center dynamic text

Microsoft Ad Center provides dynamic text which has the keyword `tag`, which you can use to dynamically create campaign URLs: `http://www.HolyHandGrenadesAreUs.com/grenade_landing_page.html?pk_campaign=Paid-Bing-TenPerCentOff&pk_kwd={keyword}`.

Considering that this is about all you get from Microsoft that is useful for campaign tracking, you are pretty limited when it comes to getting detailed data to track ROI and improve your targeting. In order to track campaigns more effectively, it is best to break up your campaigns and ad groups according to the details you want to track and manually add these campaign and ad group names to the `pk_campaign` parameter of your destination URLs.

Microsoft Ad Center Tags	
Parameter	**Value**
{keyword}	The search query a visitor used before clicking on your ad.

Using Yahoo! Search Marketing's URL tagging

Yahoo! gives you more tags than Microsoft and fewer tags than Google. You get the keyword you bid on or the raw search query. Yahoo! will also give you the match type that led to the click. Yahoo! also gives you tags for the AD ID or the Keyword ID, which are internal, dynamically generated Yahoo! IDs and are not of much use except in a software developer's environment, because they would require referencing back to Yahoo! for other details.

But that being said, you can create a campaign URL for Piwik like in the following URL:

```
http://www.HolyHandGrenadesAreUs.com/grenade_landing_page.html?
pk_campaign=Paid-Yahoo-TenPerCentOff&pk_kwd={OVKEY}-{OVMTC}
```

In this URL, I add the match type of the keyword to the keyword itself to create the `pk_kwd` parameter. This will allow us to drill down the match types that make us the most money. The `OVKEY` tag will either return `standard`, `advanced`, or `raw`.

Here is a table of Yahoo! Search Marketing tags:

Yahoo Tags	
Parameter	**Value**
`{OVKEY}` or `{YSMKEY}`	This is the keyword that the advertiser has bid on. This is not the actual user query, unless they coincide.
`{OVRAW}` or `{YSMMTC}`	This is the raw search query the visitor used at Yahoo!.
`{OVMTC}` or `{YSMADID}`	This is the match type that led to the click - standard, advanced, or raw.
`{OVADID}` or `{YSMADID}`	This is the Ad ID-the internal Yahoo! Search Marketing ID for the ad.
`{OVKWID}` or `{YSMKWID}`	This is the Keyword ID-the internal Yahoo! Search Marketing ID for the keyword.

Creating campaign URLs the easy way

Now that you know the basic structure of a campaign URL in Piwik, it is time to show you the easiest way to create them, if you are not a programmer that is. `Piwik.org` has a special form you can use to generate campaign URLs. It is called the URL Builder tool and is available at `http://piwik.org/docs/tracking-campaigns/url-builder/`. You may have also noticed the **URL Builder tool** link at the bottom of the **Campaigns** dashboard in the Piwik interface.

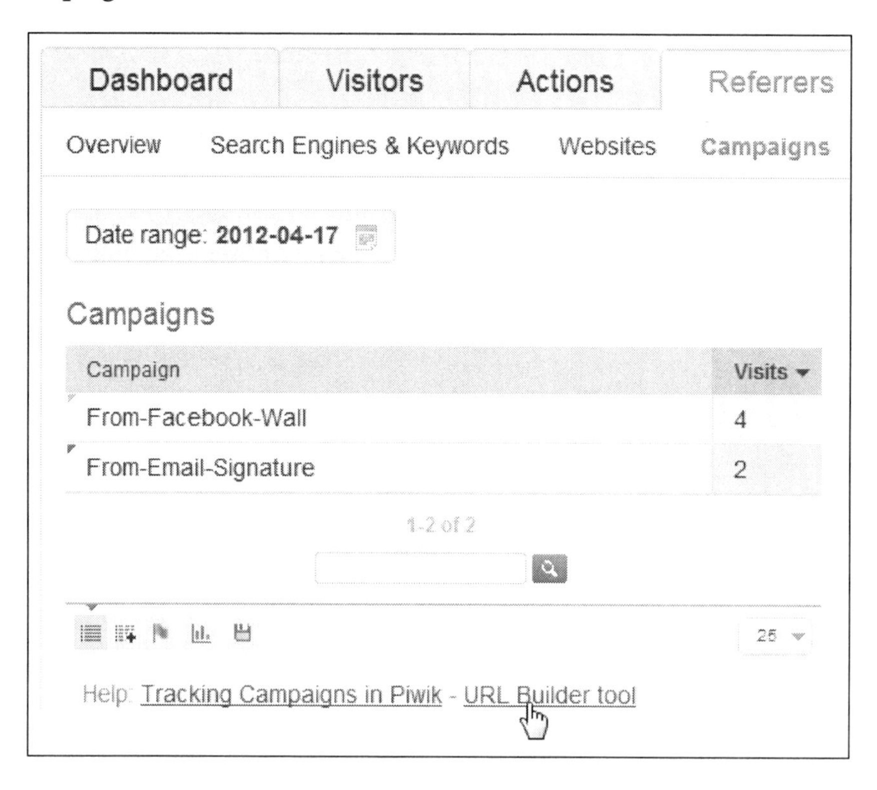

The URL Builder tool has three fields: one for **Website URL**, one for **Campaign name**, both of which are required, and one for **Campaign keyword**, which is optional.

Docs › URL Builder – Analytics Campaign Tracking

The URL Builder tool lets you generate URLs ready to use for Tracking Campaigns in Piwik. See the documentation about Campaign Tracking for more information.

Fill in the information in the form below and click the **Generate URL** button.

Step 1: Fill in the fields below. Website URL and Campaign name are required fields.

Website URL (required) http://www.holyhan *e.g. http://example.org/offer.html*

Campaign name (required) Paid-Adwords-10Perc *Email-SummerDeals, PaidAds-SummerDeals*

Campaign keyword antioch-hand-grenade *(optional) Used to track the keyword, or sub-category*

Step 2

Generate URL Clear

Step 3

http://www.holyhandgrenadesareus.com/grenade_landing_page.html

Generated URL that you can copy paste in your Campaigns, Email newsletter, Facebook Ads or tweets

Learn more about Campaign Tracking in Piwik Analytics.

So you just:

- Enter your landing page URL in the first field
- Enter the name of your campaign in the second field
- Enter the name of your keyword or other data you wish to track in the third field
- Click the **Generate URL** button

The tool will create your campaign URL for you in the field below the **Generate URL** button and you can copy and paste it wherever you need and start on the next URL.

Tracking social media campaigns

Why a special section on social media campaigns? Social media is starting to matter more than ever before. With your rank in Google depending more on social signals since the Panda series of updates began, tracking social media becomes a necessity. Social media marketing also takes time and after all time is money.

Social media has exploded in the last few years. Once, online social networks were only for geeks and now there are people who have **Facebook** accounts and don't venture out to the rest of the Internet. Every smartphone has built in social network features and there are more people browsing the Internet with phones than computers.

Another reason to track your social media campaigns with campaign parameters is because of all the software available to ingest the feeds from these social media sites. Applications such as **TweetDeck**, **Seesmic**, and others will open a browser window when you click on a link from a tweet or from Facebook and leave the referrer blank making Piwik think the visitor entered directly instead of from a social media campaign.

Social media campaigns are traditionally full of high bounce rates and awful conversion rates because a lot of social media visits occur like window shopping rather than grocery shopping. When a visit comes from a search engine, the visitor is looking for something specific. When a visit comes from social media, it comes from a stream of varied topics. By tracking your social media campaigns, you can discover what content and what style of shares bring more visitors and conversions to your site.

So let's create some social media campaign links for our holy hand grenade:

- `http://www.HolyHandGrenadesAreUs.com/grenade_landing_page.html?pk_campaign=Social-Twitter-TenPerCentOff`
- `http://www.HolyHandGrenadesAreUs.com/grenade_landing_page.html?pk_campaign=Social-Facebook-TenPerCentOff`
- `http://www.HolyHandGrenadesAreUs.com/grenade_landing_page.html?pk_campaign=Social-GooglePlus-TenPerCentOff`
- `http://www.HolyHandGrenadesAreUs.com/grenade_landing_page.html?pk_campaign=Social-Pinterest-TenPerCentOff`
- `http://www.HolyHandGrenadesAreUs.com/grenade_landing_page.html?pk_campaign=Social-StumbleUpon-TenPerCentOff-Oct102012`

If you tweet or share a link to the same post twice on two days, you may want to add a date to the campaign parameter to track each separately.

Campaign tagging and tracking tips

Here are a few tips that should lead you in the right direction when it comes to setting up your campaigns. If you are creating campaigns for a website that gets a lot of traffic, it is best to decide on the way you are going to do things when you start campaign tracking as it will be hard to retool later.

- Use as many tags as you need to fine-tune your marketing campaigns. You may start out with a Google Adwords campaign returning only keywords in your destination URL, and may later find out that you need to start tracking match type because you get a lot of clicks on one keyword and it's costing you a lot of money. Tracking match type will allow you to spend more money on certain types of matches and less on others, bringing ROI up. It is best to make sure you are tracking the variables in your marketing campaign that make a difference in advertising costs and in time.
- Be consistent with the naming convention of your Piwik campaign variables. This will help you sort and understand your campaign reports quicker and easier. If you always put dashes between sections of the `pk_campaign` parameter (that is, `?pk_campaign=MyCampaign-TheAdNetwork`), then always do so and stick to it. If you want your campaign name to have real spaces in the report for easier reporting, use `%20` to separate the words in your campaign name. You may have to change the way you create campaign names and `pk_kwd` parameters but thinking everything through thoroughly at the start will prevent a lot of headaches.
- Once you have a naming convention, write it down somewhere so that you remember and so that others can stick to your rules. You may think you won't forget, but you can never be sure.
- If you know how to use Microsoft Word, OpenOffice Calc, or Google Docs well, you can use a spreadsheet and macros to create campaign URLs in bulk, once you have a naming convention in place.
- If your campaign URL ends up too long and unruly, you may want to use a URL shortener to prevent it from getting broken in half by line wrapping in certain applications and to prevent a more inviting URL for users to click on.
- Once you create a URL for a campaign, keep it segregated to that campaign to keep your tracking accurate. You have no control over what others do. For example, someone receiving an e-mail with a link tagged for an e-mail campaign may paste that link on Facebook. But don't do it yourself.

- Combining goal tracking with campaign tracking is a one-two punch. By first setting up your goals, you can pin down those actions visitors can make that add to your business's bottom line. Combining that with campaign tracking will tell which marketing channels are contributing most to your goal conversions. If you have revenue tracking set up for your goals, even better.

Attributing visits to the correct campaign

So let's say that your link in the Holy Hand Grenades Weekly newsletter brought a visitor to your site, but he/she didn't buy. Instead, the next day, he/she went to Google and searched for "Holy Hand Grenades Are Us" because he/she remembered your brand. When the results appeared, the ad that you purchased on Adwords caught his/her eye and he/she clicked your link. The question in this situation is which campaign gets credited with the conversion?

By default, Piwik will give the conversion to the referrer of the last visit. In this case, the conversion would be credited to your Adwords campaign and not to your newsletter campaign. You can configure the Piwik tracking code to attribute the conversion the first referrer or the newsletter campaign in this example, by adding one line.

```
<!-- Piwik -->
<script type="text/javascript">
var pkBaseurl = (("https:" == document.location.protocol) ?
"https://$PIWIK_url" : "http://$PIWIK_url");
document.write(unescape("%3Cscript src='" + pkBaseurl + "piwik.js'
type='text/javascript'%3E%3C/script%3E"));
</script><script type="text/javascript">
try {
var piwikTracker = Piwik.getTracker(pkBaseurl + "piwik.php",
$SITE_ID);
piwikTracker.setConversionAttributionFirstReferrer();
piwikTracker.trackPageView();
piwikTracker.enableLinkTracking();
} catch( err ) {}
</script><noscript><p><img src="$PIWIK_url/piwik.php?idsite=1"
style="border:0" alt="" /></p></noscript>
<!-- End Piwik Tracking Code -->
```

By calling the `setConversionAttributionFirstReferrer` method right before we call `trackPageView`, we can give credit to the first referred instead of the last.

Customizing campaign parameters

So far we have mentioned the pk_campaign and pk_kwd parameters, but we have learned they are pretty flexible. By separating data with dashes or underscores, we can fit a lot into those two variables.

But Piwik also supports Google Analytics campaign parameters. What this means to you, is that if you are switching from Google Analytics to Piwik, you don't have to worry about changing the URLs for your campaigns.

Google Analytics uses four parameters: utm_campaign, utm_medium, utm_term, and utm_source. Piwik takes these parameters and converts them to pk_campaign and pk_kwd. The parameter utm_term becomes pk_kwd, and utm_campaign, utm_medium, and utm_source are joined together and are put in the pk_campaign parameter.

You can also customize the names of Piwik's campaign tracking parameters, if you just don't like pk_campaign or pk_keyword. And there are two ways to do this.

The simplest way to do this is to modify Piwik's JavaScript tracking code by setting your new parameter names before the trackPageView call:

```
<!-- Piwik -->
<script type="text/javascript">
var pkBaseurl = (("https:" == document.location.protocol) ?
"https://$PIWIK_url" : "http://$PIWIK_url");
document.write(unescape("%3Cscript src='" + pkBaseurl + "piwik.js'
type='text/javascript'%3E%3C/script%3E"));
</script><script type="text/javascript">
try {
var piwikTracker = Piwik.getTracker(pkBaseurl + "piwik.php", $SITE_
ID);
piwikTracker.setCampaignNameKey('campaign');
piwikTracker.setCampaignKeywordKey('keyword');
piwikTracker.trackPageView();
piwikTracker.enableLinkTracking();
} catch( err ) {}
</script><noscript><p><img src="$PIWIK_url/piwik.php?idsite=1"
style="border:0" alt="" /></p></noscript>
<!-- End Piwik Tracking Code -->
```

In this code, the setCampaignNameKey method changes the name of the campaign parameter from pk_campaign to campaign and the setCampaignKeywordKey method changes the name of the keyword parameter from pk_kwd to keyword. You can also designate a list of possible parameters for each value by separating these parameters with commas.

The second way to change these parameters will affect your complete Piwik installation instead of just the pages where you put modified tracking code. To do this, you must modify the `config.ini.php` file located in the `config` folder of your Piwik installation by adding the following lines to the bottom of that file:

```
[Tracker]
campaign_var_name="campaign"
campaign_keyword_var_name="keyword"
```

This will do the same thing as the previous modified tracking code, except that it will affect all sites tracked by your Piwik installation. It changes the name of the campaign parameter from `pk_campaign` to `campaign` and the name of the `keyword` parameter from `pk_kwd` to `keyword`. You can also separate the values with commas if you want to handle multiple names for either parameter.

Viewing campaign reports

Navigating back to the **Campaigns** dashboard after you have set up a few campaigns will give you an idea of what campaign tracking can tell you.

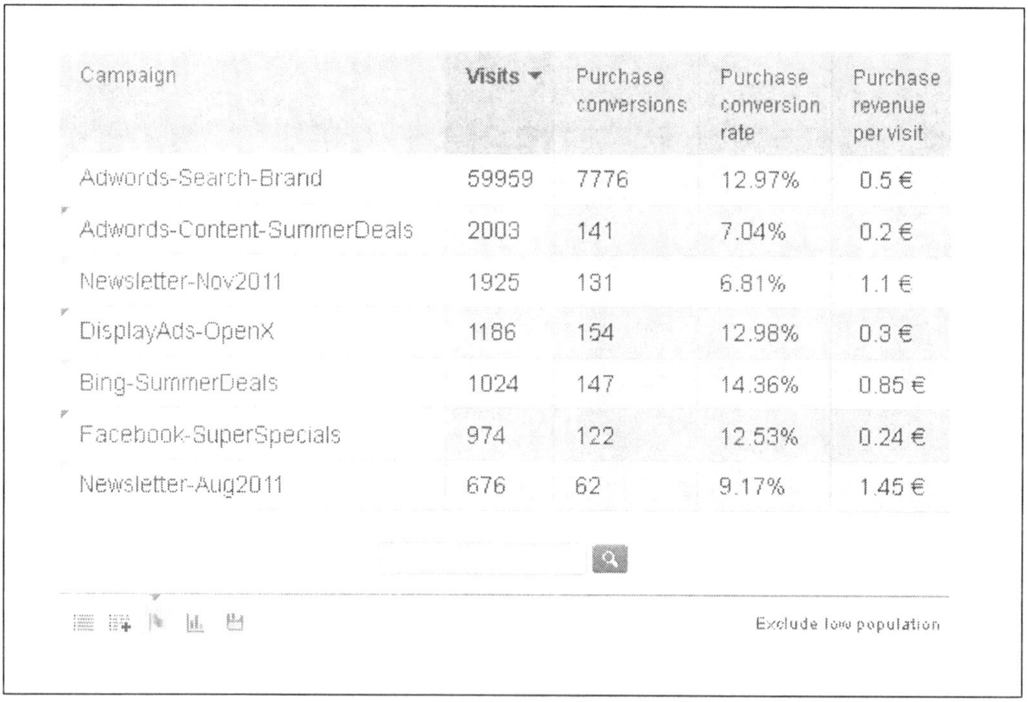

Campaign	Visits	Purchase conversions	Purchase conversion rate	Purchase revenue per visit
Adwords-Search-Brand	59959	7776	12.97%	0.5 €
Adwords-Content-SummerDeals	2003	141	7.04%	0.2 €
Newsletter-Nov2011	1925	131	6.81%	1.1 €
DisplayAds-OpenX	1186	154	12.98%	0.3 €
Bing-SummerDeals	1024	147	14.36%	0.85 €
Facebook-SuperSpecials	974	122	12.53%	0.24 €
Newsletter-Aug2011	676	62	9.17%	1.45 €

Exclude low population

You will see the campaign names on the left side of the table and beside that the total number of visits. If you have conversion tracking set up, there will also be a column for count of conversions and a column for the conversion rate of each goal you set up. And if you added revenue tracking, you will see average revenue per visit.

Campaign	Visits	Purchase conversions	Purchase conversion rate	Purchase revenue per visit
Adwords-Search-Brand	59959	7776	12.97%	0.5 €
Adwords-Content-SummerDeals	2003	141	7.04%	0.2 €
Newsletter-Nov2011	1925	131	6.81%	1.1 €

Campaign Keyword	Visits	Purchase conversions	Purchase conversion rate	Purchase revenue per visit
LearnMore	893	28	3.14 %	0.8€
LogoTop	651	56	8.6 %	1.3€
PersonnalizedGift	323	30	9.29%	1.3€
OrderNow	58	17	29%	1.8€

1-6 of 6

Campaign	Visits	Purchase conversions	Purchase conversion rate	Purchase revenue per visit
DisplayAds-OpenX	1186	154	12.98%	0.3 €
Bing-SummerDeals	1024	147	14.36%	0.85 €
Facebook-SuperSpecials	974	122	12.53%	0.24 €
Newsletter-Aug2011	676	62	9.17%	1.45 €

Exclude low population

Clicking on a campaign name in this report will break down each campaign further by the campaign keywords you set, as seen in the previous screenshot.

Summary

In this chapter, we learned that we should be tracking our marketing channels with campaign tracking in Piwik and found out that this is not hard at all. You didn't even have to create a campaign, you just added a few parameters to the URL of a web page. You also created campaign tracking URLs for your paid search ads and social media campaigns, using distinctive campaign names so you can easily tell at a glance which campaigns are performing in any one of the many Piwik widgets that show campaign data.

In the next chapter, we will learn how to track events in JavaScript, AJAX, and Flash.

6
Tracking Events

Despite the advanced tracking features of Piwik, there are still some actions on a website that may require you to do some manual work in order to track. Events in JavaScript and Flash don't cause a page load and because of that, the standard Piwik tracking code won't register any details other than a visit. In order to record user interactions with website elements such as Flash, Ajax, JavaScript, and third-party widgets, you need to use different tactics.

But, we already learned a little bit about manual triggering page views in Piwik. What exactly is an event and how does it differ from a goal? Well, sometimes they can be one and the same thing. But an event usually doesn't have a page that loads as the event happens.

For example, when a person checks out at an e-commerce site, they eventually land on a page that tells them that their credit card has been charged, their order will be shipped, and other details they need to know in order to confirm that they have completed their purchase. And on this page, you would put the tracking code that triggers a goal conversion.

Well, with events, you don't have the convenient confirmation page. An event could be a click on a JavaScript button that submits the visitor's "Like" to Facebook. Other than that one click, none of the actions occur where you can track it. But you can track that click and that is where event tracking comes in.

Fortunately, as we went over in *Chapter 3, Tracking Visitors with Piwik*, Piwik's tracking code and the HTML on the web page itself can be modified to track events manually. Here, we will go into more detail on specific types of events we can track with Piwik.

In this chapter, we will learn:

- What event tacking is used for
- How to set up event tracking in Piwik using custom variables
- How to track social media events on your website
- How to track blog commenting events
- How to track e-commerce events
- How to track Flash events in either ActionScript 2 or ActionScript 3
- How to track page loading time
- How to read custom variable reports

Tracking events with Piwik

Many of you may be familiar with event tracking with Google Analytics; and of you may not. In Google Analytics, event tracking is pretty structured. When you track an event with Google, you get five parameters:

- **Category**: The name for the group of objects you want to track
- **Action**: A string that is used to define the user in action for the category of object
- **Label**: This is optional and is for additional data
- **Value**: This is optional and is used for providing addition numerical data
- **Non-interaction**: This is optional and will not add the event hit into bounce rate calculation if set to true

We are going over a few details on event tracking with Google Analytics because the custom variable feature we will be using for event tracking in Piwik is a little less structured. And a little structure will help you drill down the details of your data more effectively from the start. You won't have to restructure and change your naming conventions later on and lose all of your historical data in the process. We don't need to look over the code for Google Analytics. Just know that it may help to set up your event tracking with a similar structure.

If you had videos on your site, enough to track, you would most likely make a category of events *Videos*. You can create as many as you need for the various objects you want to track on your site:

- Videos
- Maps
- Games
- Ads
- Blog posts (social media actions)
- Products

As for the actions that can be performed on those *Videos*, I can think of a few:

- Play
- Pause
- Stop
- Tweet
- Like
- Download

There are probably more than you can think of, but now that we have these actions we can connect them with elements of the site. As for the `label` parameter, you would probably want to use that to store the title of the movie the visitor is interacting with or the page it is located on. We will skip the `value` parameter which is for numeric data because with Piwik, you won't have a similar value. But `non-interaction` is interesting; it means that by default an action on a page counts to lower the bounce rate from that page since the user is doing something. Unfortunately, this is not a feature that we have using Piwik currently, although that could change in the future.

Okay, now that we have learned one of the ways to structure our events, let's look at the way we can track events in Piwik. There is really nothing called event tracking in Piwik, but Piwik does have custom variables which will do the same job. But, since it is not really event tracking in the truest sense of the word, the bounce rate will be unaffected by any of the custom variables collected. In other words, unlike Google Analytics, you don't get the `non-interaction` parameter you can set. But let's see what you can do with Piwik.

Custom variables are name-value pairs that you can set in Piwik. You can assign up to five custom variables for each visitor and/or each page view. The function for setting a custom variable is `setCustomVariable`. You must call it for each custom variable you set up to the limit of five.

```
piwikTracker.setCustomVariable (index, name, value, scope);
```

And here are what you set the parameters to:

- `index`: This is a number from 1 to 5 where your custom variables are stored. It should stay the same as the name of custom variable. Changing the index of a name later will reset all old data.
- `name`: This is the custom variable name or key.
- `value`: This is the value for name.
- `scope`: This parameter sets the scope of the custom variable, whether it is being tracked per visit or per page. And what scope we set depends upon what we are tracking and how complex our site is.

So how do these custom variables fit our model of event tracking? Well we have to do things a little bit differently. For most of our event tracking, we will have to set our variable scope per page. There is not enough room to store much data at the visit level. That is good for other custom tracking you may need but for event tracking you will need more space for data.

So with page level custom variables, you get five name-value sets per page. So, we would set up our variables similar to something like this for a video on the page:

- Index = 1
- Name = "Video"
- Value = "Play","Pause","Stop","Tweet","Like", and so on
- Scope = "page"

And this set of variables in using Piwik's custom variable function would look like one of the following:

- `piwikTracker.setCustomVariable(1,"Video","Play","page");`
- `piwikTracker.setCustomVariable(1,"Video","Pause","page");`
- `piwikTracker.setCustomVariable(1,"Video","Tweet","page");`

Which one you would use would depend on what action you are tracking. You would use JavaScript in the page to trigger these variables to be set, most likely by using an `onClick` event on the button. We will go into the details of various event tracking scenarios later in this chapter.

You will notice in the previous snippets of code that the `index` value of each call is `1`. We have set the index of the `"Video"` name to `1` and must stick to this now on the page or data could be overwritten. This also leaves us the two to five indexes still available for use on the same page.

That means if we have banner ads on the page, we could use one of the spare indexes to track the ads.

```
piwikTracker.setCustomVariable(2,"SidebarBanner","Click","page");
```

You will notice that Google event tracking has the `label` variable. As we are using page leveling custom variables with Piwik and the variables will be attached to the page itself, there is no need to have this extra variable in most cases. If we do need to add extra data other than an `action` value, we will have to concatenate our data to the action and use the combined value in Piwik's custom tracking's `value` variable. Most likely, if we have one banner on our video page, we will have more and to track those click events per banner, we may have to get a little creative using the following:

- `piwikTracker.setCustomVariable(2,"SidebarBanner","AddSlot1Click","page");`
- `piwikTracker.setCustomVariable(2,"SidebarBanner","AddSlot2Click","page");`
- `piwikTracker.setCustomVariable(2,"SidebarBanner","AddSlot3Click","page");`

Of course, it is up to you whether you join your data together by using CamelCase, which means joining each piece of data together after capitalizing each. This is what I did previously. You can also use spaces or underscores as long as it is understandable to you and you stick to it. Since the name and value are in quotation marks, you can use any suitable string.

And again, since these are custom variables, if you come up with a better system of setting up your event tracking that works better with your website and business model, then by all means try it. Whatever works best for you and your site is better in the long run.

So now that we have a general idea of how we will be tracking events with Piwik, let's look at some specific examples and more in depth at what events are, compared to goals or page views.

Tracking social engagement

You know that you have a Facebook "Like" button on your page, a Twitter "tweet" button, and possibly lots more buttons that do various things at other sites that you yourself have no control over and can add no tracking code to. But you can track clicks on the button itself.

You use event tracking for what you could call micro-conversions. But there is really nothing micro about them. That Facebook "Like" could end up in many more sales or conversions than a standard conversion. They could be the route on the way to one or multiple conversions. There may be a blurry line between engagement goals and micro-conversions.

And really, it is up to you what weight you give to visitor actions on your site, but use events for something smaller than you would consider a goal. If your goal is sales on your website, that Facebook "Like" should cause a spike in your sales and you will be able to correlate that to your event tracking, but the "Like" is not the end of the road, or the goal. It is a stop on the way.

If your website is a blog and your goal is to promote advertising or your services with your content, then tracking social engagement can tell you which topics have the highest social interest so that you can create similar content in the future.

So what are some other events we can track? Of course, you would want to track anything having to do with liking, tweeting, bookmarking, or somehow spreading your site on a social network. That includes Facebook, Twitter, Digg, StumbleUpon, Pinterest, and any other social network whose button you put on your site. If you spent enough time to put the buttons on your pages, you can at least track these events. And if you don't have buttons, you have to remember that each generation is using the Internet more often; smartphones make it available everywhere, and everyone is on a social network. Get with it.

And don't forget to add event tracking to any sort of *Follow Me* or *Subscribe* button. That too is an event worth tracking.

We will also look at blog comments since we can consider them to be in the social realm of our tracking.

Tracking content sharing

So let's look at a set of social sharing buttons on our website. We aren't going to blow things out of proportion by using buttons for every social network out there, just two: Twitter and Facebook. Your site may have less and should have more, but the same methods we will explore next can be used for any amount of content sharing buttons.

We are event tracking, so let's begin by defining what our custom variable data will be. We need to figure out how we are going to set up our categories of events and the actions. In this example, we will be using buttons on our Holy Hand Grenade site:

You will see our Twitter button and our Facebook button right underneath the image of our Holy Hand Grenade.

We are going to act as if our site has many more pages and events to track on it and use a naming convention that will leave room for growth. So we are going to use the category of product shares. That way we have room for video shares when we finally get that cinematographer and film our Holy Hand Grenade in action.

Now we need to define our actions. We will be adding more buttons later after we test the effectiveness of our Facebook and Twitter buttons. This means we need a separate action to distinguish each social channel.

- Share on Facebook
- Share on Twitter

And then we add more buttons:

- Share on Google+
- Share on Digg
- Share on Reddit
- Share on StumbleUpon

So let's look at the buttons in the source of the page for a minute to see what we are working with:

```
<li class="span1">
        <script type="text/javascript" src="http://platform.twitter.
com/widgets.js"></script>
        <a href="https://twitter.com/intent/
tweet?url=http%3A%2F%2Fdir23.com&text=Holy%20Hand%20Grenades"
class="twitter-share-button">Tweet</a>
      </li>

      <li class="span1"></li>

      <li class="span1">
        <script src="http://connect.facebook.net/en_US/all.
js#xfbml=1"></script>
        <fb:like href="http://dir23.com/" show_faces="false"
width="50" font=""></fb:like>
      </li>

    </ul>

      <p><a class="btn btn-primary btn-large">Buy Now >></a></p>
```

You see that the buttons are not really buttons yet, they are only HTML anchors in the code and JavaScript `includes`. Before we start looking at the code to track clicks on these buttons, we need to go over some details about the way Piwik's JavaScript works. Setting a custom variable in Piwik using an `onclick` event is a very tricky procedure. To start with, you must call more than just `setCustomVariable` because that will not work after the Piwik tracking JavaScript has loaded and `trackPageView` has been called. But there is a way around this. First, you call `setCustomVariable` and then, in that same `onclick` event, you call `trackLink`, as in the next example:

```
<p><a href="buynow.html" class="btn btn-primary btn-large" onclick="
javascript:piwikTracker.setCustomVariable(2,'Product Pricing','View
Product Price','page');piwikTracker.trackLink();">Buy Now >></a></p>
```

If you forget to add the `piwikTracker.trackLink()` call, nothing will happen and no custom variables will be set.

Now with the sharing buttons, we have another issue when it comes to tracking clicks. Most of these buttons, including Facebook, Twitter, and Google+ use JavaScript to create an **iframe** that has the button. This is a problem, because the iframe is on another domain and there is not an easy way to track clicks.

For this reason, I suggest using your social network's API functionality to create the button so that you can create a callback that will fire when someone likes or tweets your page. Another advantage to this method is that you will be sure that each tracked tweet or like will be logged accurately. Using an `on_click` event will cause a custom variable to be created with every click. If the person is not logged in to their social account at the time, the actual tweet or like will not happen until after they log in, even if they decide to do so. Facebook, Twitter, and Google+ all have APIs with this functionality.

But if you decide to try to track the click on the iframe, you can take a look at the code at `http://www.bennadel.com/blog/1752-Tracking-Google-AdSense-Clicks-With-jQuery-And-ColdFusion.htm` to see how complicated it can get. The click is not really tracked. The blur on the page is tracked, because blur usually happens if a link in the iframe is clicked and a new page is about to load.

We already have our standard Piwik tracking code on the page. This does not have to be modified in any way for event tracking. Instead we will be latching into Twitters and Facebook's APIs which we loaded in the page by including their JavaScript.

```
<script>
    twttr.events.bind('tweet', function(event) {
      piwikTracker.setCustomVariable(1,'Product Shares','Share on
Twitter','page');
      piwikTracker.trackLink();
    });
```

```
    </script>

    <script type="text/javascript">
      FB.Event.subscribe('edge.create', function(response) {
        piwikTracker.setCustomVariable(1,'Product Shares','Share on
  Facebook','page');
        piwikTracker.trackLink();
      });
    </script>
```

We add these two simple scripts to the bottom of the page. I put them right before the Piwik tracking code. The first script binds to the `tweet` event in Twitter's API and once that event fires, our Piwik code executes and sets our custom variable. Notice that here too we have to call `trackLink` right afterwards. The second script does the same thing when someone likes the page on Facebook.

It is beyond the scope of this book to go into more details about social APIs, but this code will get you started and you can do more research on your chosen social network's API on your own to see what type of event tracking will be possible. For example, with the Twitter API you can bind a function to each one of these actions: click, tweet, retweet, favorite, or follow. There are definitely more possibilities with this than there is with a simple `onclick` event.

Using event tracking on your social sharing buttons will let you know where people share your line of Holy Hand Grenades. This will help you figure out just which social networks you should have a presence on. If people on Twitter like the grenades, then you should make sure to keep your Twitter account active, and if you don't have a Twitter account and your product is going viral there, you need to get one quick and participate in the conversation about your product.

Or you may want to invest in the development of a Facebook app and you are not quite sure that it is worth the investment. Well, a little bit of event tracking will tell you if you have enough people interested in your website or products to fork over the money for an app.

Or maybe a person goes down deep into the pages of your site, digs out a gem, and it gets passed around StumbleUpon like crazy. This might indicate a page that you should feature on the home page of your website. And if it's a product page that's been hidden from light for years, maybe throw some advertising its way too.

Tracking blog comments

Commenting is a useful way to get feedback on your content and it is a feature that is built into every blogging platform. By adding a blog to your business site you can turn it into a community instead of a static business card, and adding a blog to an e-commerce website will add a useful knowledge base to what was only a showroom.

Comments are definitely something you should track with analytics. The data you receive will tell you which content engages your visitors the most. More people will bookmark, tweet, or share content than comment, because it is simply easier. So when you find a story that gets a reaction from your audience, you can focus on topics that are most likely to get comments instead of those that have not received much interaction in the past.

Now you could make commenting a goal, but this could give you a lot of goals as your content increases. It would be better to track comments as events. Your goal is to actually grow a community over time. You also could just use the actual comment count from the admin panel of your blogging platform, but it is much easier to consolidate this data in Piwik than to have to refer to more than one application for your analytics data.

So let's look at how we are going to set up the custom variables to track our blog comment events. Again, we can think in terms of categories and actions. But with comments, this is pretty simple. We could simply call our category `"Blog Comments"` and the action `"Submit Comment"`. And since we will be using page level scope, we will be able to correlate these comments directly to the content they occurred on.

So the snippet of code that will be tracking these comments will look like the following:

```
piwikTracker.setCustomVariable(1,"Blog Comments","Submit
Comment","page");
piwikTracker.trackLink();
```

Here is an example of a comment form on a WordPress blog, mine in fact:

This will be simple. Again, we will be attaching our `setCustomVariable` function to the `onclick` event of a button. This time it is the comment submit button we will be using (the button that says `Post Comment`). Here is the section of the page that has the button before we add our event tracking code.

```
<p class="form-submit">
  <input name="submit" class="sm-button" type="submit" id="submit"
value="Post Comment">
  <input type='hidden' name='comment_post_ID' value='1653'
id='comment_post_ID'>
  <input type='hidden' name='comment_parent' id='comment_parent'
value='0'>
</p>
```

We already have the parameters that we will be using and I am assuming the Piwik tracking code is in place. So all we have to do is insert our `onclick` event:

```
<p class="form-submit">
  <input name="submit" class="sm-button" type="submit"
id="submit" value="Post Comment" onclick="javascript:
piwikTracker.setCustomVariable(3,'Blog Comments','Submit
Comment','page');piwikTracker.trackLink();">
  <input type='hidden' name='comment_post_ID' value='1653'
id='comment_post_ID'>
  <input type='hidden' name='comment_parent' id='comment_parent'
value='0'>
</p>
```

Now, we will track a new blog comment every time someone clicks this button. This may be what we want to get started, but if your blog gets a lot of comment spam, this may not be the best way to do things. In the following screenshot of my WordPress admin, I currently get about 20 percent spam that my spam filtering plugin catches. And still, there will be a lot of spam in the comments that make it past this filter.

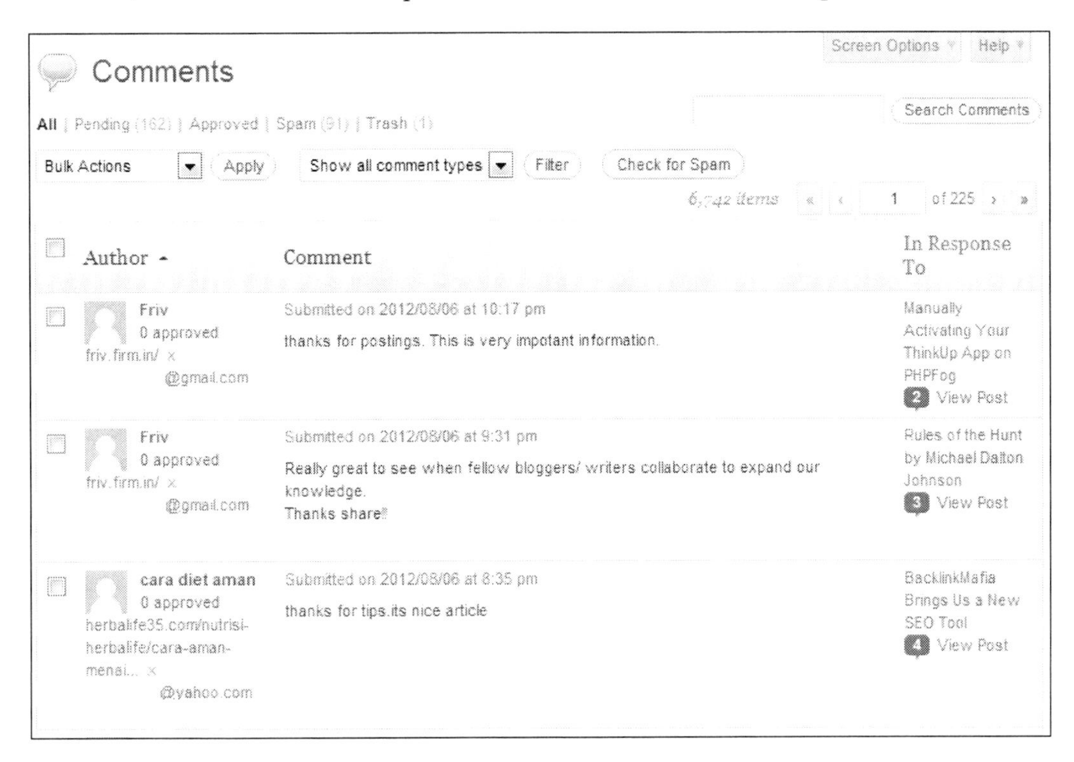

Instead of tracking with the comment submission button, it would be better in this case to track events when the comments are approved. This will involve more complex coding and would probably be best done with a plugin for your blogging platform. It is never a good practice to hack the core files of your blogging platform. For example, in WordPress, you would have to be sure to track a comment event when a comment is approved one by one, and multiple events when comments are approved in bulk. This will require more than simple JavaScript. You will have to get out your PHP programming skills.

Tracking e-commerce events

To continue with the road analogy, the road to an online purchase has many twists and forks and stops along the way. The end goal, of course, is the sale. A customer could view instructions on how to use a product, add the product to the cart, and make in to the checkout page. Each one of these steps is an event along the route that leads to a sale.

You will notice on our Holy Hand Grenade site that no price is listed on the product page; there is just a **Buy Now** button.

When someone clicks that button, they are interested in buying. They aren't buying yet, but they are at least curious about the price. Not yet a goal, but an event we want to track.

By tracking this event, we can find out what percentages of our visitors are checking out the price as well as the percentage who finally converted. If the percentage who clicked the button is high, our landing page is good. If it is lower, we can split test it with a new version, but it is good to test periodically either way to increase this click-through percentage. And if our goal conversion rate is a little low, we can play around with the price of our hand grenade or maybe experiment with making our checkout page a little less complicated.

So let's set up our custom variables to track people who check out the price of our Holy Hand Grenade. In other words, who makes it from the page (shown in the previous screenshot) and is interested enough to click the **Buy Now** button and make it to the following page:

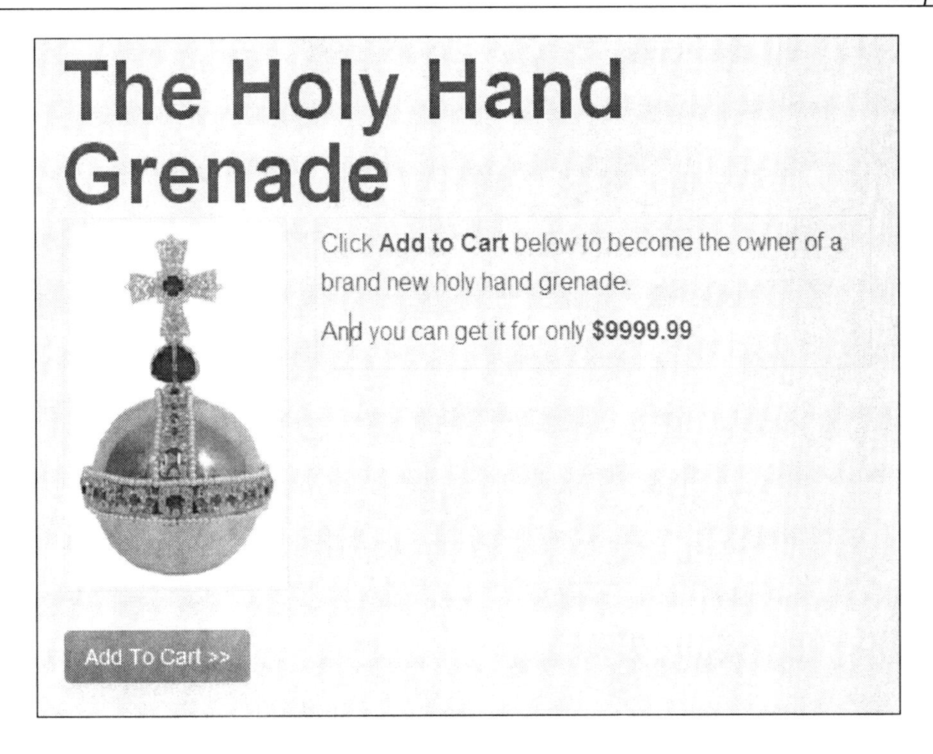

So to track this event, we are going to use a category of `"Product Pricing"` and an action of `"View Product Price"` and our snippet of JavaScript will look something like the following:

```
piwikTracker.setCustomVariable(1,"Product Pricing","View Product
Price","page");
piwikTracker.trackLink();
```

And again, we will use our handy `onclick` JavaScript event to trigger this Piwik code. Here is our button code before adding event tracking:

```
<p><a href="buynow.html" class="btn btn-primary btn-large">Buy Now
>></a></p>
```

And after we add our `onclick` event:

```
<p><a href="buynow.html" class="btn btn-primary btn-large" onclick="
javascript:piwikTracker.setCustomVariable(1,'Product Pricing','View
Product Price','page'); piwikTracker.trackLink();">Buy Now >></a></p>
```

This will tell us how many people have clicked through to see the price of our product.

If we had a full e-commerce website with hundreds or even thousands of products for sale, it would be a good idea to concatenate the product category to the action. In the previous example, we would do this if our holy hand grenade were in a `'Gold Things'` category.

```
piwikTracker.setCustomVariable(1,'Product Pricing','Gold Things-View
Product Price','page');
```

When you have thousands of products, it is good to know the best performing categories of your store. Finding top performing products is easy, especially with e-commerce tracking, which we will get to in the next chapter.

There are many other events you may want to track if you own an e-commerce website. Here are a few:

- Social media buttons
- Request a quote forms
- Save shopping cart notices
- Trial software downloads
- Video demonstrations of a product
- Related, upsell, or cross-sell products
- Live chat links
- Newsletter sign ups
- Adding a product review
- Posting a question to a forum

Which events you decide to track depends on what features you have on your website and what actions are important on the road to your goals.

Tracking Flash events

You have to give it to Flash. It has stuck around for a long time. Even when JavaScript can now do most of the interactive effects on the page, Flash is still useful when it is used in the right places. One thing Flash works well with is movies, and with movies you'll want to track plays, pauses, and stops among other things as events.

We won't go deep into Flash here, just point you in the right direction if you know enough Flash to edit ActionScript. First, you need to know what version of ActionScript you are using, either ActionScript 2 or ActionScript 3.

Tracking events with ActionScript 2

We are going to make this simple. We are only going to embed an SWF movie file into a web page with a play button, and we are going to only track clicks on this play button as an event. In this same web page, you will have your standard Piwik tracking code already in place.

In ActionScript 2, we will have to use the `getURL` method to set the custom variables we will be using to track the play events. So in your Flash application, you will want to put this code in so that an event is tracked:

```
on (release) {
   getURL ("javascript:(function(){piwikTracker.setCustomVariable
(1,"Video","Play","page");})()");
}
```

You will notice that we wrapped the Piwik function call in another anonymous JavaScript function and added an extra set of brackets at the end of this function. Doing this will cause the `setCustomVariable` function to execute immediately. There is no `onclick` event to attach to in Flash. We have to give it a little help to get the job done.

Tracking events with ActionScript 3

Okay, now with the ActionScript 3 example we are going to assume we are doing the same thing as done previously, but with ActionScript 3 code. This takes a little bit more code writing.

First, you have to reference external classes in your FLA file.

```
import flash.external.ExternalInterface
```

Then you will add an event listener to the play button in your FLA file. You will be using this `ExternalInterface` to communicate with the Piwik tracking code already in the page the video is located.

```
playBtn.addEventListener(
MouseEvent.CLICK, ExternalInterface.call('piwikTracker.
setCustomVariable', 1,'Video', 'Play', 'page'));
```

Then in the SWF embed code, you will have to allow all of this to happen by setting `allowScriptAccess` to `always` in two locations.

```
<object ...
    <param  name="allowScriptAccess" value="always"  />
    <!--  {THE_REST_OF_THE_OBJECT_HERE}   -->
    <embed ...
```

```
        allowScriptAccess="always"
        <!-- {THE_REST_OF_THE_EMBED_HERE} -->
      </embed>
  </object>
```

If you know Flash and ActionScript, this should be a pretty simple addition to your code. You can use similar code to call other methods in the `piwikTracker` object.

Tracking page load time

With page speed being a factor in the rank of your website on Google, tracking the load time of your web pages may be something you create an event out of. And Google is not the only reason you should know how long it takes your pages to load. There is a method behind the Google algorithm. Visitors don't like slow pages. They want their content now. After all, they could just search again and find another page that doesn't waste a whole five seconds of their time.

This is going to require an extra bit of JavaScript though. We will be using the JavaScript `Date()` method to generate a timestamp at the top of the page. And then at the bottom of the page, by using the `window.onload` JavaScript event, we will wait for the page to load before we create another timestamp. We will use the difference in these two timestamps to calculate the load time of the page and save this as a custom variable.

```
<html>
  <head>
  <script type = "text/javascript">
    var page_load_start = new Date();
  </script>
  <title>Title</title>
  </head>
  <body>
  <h1>The Header</h1>
  <p>The Body</p>
  <script type = "text/javascript">
    var _paq = _paq || [];
    window.onload = (function () {
      var page_load_end = new Date();
      var load_time = page_load_end.getTime() - page_load_start.
getTime();
      var u = ("https:" == document.location.protocol) ?
"https://YOUR_PIWIK_URL" : "http://YOUR_PIWIK_URL";
        _paq.push(['setSiteId', YOUR_SITE_ID]);
        _paq.push(['setTrackerUrl', u + 'piwik.php']);
        _paq.push(['setCustomVariable', 1, 'Landing Page Time',
load_time, 'page']);
```

```
        _paq.push(['trackPageView']);
        _paq.push(['enableLinkTracking']);
        var d = document,
        g = d.createElement('script'),
        s = d.getElementsByTagName('script')[0];
        g.type = 'text/javascript';
        g.defer = true;
        g.async = true;
        g.src = u + 'piwik.js';
        s.parentNode.insertBefore(g, s);
    });
  </script>
  </body>
</html>
```

So we create a `page_load_start` time in the head of the page. Then we use the asynchronous version of the Piwik tracking code. In this same bunch of code right before the ending body tag, we set the `page_load_end` time and subtract `page_load_start` time from it to get `load_time`. You will also notice that we set the category of our event to `'Landing Page Time'`, and the action, although more of a just a value in this case, to `load_time`. The landing page time will show up in your reports in milliseconds.

Date range: **2012-05-02**

Custom Variables

Custom Variable name		Unique visitors
Landing Page Time		-
Custom Variable value	**Visits**	Actions
65	1	1
381	1	1
423	1	1
441	1	1
443	1	1
457	1	1
551	1	1
578	1	1
579	1	1
618	1	1

1-10 of 22 Next ›

By implementing this load time event tracker across your website, you can have up to the minute data on the load time for individual pages. This could be used to find which pages and content need optimization and help you determine high traffic times when your server may not be able to handle the load and start responding more slowly.

Reading custom variable reports

You will find the custom variables report by clicking on the **Visitors** menu and then choosing **Custom Variables**:

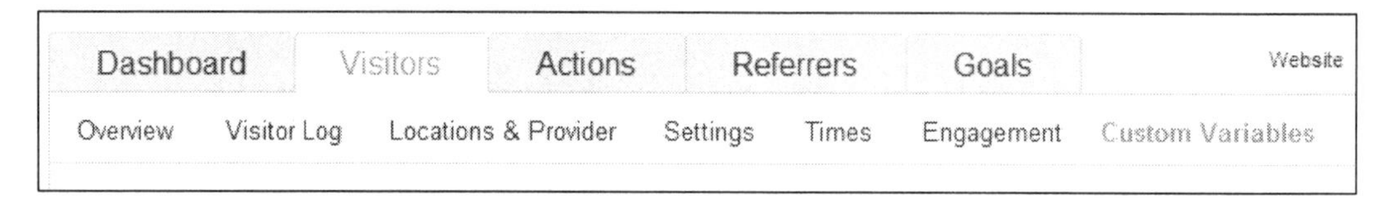

This report will be broken down by the custom variable name. By clicking on each name or event category you can find the values or actions that we have set, along with the following data in a table:

- Unique visitors
- Visits
- Pages
- Time on site
- Bounce rate
- Conversion rate
- Revenue

For custom variables that have the page level of scope, you will get this data:

- Unique visitors
- Visits
- Pages

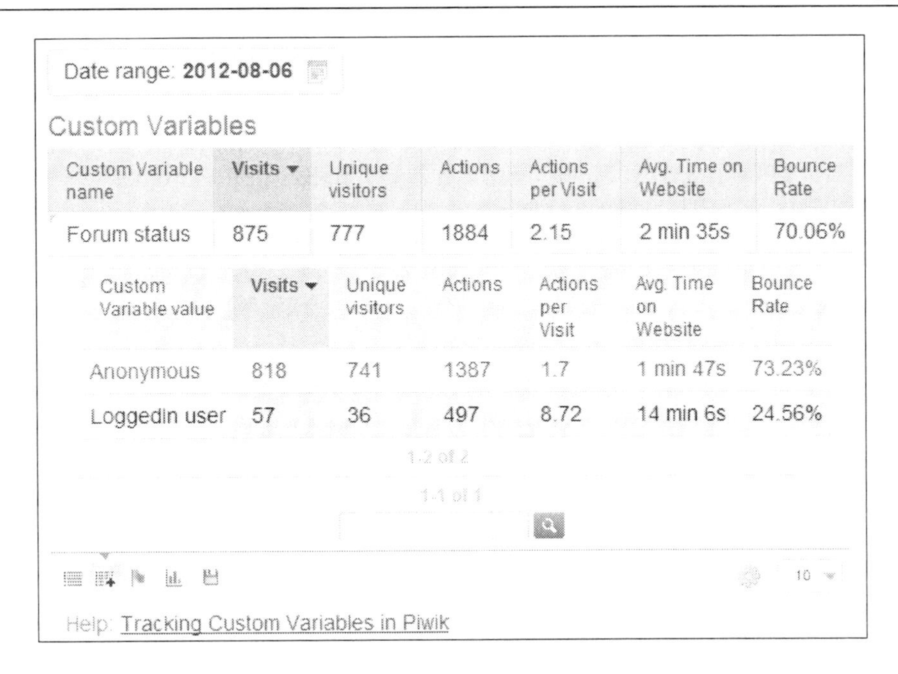

Date range: **2012-08-06**

Custom Variables

Custom Variable name	Visits	Unique visitors	Actions	Actions per Visit	Avg. Time on Website	Bounce Rate
Forum status	875	777	1884	2.15	2 min 35s	70.06%

Custom Variable value	Visits	Unique visitors	Actions	Actions per Visit	Avg. Time on Website	Bounce Rate
Anonymous	818	741	1387	1.7	1 min 47s	73.23%
LoggedIn user	57	36	497	8.72	14 min 6s	24.56%

1-2 of 2

1-1 of 1

Help: Tracking Custom Variables in Piwik

You can also find custom variables by choosing the **Visitors** menu again and choosing the **Visitor Log** report. Custom variables with the scope of visit are listed on the left-hand side of each entry, as shown in the left hand column directly under the date and time of the visit, as you can see in the following screenshot:

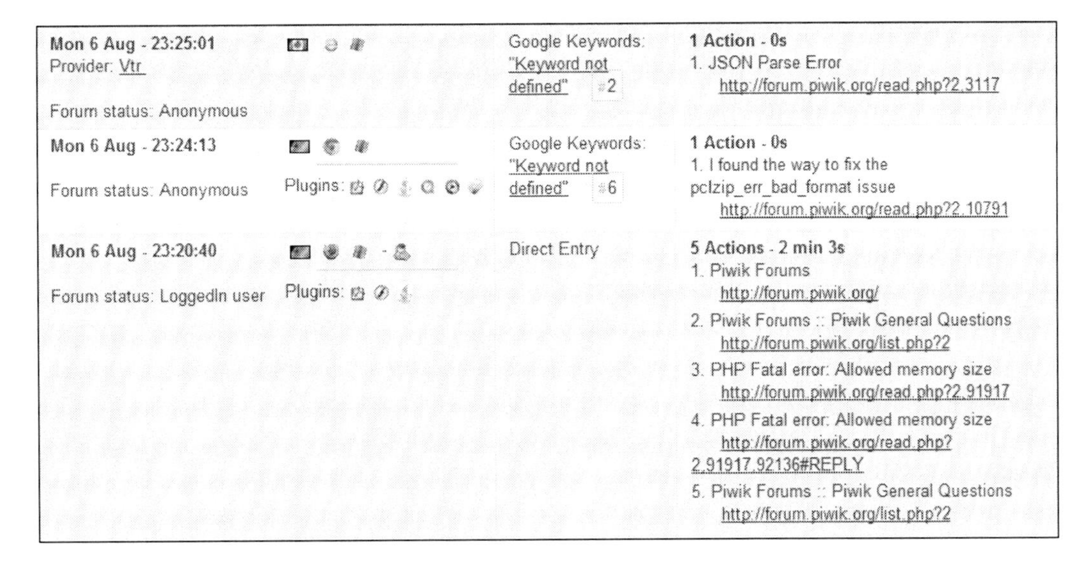

You can also view custom variables which have the page level of scope by hovering over the page URL or page title in the **Visitor Log**.

Other uses for custom variables

This chapter was about event tracking, but we went into some detail about which custom variables in Piwik are used. But they are custom variables, so you can use them for a lot more than just event tracking. Feel free to use them wherever you need more data about a visitor or a page view.

If you want to see which users have logged into your site and which users haven't, you may want to set a custom variable called "User status" with a scope of "visit" and a value of either "Logged In" or "Anonymous".

If you want to discover how many visits you get to a category of pages, you could create a custom variable called "Category View" with a scope of "page" and the value could be the category of the current page or post.

And if you want to track how active your visitors are, you could create a custom variable called "Customer Engagement" with a scope of "visit" and a value of "New", "Engaged", or "Customer".

The only limitation you have with custom variables is that you can track only five custom variables per visits and up to five per page view. But other than that, you have many options when it comes to using Piwik's custom variables.

Summary

In this chapter, we used the most custom code so far in the book, even going as far as adding custom JavaScript to track page load time. We learned that events are something less than goals, but are stops on the road to goals and are worth tracking in their own right. We learned how to use Piwik's custom variable feature for event tracking and used it to track social media events, blog comments, e-commerce events, and Flash events.

In the next chapter, we will dive into e-commerce tracking and how Piwik is a great tool for keeping track of sales and ROI on a website with hundreds or thousands of products.

7
E-commerce Tracking

No one knows the need for web analytics more than the e-commerce website owner, web master, or SEO. You are in the customer service business just like any retail store. A customer may not come back to a brick and mortar store because its service is bad. Well, when you have an e-commerce website, most of your customer service will be done by your site itself, whether you like it or not. Unless a customer calls or e-mails you for help, your store will show the customer where the product they are looking for is, will give them details on how to use it, and will be their cashier when and if they decide to check out.

Tracking the activity on your e-commerce website is crucial in guaranteeing that its customer service is constantly improving. And how do you improve a website's customer service? Well, first you have to discover what is making your visitors leave before they become customers. If your checkout form is too complicated or takes too long to load, it is the same thing as a long line at a supermarket. So you simplify your checkout form and see if less of your shopping carts get abandoned.

There are many details that can drive your visitors away and by tracking e-commerce actions, you can make changes to your site and have the data you need to know if your changes were the right thing to do.

In this chapter, we will learn:

- How to enable e-commerce tracking for your website
- How to track orders and items purchased in Piwik
- How to track shopping carts and the items in the products in those carts
- How to track product and product category page views
- How to write an e-commerce plugin for ZenCart or your chosen platform
- How to read and use Piwik's e-commerce reports

Enabling e-commerce tracking for your website

By default, when you add a new website to track in Piwik, e-commerce tracking is not active. But it is pretty simple to activate it. Just click on the **Settings** link in the top-right corner of Piwik's interface.

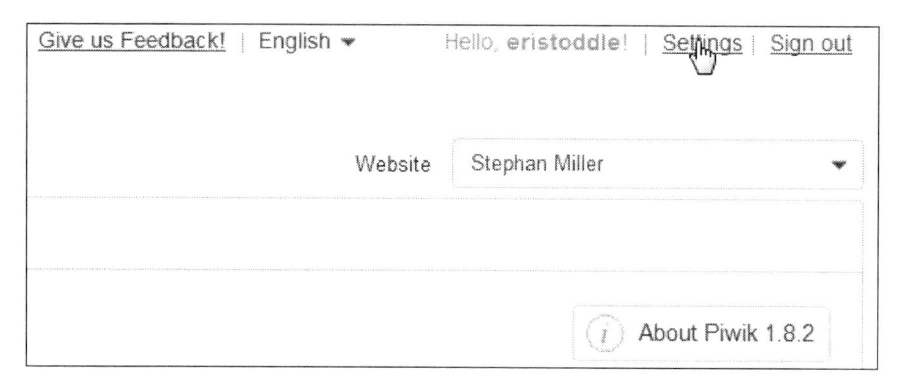

From there, choose **Websites** from the menu. You will see a listing of all the websites you track in Piwik. Scroll down to the site you want to activate tracking on.

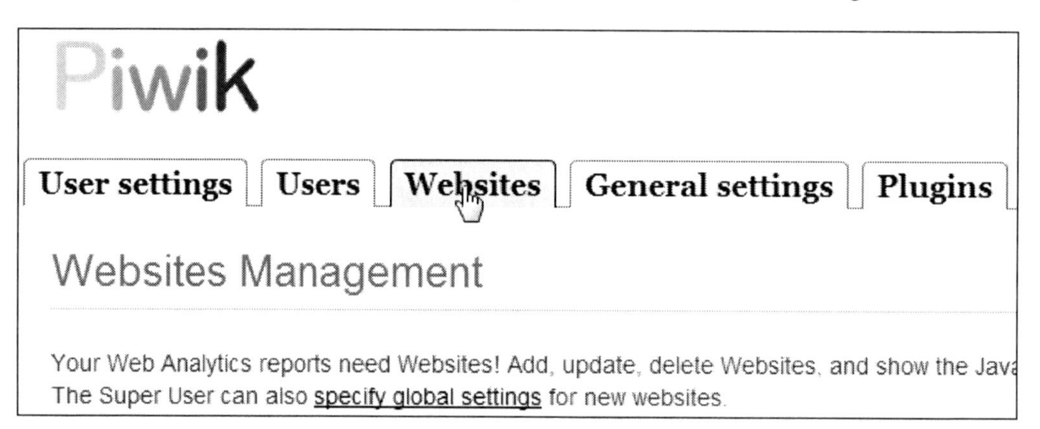

Click on the **Edit** link on the right-hand side of the website's row.

Excluded Parameters	Time zone	Currency	Ecommerce			JavaScript Tracking Code
	America/Chicago	USD	-	Edit	Delete	View Tracking code
	America/Chicago	USD	-	Edit	Delete	View Tracking code
	America/Chicago	USD	-	Edit	Delete	View Tracking code
	America/Chicago	USD	-	Edit	Delete	View Tracking code

Then the table row will expand so that you can edit it. A drop-down field will appear in the **Ecommerce** column. Choose the `Ecommerce enabled` option and then click on the **Save** button to save your changes.

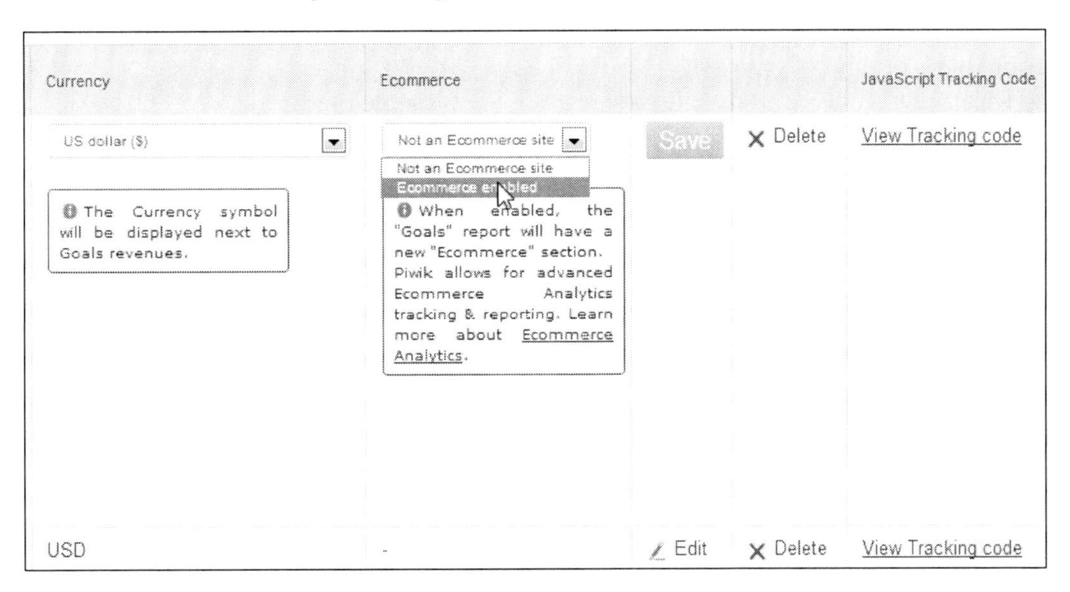

Now e-commerce tracking is enabled for your website. You will notice that the **Goals** tab in Piwik's main menu has become **Ecommerce & Goals**. And now that we have enabled our tracking, it is time to add code to our website to use it.

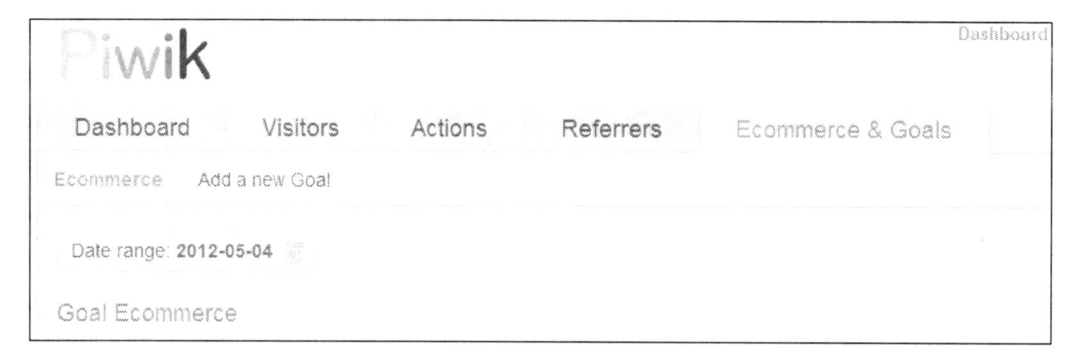

E-commerce tracking code is a bit more complex than the standard tracking code. Nothing is going to happen automatically by adding the standard Piwik JavaScript code to the bottom of your page. You will have to write some code, pay someone else to write some code, or find a plugin for your e-commerce platform.

You can think of e-commerce tracking as advanced goal tracking, and for complete tracking of your e-commerce website you should add event tracking to events such as product information downloads and other e-commerce events, which we covered in *Chapter 6, Tracking Events*, as well as goal tracking for things such as newsletter subscriptions and news or blog feed subscriptions. There are three specific types of tracking available for e-commerce using Piwik:

- Orders and products purchased
- Add to shopping cart actions and the products involved
- Product and category page views

The data that results from this tracking is phenomenal though. You will have the information you need to improve the sales of your products at your fingertips. You will know which products you sell the most of and which bring in the highest dollar amounts. You will learn what your best producing categories are and the conversion rate of your product pages. You will know how long a customer took to make a purchase and just what path they took through your site to do so. And you can take this knowledge and use it to increase conversion rates and sales.

Tracking orders and products purchased

In the very least, you need to know how well your products are selling, so we will begin with tracking our sales. This is the base metric of all of our e-commerce tracking data. Your shopping cart itself will give you data on sales, but most shopping carts don't have a way of correlating this with your visitor data the way Piwik can. We will learn the revenue of each product, how many we have sold, and how many unique purchases of that product we have had. If our e-commerce shop has categories, we can track which categories produce sales and which need a little work.

In order to do this, we need to tell Piwik that we made a sale right before we call `trackPageView()`. We do this with two steps:

1. Add the item or items sold using `addEcommerceItem(Sku,ProductName,Category,Price,Quantity)` and call it once for each SKU or Stock Keeping Unit (that is, your internal product number) sold in the order. With this function you will be able to tell Piwik the product's SKU, its name, its category, its price, and how many you sold.
2. Create an e-commerce order in Piwik with `trackEcommerceOrder(OrderID,GrandTotal,SubTotal,Tax,Shipping,Discount)` which can hold the ID your e-commerce platform gave the order, the grand total of the order, the subtotal, the tax, the shipping, and whether or not the order was given a discount.

In you are familiar with Google Analytics e-commerce tracking, you will notice that Google's `_addTrans()` and `_trackTrans()` get combined into one function in Piwik.

Now where you add this code depends on how your e-commerce platform works. Many websites have a "checkout success" page that does two jobs of notifying the customer that their payment has processed and of converting a shopping cart object into an order object in one way or another. The data you need to track the order in Piwik may be stored in a cookie or a session object. Or you may get only the order ID from the checkout success page and have to write some PHP code to get the order information you need from the database using that ID.

Here is an example of the JavaScript code needed to track an e-commerce transaction in Piwik. Most likely, you will have to use other code, such as PHP, to dynamically generate the sections of the code that track your order based on the data on your checkout success page. We will learn one way of doing this by writing a Piwik plugin for ZenCart, an open source e-commerce platform, later on in the chapter. But for now, let's learn how this code works.

```
<!--Piwik-->
  <script type = "text/javascript">
    var pkBaseURL = (("https:" == document.location.protocol) ?
      "https://$PIWIK_URL" : "http://$PIWIK_URL");
    document.write(unescape("%3Cscript src='" + pkBaseURL +
      "piwik.js' type='text/javascript'%3E%3C/script%3E"));
  </script>
  <script type = "text/javascript">
    try {
      var piwikTracker = Piwik.getTracker(pkBaseURL + "piwik.php",
        $SITE_ID);
      piwikTracker.addEcommerceItem(
        "M-2542", //sku
        "Holy Hand Grenade", //name
        "Gold Things", //category
        14.99, //price
        1); //quantity
      piwikTracker.addEcommerceItem(
        "B-2535", //sku
        "Holy Hand Grenade Rattle", //name
        "Gold Things", //category
        7.49, //price
        2); //quantity
      piwikTracker.trackEcommerceOrder(
        "000005236", //order id
        38.97, //grand total
        29.97, //sub total
        5.5, //tax
        4.5, //shipping
        false); //discount offered
      piwikTracker.trackPageView();
      piwikTracker.enableLinkTracking();
    } catch (err) {}
  </script>
  <noscript><p><img src ="$PIWIK_URL/piwik.php?idsite=1" style =
    "border:0" alt = ""/></p></noscript>
<!--End Piwik Tracking Code-->
```

This is the code resulting from tracking an order with two products in it. You will notice it begins and ends like the Piwik code you already have posted in your website. But between the creation of the `piwikTracker` object and when we call `piwikTracker.trackPageView()` there are three more functions.

The first two are `addEcommerceItem` functions. We add two separate line items from a customer's shopping cart. Each function takes five parameters for this order as follows:

- **SKU** (required): This actually stands for Stock Keeping Unit, but it is just whatever number or string you use to identify a unique product. You can use any string, such as a UPC or a combination of brand and manufacturer's part number.
- **Product Name** (optional): This is the name of the product. You can make it the same name you use in your shopping cart or use a custom name if you choose.
- **Category** (optional): This parameter is obvious; the category you list your product under. When writing code to track categories in a site with a lot of categories and subcategories, you may want to create a breadcrumb type category list to send back to Piwik such as, "Gold Things\For The Baby" and "Gold Things\For Adults". If you had a subcategory of "For the Baby" under another category of "Silver Things", and only sent the subcategory to Piwik, all of your gold and silver baby things would be thrown in the same category. Plus if your category only holds subcategories, you will now be able to track sales across your top level categories.
- **Price** (optional): This is the price of unit of the product, not the total of the product prices if the customer bought more than one. This value must be an integer or float, not a string. So you can use 5.67, 9.9, and 7, but you cannot send Piwik values such as "$5.67", "14.4", or "7". In other words, just numbers and a decimal point, nothing that has to go in quotes. If you must use values in quotes such as "5.99", then you can use the JavaScript `parseFloat` function to convert the value into `float` such as `newValue = parseFloat("5.99");` and `newValue` will be a `float` instead of a string.
- **Quantity** (optional): This is how many of the product that was sold in this order line. It is an `int` value.

The final function is the `trackEcommerceOrder` function. This will give Piwik the details of the order as a whole. This function takes up to six parameters as follows:

- **Order ID** (required): This is the ID of the order in your e-commerce website. It may be the auto incrementing ID in your `orders` database table.
- **Grand Total** (required): This is the grand total of the order. It must be a `float` or `int` value and not a string, as discussed earlier.

- **Subtotal** (optional): This is the total before taxes and shipping. It must also be a `float` or `int` value.
- **Tax** (optional): This is the sales tax applied to the order. It must also be a `float` or `int` value.
- **Shipping** (optional): This is the shipping you charged your customer. It must also be a `float` or `int` value.
- **Discount** (optional): This is a `true` or `false` value indicating whether or not a discount was applied to the order.

Also note that any of the optional parameters in our tracking code can be set to `false` if needed.

Tracking shopping carts and items in them

Tracking shopping cart updates in your e-commerce website will allow you to track shopping cart abandonment. Customers may leave your website before checking out for many reasons. Maybe your shipping charge is too high. Maybe your checkout forms are too complicated and you need to streamline them a bit. Maybe the customer is actually saving the cart for later. Whatever the reason, by having access to stats on lost sales, you can work to minimize the amount of shopping carts that are abandoned by making changes to your site and tracking the effect it has on your abandoned carts.

There are two Piwik functions you will be using to track your shopping carts. They are as follows:

- `addEcommerceItem(productSKU, productName, productCategory, price, quantity)`: This is the same function we use to add items to an order that we discussed in the section before this. The only required parameter is the product SKU. The rest of the parameters are optional. The product SKU, product name and product category can be a string. The price can be a `float` or an `int` value. And the quantity must be an `int` value.
- `trackEcommerceCartUpdate(cartTotal)`: This function takes the total of all products in the shopping cart and gives your Piwik installation the data it needed to track the dollar value of abandoned carts. And this has to be a `float` or an `int` value, not a string.

And here is an example of how we would use these functions in our Piwik tracking code:

```
<!--Piwik-->
  <script type = "text/javascript">
    var pkBaseURL = (("https:" == document.location.protocol) ?
      "https://$PIWIK_URL" : "http://$PIWIK_URL");
    document.write(unescape("%3Cscript src='" + pkBaseURL +
      "piwik.js' type='text/javascript'%3E%3C/script%3E"));
  </script>
  <script type = "text/javascript">
    try {
      var piwikTracker = Piwik.getTracker(pkBaseURL + "piwik.php",
        $SITE_ID);
      piwikTracker.addEcommerceItem(
        "M-2542", //sku
        "Holy Hand Grenade", //name
        "Gold Things", //category
        14.99, //price
        1); //quantity
      piwikTracker.addEcommerceItem(
        "B-2535", //sku
        "Holy Hand Grenade Rattle", //name
        "Gold Things", //category
        7.49, //price
        2); //quantity
      piwikTracker.trackEcommerceCartUpdate(29.97); //cart total
      piwikTracker.trackPageView();
      piwikTracker.enableLinkTracking();
    } catch (err) {}
  </script>
  <noscript><p><img src ="$PIWIK_URL/piwik.php?idsite=1" style =
    "border:0" alt = ""/></p></noscript>
<!--End Piwik Tracking Code-->
```

Again, the e-commerce functions are inserted after we create `piwikTracker` and before we called `piwikTracker.trackPageView`. In this cart, we have the same two items we had in our order, so we use `addEcommerceItem` in the exact same way and with the same parameters as we did in our order tracking example. And after that we call `piwikTracker.trackEcommerceCartUpdate` with the total of the cart which is `29.97`.

Tracking product and category page views

Tracking shopping carts gives Piwik the information it needs to calculate lost sales. But in order to track the conversion rate of your product or category pages, you need to track the views those pages get. This conversion rate will be another tool to help you increase sales on your website as you make changes to it.

And your Piwik tracker actually has one function that will do both jobs.

```
setEcommerceView(productSKU, productName, categoryName, price)
```

This function takes the SKU of your product, which is the only required parameter for product page tracking, your product's name, the name of the category it is in, and its price. The price again has to be an `int` or a `float` value. The rest of the parameters are string. Here is an example of how we use this function:

```
<!--Piwik-->
  <script type = "text/javascript">
    var pkBaseURL = (("https:" == document.location.protocol) ?
      "https://$PIWIK_URL" : "http://$PIWIK_URL");
    document.write(unescape("%3Cscript src='" + pkBaseURL +
      "piwik.js' type='text/javascript'%3E%3C/script%3E"));
  </script>
  <script type = "text/javascript">
    try {
      var piwikTracker = Piwik.getTracker(pkBaseURL + "piwik.php",
        $SITE_ID);
      piwikTracker.addEcommerceView(
        "M-2542", //sku
        "Holy Hand Grenade", //name
        "Gold Things", //category
        14.99); //price
      piwikTracker.trackPageView();
      piwikTracker.enableLinkTracking();
    } catch (err) {}
  </script>
  <noscript><p><img src ="$PIWIK_URL/piwik.php?idsite=1" style =
    "border:0" alt = ""/></p></noscript>
<!--End Piwik Tracking Code-->
```

We call it right before `piwikTracker.trackPageView`. And we use the same function to track a category page view.

```
piwikTracker.addEcommerceView(
      false, //no sku
      false, //no name
      "Gold Things", //category
      false); //no price
```

Notice that any parameter that did not apply, we simply set to `false`. This is a Boolean value and has no quotes.

Adding Piwik e-commerce tracking to ZenCart

You may be able to find a plugin that adds Piwik's e-commerce tracking to the shopping cart software that you use. But often you will be faced with writing your own code for your e-commerce platform. If you know your shopping cart well enough to write custom code for it, it is really not that hard to integrate Piwik tracking and the payoff is worth the work.

We are going to write a plugin for ZenCart. When I was writing this book, I couldn't find a plugin for the ZenCart installation I was using to test Piwik, so I figured we could write one. ZenCart is an open source e-commerce shopping cart that branched from osCommerce in 2003. osCommerce is still the more popular of the two platforms, but I prefer ZenCart for ease of modification.

Although we will be writing a plugin for ZenCart, you can use similar logic when writing custom code for your e-commerce platform. If we look back over the previous code, we can see that we need to find four types of pages on our site to use Piwik's e-commerce tracking. These pages are as follows:

- **The Checkout Success page**: This is the page where customers land after they have made a payment. We will need to get the details of the sale from this page to send to our Piwik installation.
- **The Shopping Cart page**: Whatever page on your site that shows your customer the list of products they are purchasing. We will need to know when the cart is updated and what products were added.
- **The Category pages**: We will need to know when these pages are viewed. It will give us the information we need to calculate conversion rate. In e-commerce platforms, one page will usually control all categories and be updated from the database based on category parameters in the URL.

- **The Product pages**: We also need to know when these pages are viewed for calculating conversion rates. These also are usually on PHP in most shopping carts. Information on the page is dynamically updated based on product ID parameters in the URL.

If we wanted to just hack away at our platform, we could find these pages and put our custom PHP and JavaScript code right in them. But most open source platforms have a system of plugins. Plugins allow developers to write add-ons to software without editing the core files of the system. If a plugin causes an error, the plugin can be deactivated and the system itself can go on as normal. And the software itself can be updated without removing any code modifications. If we were to hack core files to do new things, an update would remove all modifications.

Creating functions in PHP to mirror Piwik's functions

So let's think about how we want our plugin to work. It has to do so many things. It has to have at least five different types of JavaScript code—one for each of our e-commerce tracking functions and one for regular old tracking. But really the code is not that different. It all has the same code as the regular tracking. We will just have to add extra functions right before we call `trackPageView()` depending on what page we landed on.

So we can just create a function in PHP for each type of JavaScript line we have to write and have each function return the JavaScript code to us so we can print it out when needed with the rest of our Piwik JavaScript at the bottom of the page. We need functions that will do the following things for us:

- We need a function to log the category page
- We need a function to log the product page
- We need a function to log the cart
- We need a function to log orders

You will notice there is no function for standard tracking, because for that we can use the same code on every page. It does not have to be dynamically generated. Also, we are not writing a fully-fledged plugin where the ZenCart store owner can edit his/her details in the backend. That would overcomplicate things.

First let's look at an easier function to write. We are going to write a simple PHP function that will return the JavaScript code to set a custom variable in Piwik. We will make this PHP function accept the parameters of `$index`, `$key`, and `$value`.

```
function log_custom_variable($index,$key,$value) {

  return 'piwikTracker.setCustomVariable
    ('.$index.',"'.$key.'","'.$value.'","visit");' . "\n";

}
```

So when we give `log_custom_variable` 1 for an `$index`, `"Video"` for a `$key` and `"Play"` for a `$value`, it will return the following string:

```
piwikTracker.setCustomVariable(1,"Video","Play");
```

This is a line of JavaScript we can print in the middle of our Piwik tracking code that will set our custom variable for us and we can reuse for whatever custom variables we need to track throughout our site. By using PHP functions such as this we can create a bridge between our server-side data and the JavaScript that must be executed on the client's browser.

So let's look at our e-commerce tracking functions. In a ZenCart installation, these functions will be in a file we will call `zenpiwik.php`. And we would upload this file to `/includes/functions/extra_functions/` folder of our ZenCart installation. Functions in the files of this folder will automatically be loaded by ZenCart and will be available for use by the code we will use to print the extra lines in our Piwik tracking JavaScript. For other e-commerce platforms you may have to include a function file such as this manually by using `include` or `require`, and of course, you would have different database calls than those given next.

First, we will take a look at the function that will dynamically generate the code to track category page views.

```
function log_category($categories_id,$language_id) {
  global $db;

  $categories_query = "select categories_name from " .
    TABLE_CATEGORIES_DESCRIPTION . " where categories_id = " .
    (int)$categories_id . " and language_id = " .
    (int)$language_id;
  $categories = $db->Execute($categories_query);

  if ($categories->RecordCount() == 1) {
    return 'piwikTracker.setEcommerceView(productSku =
      false,productName = false,category = "'.$categories-
      >fields['categories_name'].'");' . "\n";
  }

}
```

The two parameters this function receives are the `$categories_id` and the `$language_id`. The `$language_id` parameter is something necessary for ZenCart to choose the correct language for the web page. The category ID is the important part. Our ZenCart installation has this ID available when the category page is loaded, but it is only available to the server-side PHP code and not yet to the JavaScript. What we really want is a category name.

So we query the database for the name of the category with the next three lines. We then check if we actually got any results from the database with `if ($categories->RecordCount() == 1)`. And if we get a result, the function returns the following string, if we gave it a category ID that mapped to our "Gold Things" category:

```
piwikTracker.setEcommerceView(productSku = false,productName =
  false,category = "Gold Things");
```

The database calls may be different for your e-commerce website, but you can use the same concept and just change the queries.

And here is the function that will return the line of JavaScript code we need to track our product page views:

```
function log_product($products_id,$language_id) {
  global $db;

  $products_query = "select p.products_model, pd.products_name,
    cd.categories_name from " . TABLE_PRODUCTS . " p, " .
    TABLE_PRODUCTS_DESCRIPTION . " pd, " .
    TABLE_PRODUCTS_TO_CATEGORIES . " p2c, ".
    TABLE_CATEGORIES_DESCRIPTION ." cd WHERE p.products_id =
    pd.products_id and p2c.categories_id = cd.categories_id and
    p.products_id = " . (int)$products_id . " and pd.language_id
    =".(int)$language_id." and cd.language_id
    =".(int)$language_id;
  $products = $db->Execute($products_query);

  if ($products->RecordCount() == 1) {
    return 'piwikTracker.setEcommerceView("'.$products-
    >fields['products_model'].'","'.$products-
    >fields['products_name'].'","'.$products-
    >fields['categories_name'].'");' . "\n";
  }

}
```

It is very similar to the `log_category` function. But instead of a category ID, this function receives the product ID. This database query is more complex because we not only want the product SKU and name, but also the product category. So we connect multiple tables in the database with a `join` statement and then query using the product ID. For other e-commerce platforms, it is likely you will have to use a similar `join` query with your database tables. And again the results are checked and if we have a result, a string like the following will be returned:

```
piwikTracker.setEcommerceView("S-4003","Sterling Silver Holy Hand
  Grenade","Silver Things");
```

Now it's time for a function that is a bit more complex. The `log_cart` function takes an array of products that ZenCart uses to hold the data on items in the shopping cart or `$products` and the total of the cart, or `$total`.

```
function log_cart($products,$total,$language_id) {
  global $db;

  for ($i=0, $n=sizeof($products); $i<$n; $i++) {

    if (!is_null($products[$i]['model'])) {
      $categories_query = "select cd.categories_name from " .
        TABLE_CATEGORIES_DESCRIPTION ." cd, ".
        TABLE_PRODUCTS_TO_CATEGORIES . " p2c
        WHERE cd.categories_id = p2c.categories_id and
        p2c.products_id = " . (int)$products[$i]['id'] . "
        and cd.language_id =".(int)$language_id;

      $categories = $db->Execute($categories_query);
      $string .= 'piwikTracker.addEcommerceItem
        ("'.$products[$i]['model'].'",
        "'.$products[$i]['name'].'",
        "'.$categories->fields['categories_name'].'",
        '.$products[$i]['final_price'].',
        '.$products[$i]['quantity'].');' . "\n";

    }

  }

  $string .= 'piwikTracker.trackEcommerceCartUpdate
    ('.$total.');' . "\n";

  return $string;
}
```

In this function, we loop through the array that ZenCart gives and check if the "model" key in the array contains a value. In ZenCart, this is our SKU. If this key exists, the database is queried to find the product category. From the results of this data, we create a string of Piwik JavaScript for tracking the product and concatenate it to our `$string` variable. This variable grows in length as a new line of code is added for each product. When we are done looping through the products, we add the final string to the `$string` value, which tracks the total value of the cart. A result would look something like the following:

```
piwikTracker.addEcommerceItem("M-2542", "Holy Hand Grenade", "Gold
  Things", 14.99,  1);
piwikTracker.addEcommerceItem("B-2535","Holy Hand Grenade
  Rattle","Gold Things",7.49, 2);
piwikTracker. trackEcommerceCartUpdate(22.41);
```

And finally, we have the function we will use to track the actual orders. It is the most complex of them all, because it requires much more data. Again ZenCart requires `$language_id` as it did in every function. This time its parameters include the last ID inserted into the order database or `$insert_id`, the result of the database call to the orders table or `$order`, and the array of products in the order or `$products`.

```
function log_order($insert_id,$order,$products,$language_id) {
  global $db;

  foreach ($products as $p) {

    if (!is_null($p['products_id'])) {
      $categories_query = "select cd.categories_name from " .
        TABLE_CATEGORIES_DESCRIPTION ." cd, ".
        TABLE_PRODUCTS_TO_CATEGORIES . " p2c
        WHERE cd.categories_id = p2c.categories_id and
        p2c.products_id = " . (int)$p['products_id'] . " and
        cd.language_id =".(int)$language_id;
      $categories = $db->Execute($categories_query);

      $order_product_query = "select products_model, products_tax,
        products_quantity, final_price from " .
        TABLE_ORDERS_PRODUCTS . "
        where orders_id = " . (int)$insert_id . " and
        products_id = " . (int)$p['products_id'];
      $order_product = $db->Execute($order_product_query);

      $string .= 'piwikTracker.addEcommerceItem
        ("'.$order_product->fields['products_model'].'",
        "'.$p['products_name'].'",
        "'.$categories->fields['categories_name'].'",
        '.(float)$order_product->fields['final_price'].',
        '.$order_product->fields['products_quantity'].');' . "\n";
```

```
        }

    }

    $st_result = $db->Execute("SELECT ROUND(value, 2) subtotal FROM
      ". TABLE_ORDERS_TOTAL ." WHERE class='ot_subtotal' AND
      orders_id = ". $order->fields['orders_id']);
    $subtotal = $st_result->fields['subtotal'];
    $shipping = (float)$order->fields['order_total'] -
      (float)$order->fields['order_tax'] -
      (float)$st_result->fields['subtotal'];

    $string .= 'piwikTracker.trackEcommerceOrder
      ("'.$insert_id.'",'.$order->fields['order_total'].',
      '.$subtotal.','.$order->fields['order_tax'].',
      '.$shipping.',false);' . "\n";

    return $string;

  }
```

This works for ZenCart, but on another e-commerce platform, it could be quite different. In fact, it could be even simpler. So I will go over the basics of what this does.

The `$insert_id` is the last ID inserted into the order database. This will be the `orderID` value we need to track the e-commerce order. From the `$order` object, we get the rest of the data we need for the `trackEcommerceOrder` function in Piwik. And again we loop through the products array creating a string of JavaScript code for tracking that product with Piwik. And when all of this is done, it returns a string like the following:

```
piwikTracker.addEcommerceItem("M-2542", "Holy Hand Grenade",
  "Gold Things", 14.99, 1);
piwikTracker.addEcommerceItem("B-2535","Holy Hand Grenade
  Rattle","Gold Things",7.49, 2);
piwikTracker.trackEcommerceOrder(169,30.41,22.41,0,8.00,false);
```

We just hardcoded the discount value to `false` because we won't be giving discounts, but you could have your own function check if a discount has been given to the order and set this value to `true` if it has been.

Now that we have the PHP functions that return the lines of JavaScript code we need to track our e-commerce actions, it's time to use them.

Mixing PHP and JavaScript

What we need to do in the middle of our standard Piwik tracking code is check if it is a category page, shopping cart page, or checkout success page and if it is one of these pages, print the correct JavaScript code.

I am going to simplify the code I wrote for ZenCart here. It involves adding data to the PHP `$_SESSION` variable before printing it to Piwik's tracking code. The full working ZenCart plugin with a README file is available in the code files of the book. But we just want to learn about the details of Piwik e-commerce tracking and not the inner workings of one specific e-commerce shopping cart. This is not production code. So here is the slightly simplified code:

```
<!-- Piwik with E-Commerce Tracking-->
  <script type="text/javascript">
    var pkBaseURL = (("https:" == document.location.protocol) ?
      "https://YOUR_PIWIK_URL: "http://YOUR_PIWIK_URL/piwik/");
    document.write(unescape("%3Cscript src='" + pkBaseURL +
      "piwik.js' type='text/javascript'%3E%3C/script%3E"));
  </script>
  <script type="text/javascript">
    try {
      var piwikTracker = Piwik.getTracker(pkBaseURL + "piwik.php",
        YOUR_PIWIK_ID);
      <?php
        if (($current_page_base == FILENAME_DEFAULT) &&
          zen_not_null($current_category_id)) {
          if ($log_category = log_category((int)
            $current_category_id,$_SESSION['languages_id'])) {
            echo $log_category;
          }
        }
        if ($current_page_base == FILENAME_PRODUCT_INFO) {
          if ($log_product =
            log_product((int)$_GET['products_id'],
            $_SESSION['languages_id'])) {
            echo $log_product;
          }
        }
        if ($current_page_base == FILENAME_SHOPPING_CART) {
          echo $log_cart($products,$total,$language_id);
        }
```

```
        if ($current_page_base == FILENAME_CHECKOUT_SUCCESS) {
          echo $log_order
            ($insert_id,$order,$products,$language_id);
        }
      ?>
      piwikTracker.trackPageView();
      piwikTracker.enableLinkTracking();
      piwikTracker.setConversionAttributionFirstReferrer();
    } catch( err ) {}
  </script>
  <noscript><p><img src="http://YOUR_PIWIK_URL/piwik.php?idsite=
    YOUR_PIWIK_ID" style="border:0" alt="" /></p></noscript>
<!-- End Piwik E-Commerce Tracking Tracking Code -->
```

We will focus on the PHP code that starts right after the `piwikTracker` object is created and ends before `piwikTracker.trackPageView` is called. Let's take a look at what this code does:

1. The first `if` construct checks if a `$category_id` is set for the page and if so we echo the results of the `log_category` function.
2. Then we check if the page is a product info page and if so, we print the results of the `log_product` function.
3. Next we check if it is the shopping cart page and print the string that the `log_cart` function returns if this is true.
4. And finally, we check if the current page is the checkout success page and if it is, we echo the string it returns.

This example module should lead you in the right direction if you need to write a custom plugin or module for your shopping cart website. If you use ZenCart, you're in luck. The plugin in the example code available from the Packt website is a working example. I also have a more advanced version of this plugin available on Github with admin configuration settings and a Piwik dashboard embedded in a page in the admin section of the site. You can get the version of the plugin for ZenCart 1.3.9 and older at `https://github.com/eristoddle/Piwik-Ecommerce-for-Zen-Cart` and the version for ZenCart 1.5 at `https://github.com/eristoddle/Piwik-Ecommerce-for-Zen-Cart-1.5`.

Reading and using Piwik's e-commerce reports

Once you turn on e-commerce tracking and add the code you need to your website, Piwik will provide a plethora of reports on the customers and sales at your shopping cart site. As we said earlier, activating e-commerce in Piwik changes the **Goals** tab to the **Ecommerce & Goals** tab. When you click on the tab, the first report you will see is an overview of your e-commerce goals.

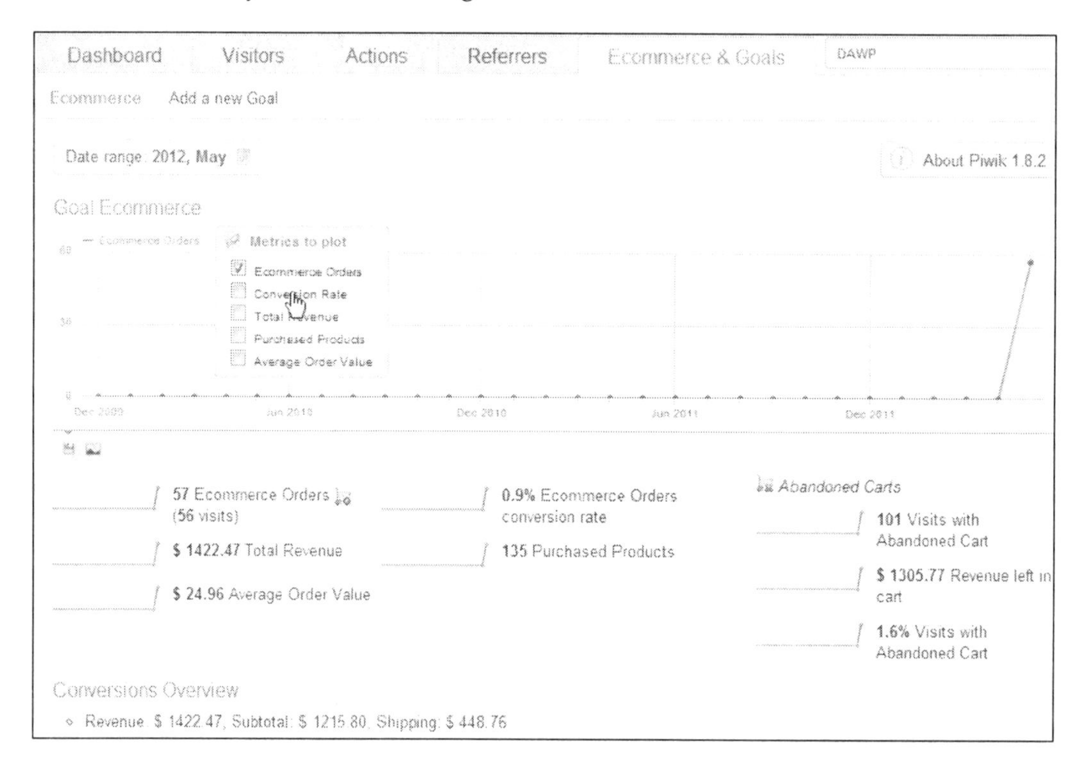

At the top will be a chart that by default will show a count of orders across the date range you have chosen. It will give you a good indication of whether sales are increasing, decreasing, or plateauing. If you want to chart more metrics such as conversion rate, total revenue, or average order value, you can click on the graph icon in the top-left corner of the chart. You can choose one, more, or all of these metrics to plot and each will display data with a different color line.

The smaller charts below also give you these metrics along with data on your abandoned carts. Clicking on any one of the smaller graphs will activate the same metric on the larger graph so you can then see the data in more detail. And below that, under **Conversions Overview**, you will get the total for revenue, the total of your subtotals, total tax, and total shipping for the date range you selected. You can quickly cycle through your date range selection to get a broad overview of your sales over the last day, week, or month.

Below this area are a lot more reports. These reports are represented by tables because they contain a lot more metrics. The default report is your sales by product SKU, shown next. This report will tell you what your top performing SKUs are for the date range you have chosen. You can sort this and the other report tables by any metric you choose. Just click on the column heading. We have sorted by **Product Revenue** in the next screenshot. These metrics are:

- **Product Revenue**: This will tell you the total revenue for the SKU listed. One high dollar product sale or a lot of sales of a low priced item could make a product jump to the top of this list.
- **Quantity**: This metric will tell you the total quantity sold of the SKU. You can find out which products are the most popular on your site by sorting this column.
- **Unique Purchases**: This will tell you how many different people bought the listed SKU. If a lot of you customers are buying a product, you want to keep it in stock and you can use this report to see just how many you need in stock for a weeks or month's worth of customers depending on the date range you choose.
- **Average Price**: This is just like it sounds. This is the average price that the SKU sold for. If you changed the price of the product during the date range chosen, it may not match up to the current price. Its value is **Product Revenue** divided by **Quantity**.
- **Average Quantity**: Do people buy a lot of a certain SKU in bulk quantities? This metric will tell you that. Maybe you should package your products in different ways? Maybe create a four pack if the average quantity is four or four items? Or start offering bulk discounts?
- **Visits**: This metric will how many visits there were to the product page in the date range chosen. The following example is from a live site selling thousands of very specific parts. When a person lands on a product page that matches the part he/she needs, he/she buys it.

- **Conversion Rate**: The conversion rate is the percentage of visits to the SKU's product page on the site that resulted in a sale. With this number you can tell which items in your e-commerce shop almost sell themselves and which may need a little more description or better copy. In our screenshot, the conversion rate is not bad at all, because these are very specific items that people usually buy if they make it to the product page and it matches their need.

Product SKU	Product Revenue	Quantity	Unique Purchases	Average Price	Average Quantity	Visits	Conversion Rate
F-2749	$ 39.90	10	1	$ 3.99	10	1	100%
D-1858	$ 30.98	2	1	$ 15.49	2	1	100%
A-189	$ 28.17	1	1	$ 28.17	1	1	100%
B-656	$ 26.88	2	1	$ 13.44	2	2	50%
M-6090	$ 23.96	4	1	$ 5.99	4	1	100%
C-1110	$ 9.99	1	1	$ 9.99	1	1	100%
M-6092	$ 2.89	1	1	$ 2.89	1	1	100%
B-623	$ 2.64	1	1	$ 2.64	1	1	100%
M-6023	$ 2.49	1	1	$ 2.49	1	1	100%
M-6040	$ 1.79	1	1	$ 1.79	1	1	100%

Along the left side of the page, you will notice 19 more reports you have access to. By choosing one of these reports, you can take different cross sections of your visitors and have access to the same metrics we just discussed. The following is basically the same report as given earlier, but presents the product name instead of the product SKU and can be accessed by clicking on the **Product Name** link. And here we have the same metrics to examine as we did in the last example.

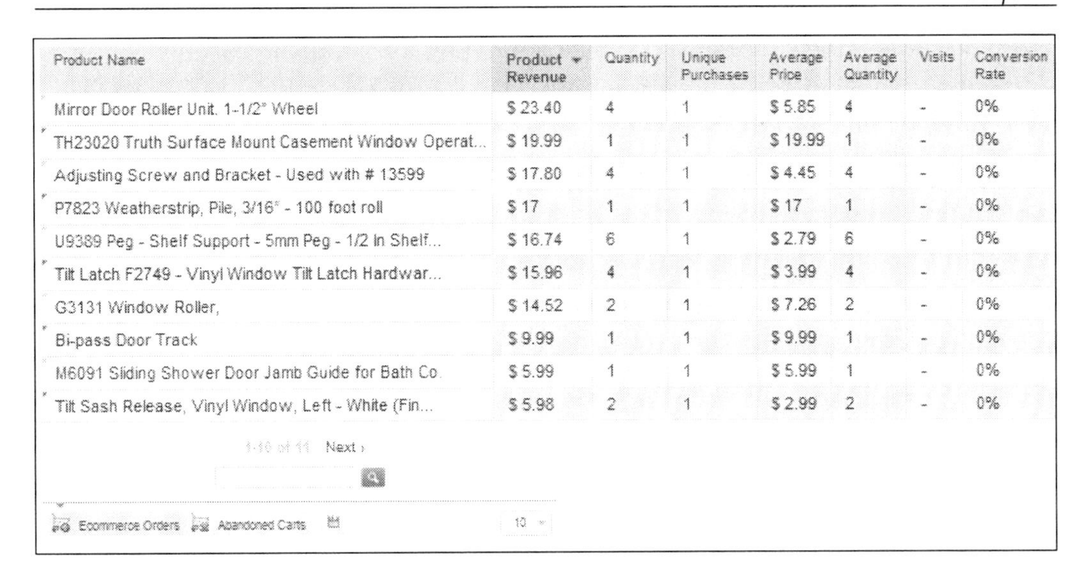

Product Name	Product Revenue	Quantity	Unique Purchases	Average Price	Average Quantity	Visits	Conversion Rate
Mirror Door Roller Unit. 1-1/2" Wheel	$ 23.40	4	1	$ 5.85	4	-	0%
TH23020 Truth Surface Mount Casement Window Operat...	$ 19.99	1	1	$ 19.99	1	-	0%
Adjusting Screw and Bracket - Used with # 13599	$ 17.80	4	1	$ 4.45	4	-	0%
P7823 Weatherstrip, Pile, 3/16" - 100 foot roll	$ 17	1	1	$ 17	1	-	0%
U9389 Peg - Shelf Support - 5mm Peg - 1/2 In Shelf...	$ 16.74	6	1	$ 2.79	6	-	0%
Tilt Latch F2749 - Vinyl Window Tilt Latch Hardwar...	$ 15.96	4	1	$ 3.99	4	-	0%
G3131 Window Roller,	$ 14.52	2	1	$ 7.26	2	-	0%
Bi-pass Door Track	$ 9.99	1	1	$ 9.99	1	-	0%
M6091 Sliding Shower Door Jamb Guide for Bath Co.	$ 5.99	1	1	$ 5.99	1	-	0%
Tilt Sash Release, Vinyl Window, Left - White (Fin...	$ 5.98	2	1	$ 2.99	2	-	0%

1-10 of 11 Next ›

Ecommerce Orders Abandoned Carts 10

After that is the **Product Category**. This report will give you our standard metrics report **Product Revenue**, **Quantity**, **Unique Purchases**, **Average Price**, **Average Quantity**, **Visits**, and **Conversion Rate**. But this data is now broken up by complete categories of products instead of single products. Using this reports data, you can discover your top revenue generating or selling categories.

Product Category	Product Revenue	Quantity	Unique Purchases	Average Price	Average Quantity	Visits	Conversion Rate
Internal	$ 49.98	2	1	$ 24.99	2	-	0%
Nylon	$ 30.98	2	1	$ 15.49	2	-	0%
Towel Bars and Brackets	$ 29.98	2	1	$ 29.98	2	-	0%
Rollers	$ 12.78	2	1	$ 6.39	2	-	0%
Sweeps and Splash Guards	$ 3.49	1	1	$ 3.49	1	-	0%
Pegs and Plugs	$ 2.79	1	1	$ 2.79	1	-	0%
Catches and Bumpers	$ 1.59	1	1	$ 1.59	1	19	5.26%
Door Protectors and Latch Shields	$ 0	-	-	$ 0	0	2	0%
Cylinder Locks	$ 0	-	-	$ 0	0	2	0%
Guides, Corners, and Accessories	$ 0	-	-	$ 0	0	2	0%

The link below is the `Ecommerce Log` which provides a lot of data. The only difference between the data it presents and what is available in the **Visitor Log** of the **Visitors** menu is that this report contains only those visitors that have completed e-commerce goals or have abandoned their cart. If you have today's date selected, then this log will be real time, but for any date in the past, it will display the archived data from that date.

The e-commerce log is handy for looking at your sales on a customer to customer basis. The combination of client side JavaScript and data from your website results in a very detailed set of data. You can see in the following screenshot, in the third entry, some actually used an iPhone to purchase. Maybe we need to start thinking about adding responsive design to our site.

Date	Referrer URL	Actions
Sat 12 May 21:07:55 IP: 75.54.78.254 Provider: Sbcglobal	Google Keywords: "sterling shower door replacement parts"	**17 Actions - 18 min 26s** 1. **Ecommerce order** (2912) Revenue: **$ 9.54**, Quantity: 1 • M-6014: M6014 Shower Door Catch, Stainless w/Nylon Tip (Catches and Bumpers), Quantity: 1, Price: $ 1.59
Sat 12 May 19:54:30 IP: 72.60.182.107 Provider: Spcsdns	Google Keywords: "patio door wheels"	**11 Actions - 29 min 19s** 1. **Ecommerce order** (2911) Revenue: **$ 20.73**, Quantity: 2 • D-1797: Roller 1-1/2 inch (Rollers), Quantity: 2, Price: $ 6.39
Sat 12 May 17:11:45 IP: 71.90.102.204 Provider: Charter	Google Keywords: "prime line shelf locking shelf 3/4"	**10 Actions - 4 min 48s** 1. **Ecommerce order** (2909) Revenue: **$ 10.74**, Quantity: 1 • U-9396: U9396 Peg - Shelf Support - 5mm Peg - 3/4 In Shelf - Brown (Pegs and Plugs), Quantity: 1, Price: $ 2.79

You will also see in the **Actions** column that a lot of the details of the orders are there including the order ID, total revenue, quantity sold, as well as the details of the products that were sold. As for abandoned carts, you will get the revenue left in the cart, how many products were abandoned, and details on each of the products. You will also see the same data now in your **Visitor Log** when a visitor has completed an e-commerce action.

Below that report is the **Keywords** report. From this report you will discover which of your keywords are performing the best, so you can optimize your pages for them.

After that is the **Search Engines** report as shown next. Both the **Keywords** report and the **Search Engines** report show the same set of metrics in their respective tables. These metrics are a bit different because instead of comparing our revenue by products, we will now be comparing it by referrers. Here we have:

- **Visits**: This column will tell you how many visits you got from the search engine or other referrer
- **Ecommerce Orders**: This will tell you just how many actual orders resulted from people who came from the listed search engine or keyword
- **Total Revenue**: This column will tell you the total money you have made in sales from each listed referrer
- **Ecommerce order conversion rate**: This column will tell you the conversion rate of visits coming from the traffic source
- **Average Order Value**: This column will tell you the average order value from the listed search engine or referrer
- **Purchased Products**: This column will give you a count of products that were purchased by visitors from the listed referrer
- **Revenue for Visit**: This is the average revenue per visit that came from the listed referrer

Search Engine	Visits	Ecommerce Orders	Total Revenue	Ecommerce order conversion rate	Average Order Value	Purchased Products	Revenue per Visit
Google	443	6	$ 129.30	1.35%	$ 21.60	9	$ 0.30
Google Shopping	9	1	$ 57.90	11.11%	$ 57.90	2	$ 6.40
AOL	10	0	$ 0	0%	$ 0	0	$ 0
Ask	35	0	$ 0	0%	$ 0	0	$ 0
Babylon	2	0	$ 0	0%	$ 0	0	$ 0
Bing	22	0	$ 0	0%	$ 0	0	$ 0
Bing Images	1	0	$ 0	0%	$ 0	0	$ 0
blekko	1	0	$ 0	0%	$ 0	0	$ 0
Comcast	15	0	$ 0	0%	$ 0	0	$ 0
Google Custom Search	3	0	$ 0	0%	$ 0	0	$ 0
Google Images	8	0	$ 0	0%	$ 0	0	$ 0
Google Video	1	0	$ 0	0%	$ 0	0	$ 0
InfoSpace	3	0	$ 0	0%	$ 0	0	$ 0
MyWebSearch	8	0	$ 0	0%	$ 0	0	$ 0
Yahoo!	19	0	$ 0	0%	$ 0	0	$ 0
Yahoo! Images	1	0	$ 0	0%	$ 0	0	$ 0

From the look of this report, Google is the top when it comes to making sales, but Ask is sending more traffic than Yahoo. Interesting!

Next is the **Websites** report which will show you which websites are bringing you the traffic that converts. It contains the same metrics in its table as the **Keywords** or **Search Engines** reports.

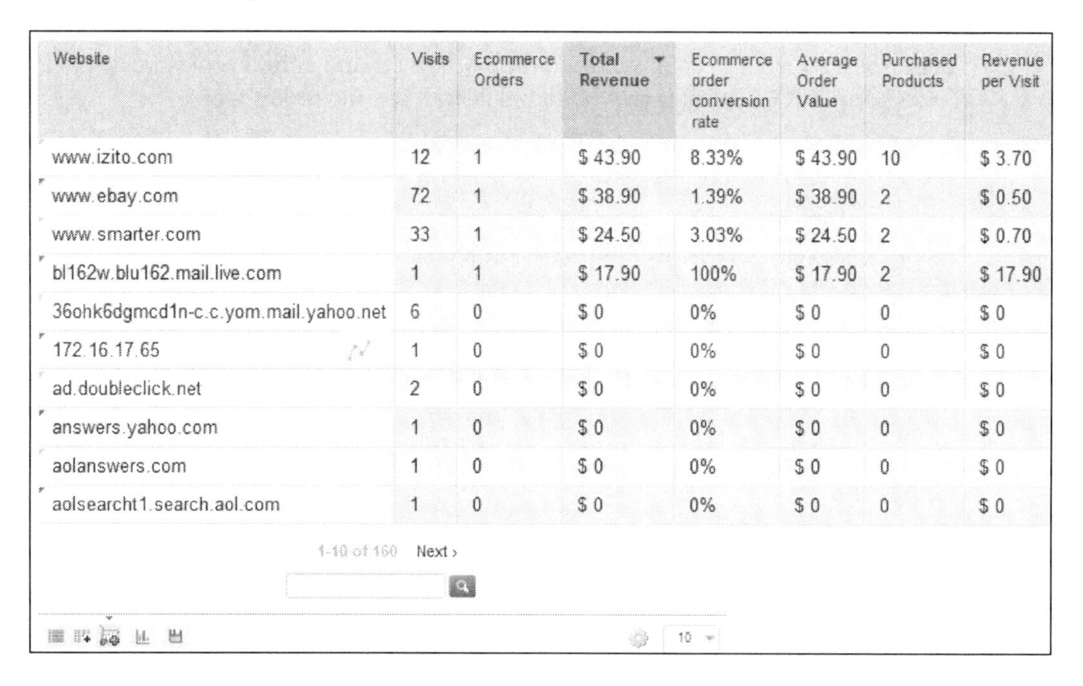

Website	Visits	Ecommerce Orders	Total Revenue	Ecommerce order conversion rate	Average Order Value	Purchased Products	Revenue per Visit
www.izito.com	12	1	$ 43.90	8.33%	$ 43.90	10	$ 3.70
www.ebay.com	72	1	$ 38.90	1.39%	$ 38.90	2	$ 0.50
www.smarter.com	33	1	$ 24.50	3.03%	$ 24.50	2	$ 0.70
bl162w.blu162.mail.live.com	1	1	$ 17.90	100%	$ 17.90	2	$ 17.90
36ohk6dgmcd1n-c.c.yom.mail.yahoo.net	6	0	$ 0	0%	$ 0	0	$ 0
172.16.17.65	1	0	$ 0	0%	$ 0	0	$ 0
ad.doubleclick.net	2	0	$ 0	0%	$ 0	0	$ 0
answers.yahoo.com	1	0	$ 0	0%	$ 0	0	$ 0
aolanswers.com	1	0	$ 0	0%	$ 0	0	$ 0
aolsearcht1.search.aol.com	1	0	$ 0	0%	$ 0	0	$ 0

1-10 of 160 Next ›

I didn't know that `smarter.com` existed before this report. And there was actually a sale from the website, which made me go take a look to see what type of site was giving us a new sale.

After that is the **Referrer Type** report, which will tell us how search engine visitors, direct entry visitors, and visitors referred from other websites stack up as a whole when it comes to e-commerce actions. Again, we have the same metrics here as in all the referrer based reports.

Referrer Type	Visits	Ecommerce Orders	Total Revenue	Ecommerce order conversion rate	Average Order Value	Purchased Products	Revenue per Visit
Search Engines	4789	45	$ 1067.70	0.94%	$ 23.70	102	$ 0.20
Direct Entry	889	8	$ 229.50	0.9%	$ 28.70	17	$ 0.30
Websites	846	4	$ 125.20	0.47%	$ 31.30	16	$ 0.10

A newer report in Piwik, that came along with the last update, was the **Visits to Conversion** report. It is a very simple report that tells you how many visits it takes to your e-commerce site before a sale happens. In the next screenshot we see that a majority of the sales happen on the first visit. That's a good thing. But three of the sales took 15-25 visits to complete. That could indicate a lot of price shopping or a few customers having a difficulty finding the right item.

Visits to Conversion	Conversions
1 visit	42
2 visits	9
3 visits	1
4 visits	0
5 visits	0
6 visits	0
7 visits	0
8 visits	1
9-14 visits	1
15-25 visits	3
26-50 visits	0
51-100 visits	0
101+ visits	0

Another new report similar to the last is the **Days to Conversion** report. With it we can see how many days it took visitors on our site to make a purchase. Again, our example screenshot looks pretty good. Most of our visitors buy the day they land on our site, but a few took a week or more to make a purchase.

Days to Conversion	Conversions
0 days	46
1 day	5
2 days	3
3 days	0
4 days	0
5 days	0
6 days	0
7 days	0
8-14 days	3

After that, we can see a report that gives us our e-commerce data by **Country**. You may assume you sell to one country and it's where all of your income is coming from. But you may be surprised at the profit you can make by opening up your online shop to other countries. It has the same metrics displayed as our referrer reports: **Visits, Ecommerce Orders, Total Revenue, Ecommerce order conversion rate, Average Order Value, Purchased Products**, and **Revenue per Visit**.

Country	Visits	Ecommerce Orders	Total Revenue	Ecommerce order conversion rate	Average Order Value	Purchased Products	Revenue per Visit
United States	6253	55	$ 1370.40	0.88%	$ 24.90	133	$ 0.20
Canada	57	1	$ 31.60	1.75%	$ 31.60	1	$ 0.60
Korea, Republic of	3	1	$ 20.40	33.33%	$ 20.40	1	$ 6.80
Australia	36	0	$ 0	0%	$ 0	0	$ 0
Belgium	1	0	$ 0	0%	$ 0	0	$ 0

1-5 of 38 Next ›

After that is the **Continent** report which will show you e-commerce data by continents. This is followed by the **Custom Variable** report which will show you the same data grouped by custom variables you have set. And the last report shows the server time sales were made. These last three reports also use the same metrics as the referrer reports.

Server time	Visits	Ecommerce Orders	Total Revenue	Ecommerce order conversion rate	Average Order Value	Purchased Products	Revenue per Visit
15h	450	9	$ 231	2%	$ 25.70	23	$ 0.50
12h	437	8	$ 189.10	1.83%	$ 23.60	13	$ 0.40
16h	444	4	$ 167.90	0.9%	$ 42	23	$ 0.40
19h	475	5	$ 159.20	1.05%	$ 31.80	13	$ 0.30
17h	411	6	$ 148.90	1.46%	$ 24.80	26	$ 0.40
20h	440	4	$ 104.70	0.91%	$ 26.20	9	$ 0.20
21h	372	3	$ 73.40	0.81%	$ 24.50	6	$ 0.20
14h	443	3	$ 70.10	0.68%	$ 23.40	4	$ 0.20
11h	398	3	$ 51.20	0.75%	$ 17.10	2	$ 0.10
13h	412	4	$ 48.70	0.97%	$ 12.20	2	$ 0.10
0h	130	1	$ 38.90	0.77%	$ 38.90	2	$ 0.30
6h	86	1	$ 31.60	1.16%	$ 31.60	1	$ 0.40

From the previous report, it looks like our site is most active at 7 p.m. server time.

A note about SSL

If you use Piwik for an e-commerce site, your website is most likely secure. There are some instances where it may not necessarily need to be, like if you use an off-site payment processor that actually takes credit card details on their page. But other than cases like this, your e-commerce site should be secured by a valid security certificate.

Because your e-commerce site is secure, you will need your Piwik installation to be secure also. If it is running on the same domain as your e-commerce website, you will have no worries. But if you are running the Piwik installation you use to track your e-commerce website on another server and domain, you will have to get a security certificate for your Piwik installation and have `mod_ssl` installed. Otherwise, when a visitor is on a secure part of your website and this part of the Piwik code executes, there will be an issue.

```
var pkBaseURL = (("https:" == document.location.protocol) ?
  "https://YOUR_PIWIK_URL" : "http:// YOUR_PIWIK_URL");
```

The code will never be able to load the secure URL because it doesn't exist. Not only will there be no tracking but it will most likely slow down the visitor's browser as it tries to load the URL.

One option is to do something like this:

```
var pkBaseURL = "http:// YOUR_PIWIK_URL";
```

But this will cause an error in the user's browser because he/she will be on a secure page and that secure page will be trying to load JavaScript from an unsecure connection. So I would not suggest doing this. The best options are to use a Piwik installation located on the same domain as the secure website you are tracking, or to get a certificate for your Piwik domain.

Summary

In this chapter we learned about e-commerce tracking in Piwik and how to enable it. We learned about tracking orders, products purchased, category page views, product page views, and shopping carts. We also wrote a plugin for ZenCart and learned how we could have PHP on our server write the JavaScript needed on the client side dynamically based on the details of the web page. And finally we went through the multitude of reports that you can use to improve sales and conversions on your website.

In the next chapter, we will learn about website and user administration for those of you who will be providing Piwik as a service for users.

8
Piwik Website and User Administration

Piwik was designed for multiple users and multiple websites. And this makes it easy for a developer who has installed Piwik to provide analytics as a service for their clients or customers. By installing or writing custom plugins you can customize your Piwik installation for your customer's needs, providing more features and data than a standard installation of Piwik. Piwik also gives you the option, out of the box, to customize the logo in the interface and in reports, so that you can brand your website analytics service.

In this chapter we will learn how to:

- Change your own Super User settings
- Change anonymous user settings
- Add and edit users
- Set user permissions
- Add a website
- Track multiple domains or subdomains in the same website
- Use Piwik in an intranet
- Turn Piwik into a white label analytics service
- Install a Piwik plugin
- Give users the ability to sign up by themselves

Changing your Super User settings

You can change your user settings at any time by clicking on the **Settings** link in the top-right menu of Piwik, as shown in the following screenshot:

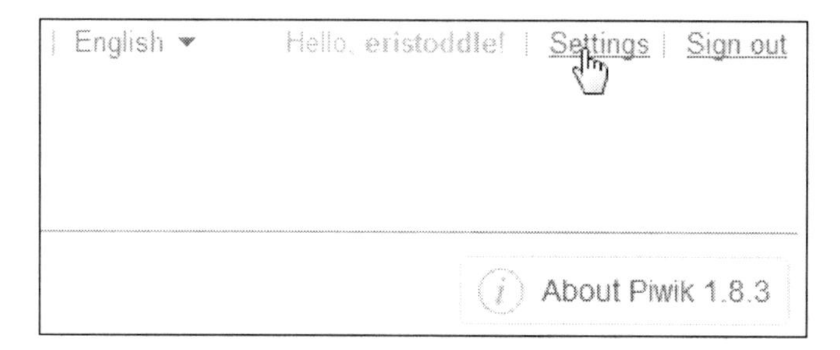

The first page that loads is the one to edit your user settings. At the top is where you can change your basic settings. This is shown in the following screenshot:

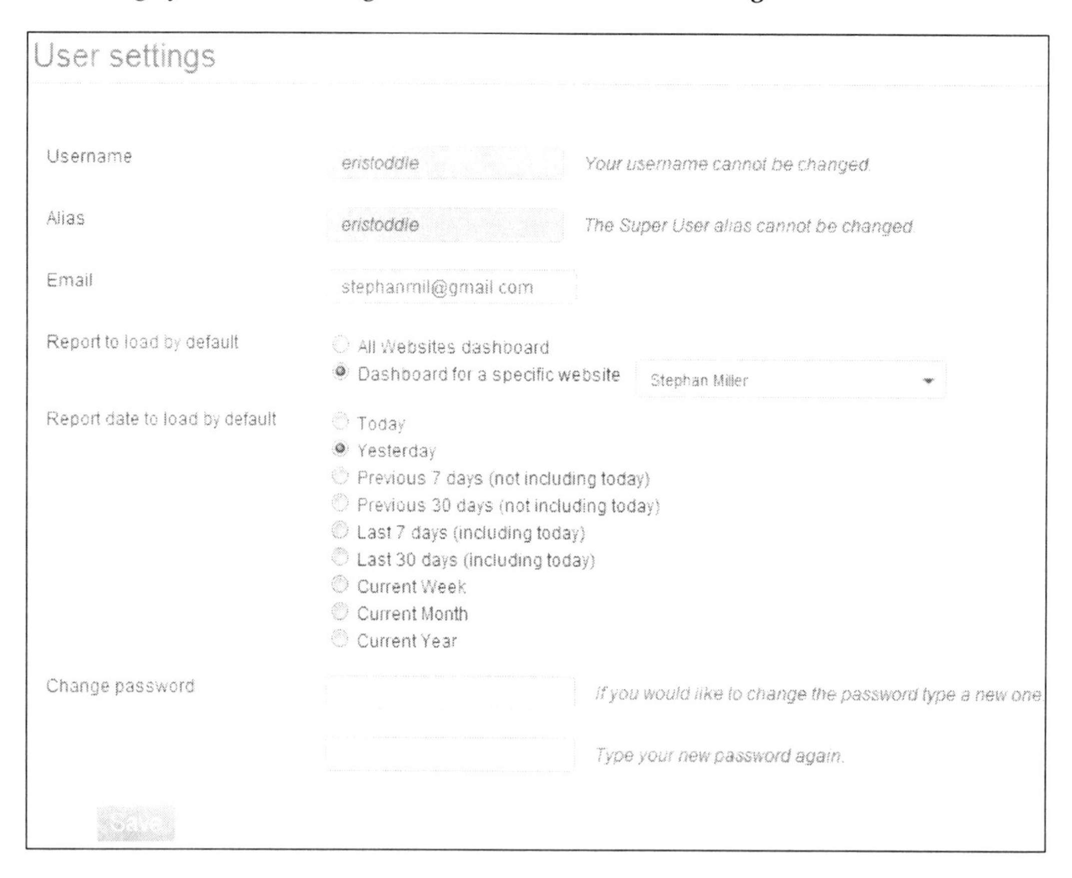

Here you can change your e-mail address and password. Once you change your password, your API token for Piwik will be reset and you must add your new API key to any software that requires it.

You can also set the default reports to load in your dashboard. You can choose the **All Websites dashboard** or the **Dashboard for a specific website**. Below that you can set the date and date range you want the reports in your dashboard to load by default, as shown in the following screenshot:

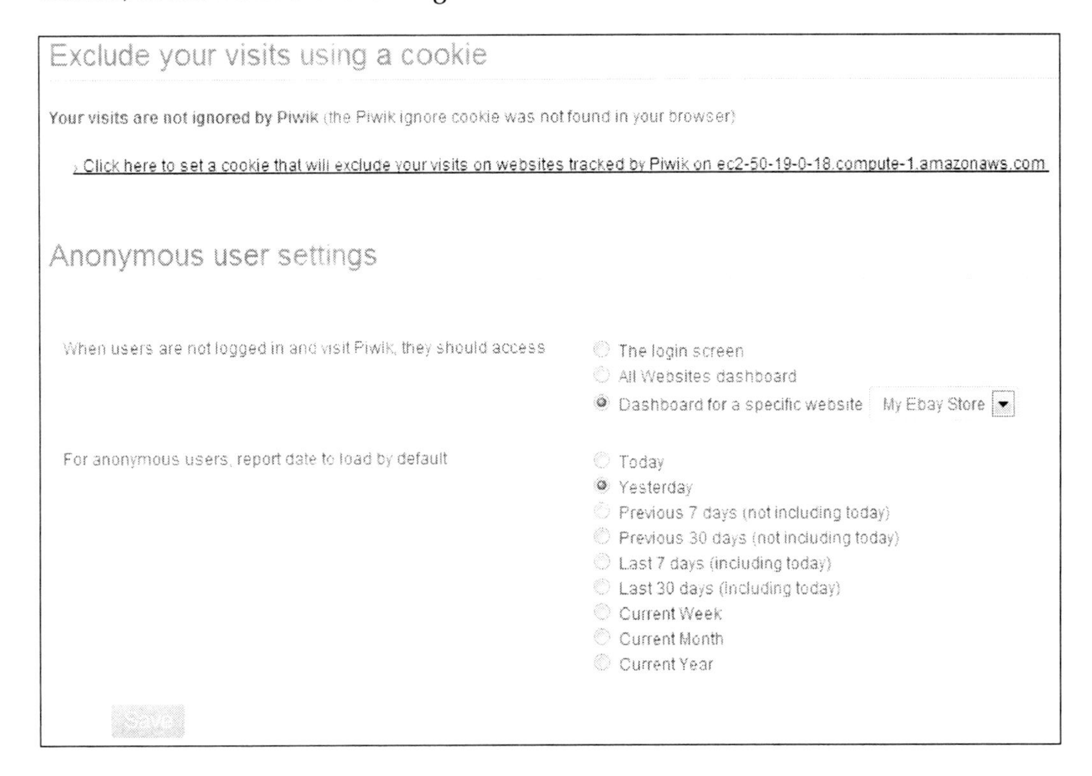

Below that is a link, that when clicked on, will exclude you from being tracked by your Piwik installation. You just click on the link and Piwik will set a cookie in your browser to tell Piwik to ignore you. Note that you will have to set this cookie in each browser that you use. You would want to check this during production so that you don't inadvertently become your site's biggest fan. But while developing your site or app, it is better to leave this unchecked for testing purposes.

The next form deals with the *anonymous user*. This is the other user that gets created when you install Piwik. This user is any user not logged into Piwik. There are many reasons you may want the general public to access your stats. If you are selling advertising, potential advertisers may want to know the type of traffic you are getting. Or you may just want to brag about your traffic growth. But here is where you set the default reports any anonymous user will see. Anonymous user access is set on a site-by-site basis in Piwik, so these settings are only global defaults for the websites that anonymous users currently have access to.

Creating users in Piwik

In order to add users in Piwik, you need to be a Super User. And we add users by first accessing the **Settings** link in the top right-hand side menu in Piwik.

On the **Settings** page, choose the **Users** menu, as shown in the following screenshot:

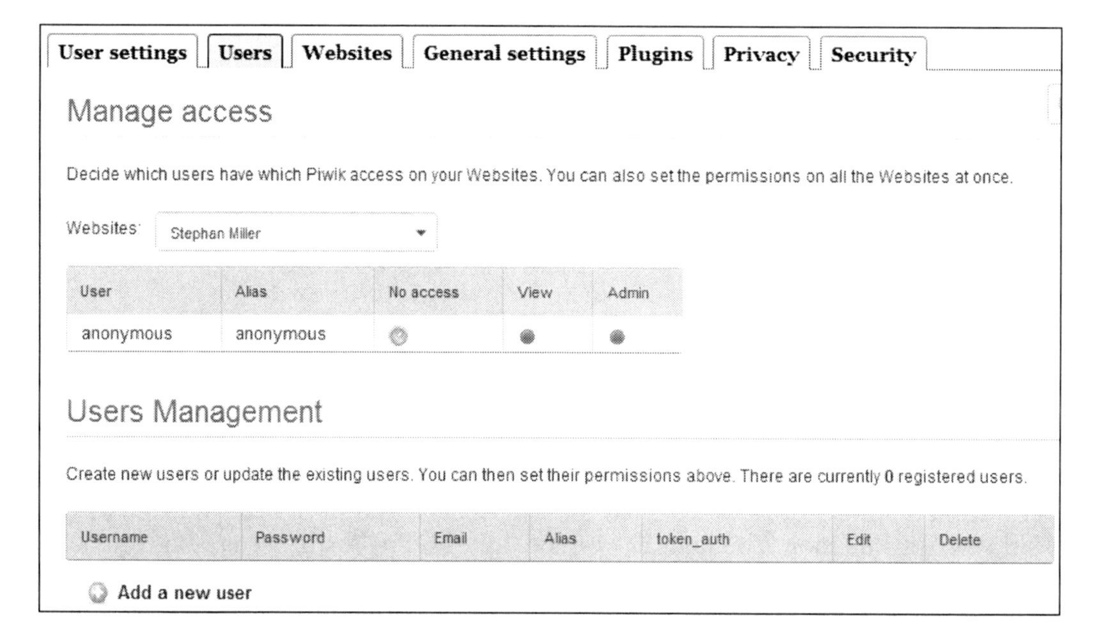

Down near the bottom, you will see the **Add a new user** link which you will be clicking on to add your user.

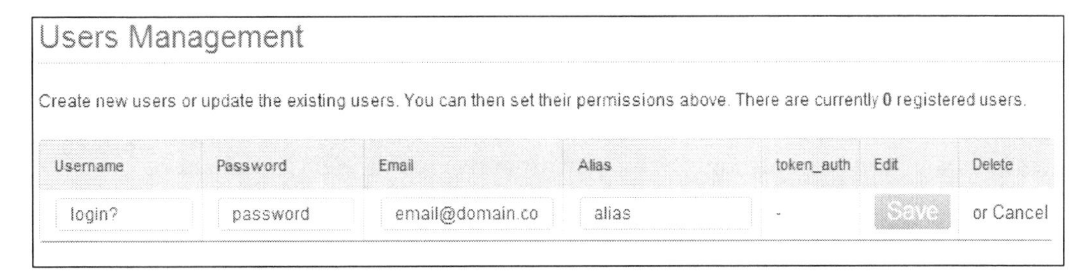

And then just fill out the form with a **Username**, a **Password**, the **Email** address of the user you are adding, and an **Alias**. The **Alias** field is not required and will be replaced with the **Username** if left empty. But if you plan on adding quite a few users, it would be a good idea to enter the user's real name or company name in the **Alias** token to help you more readily identify your users after usernames start stacking up. If you are creating a user specifically for API access purposes, the **Alias** field is a handy place to put the name or domain of your application. When you are done filling out the form, click on the **Save** button to save your new user.

Once that is done, you will see your added user listed under the **User Management** menu along with their new authorization token for the Piwik API. This is shown in the following screenshot:

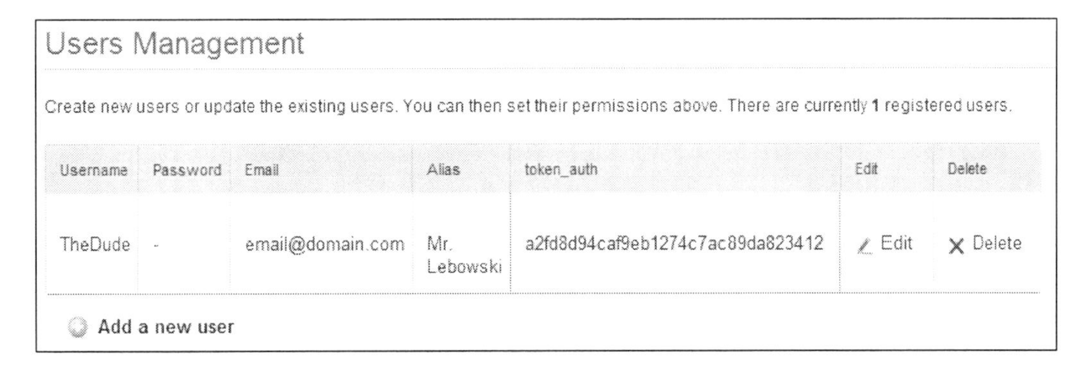

If you need to edit this user in the future, you can click on the **Edit** link at the right-hand side end of that user's row to change their password, e-mail, or alias name. Their username will have to remain the same. Changing their password will automatically change their authorization token to another random string.

Managing website access

When you first create a new user in Piwik, that user doesn't have permission to view or do anything, just like our anonymous user. You have to create those permissions. You may have noticed that the **Manage access** section of the **Users** panel also has a table of users, each with green check mark under the **No access** column and a red circle under the other two columns, as shown in the following screenshot. These not only signify the permissions for the users but are also buttons to change those permissions.

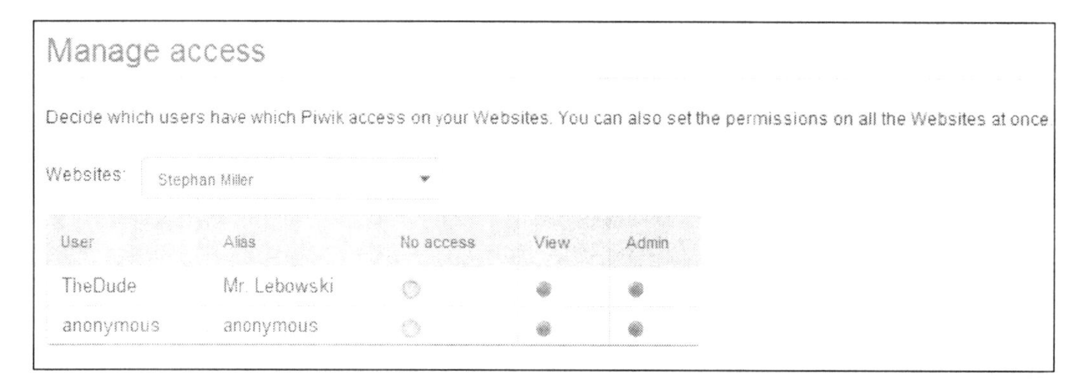

The **Websites** drop-down field determines the scope of the permissions you are giving to each user. You can give users access and admin rights on a site-by-site basis, or change their permissions on all sites at once by choosing **Apply to all websites** in the drop-down. When you do choose to make changes to permissions on all websites, Piwik will warn you with a pop-up.

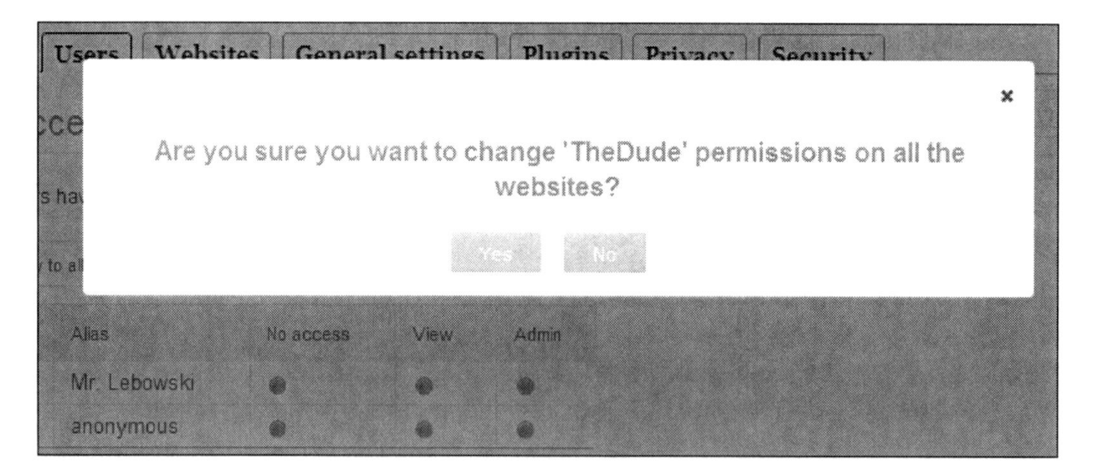

The **View** and **Admin** buttons can be switched on and off by clicking on them. The **No access** buttons are purely off switches. When the **No access** button is red, the user has some sort of access to the site's stats and this access can be turned off with one click. When it is green, they don't have access and clicking the green check mark does nothing. Once you change permissions, Piwik will notify you that the action has been completed.

So with us throwing all these permissions around, it would be good to know what type of permissions we are giving. Let's start with our own permissions for the Super User. You will notice that your username was not in either of these user tables. You will also notice the anonymous user popping up in these tables. The anonymous user's permissions can be set just like any other users.

Who is a Super User?

Since you just installed Piwik, you are the Super User of the installation. Let's see what being a Super User means.

- A Super User is the only user that can create users
- A Super User is the only user that can create websites
- A Super User is the only user that can install plugins
- There is only one Super User per Piwik installation
- A Super User is created during the installation process
- A Super User's username and password are in the `config/config.ini.php` file while other others credentials are stored in the database

What are admin permissions?

A Super User can do a lot. But just what can an admin do?

- Admins can edit their website's settings
- They can grant admin and view settings to other users for the websites they have the admin permissions for
- Admins can also create users for the websites they administrate and make those users admin of these same sites, if they so choose
- They cannot add websites or install plugins

What are view permissions?

- A user with view permission for a website(s) can view all the reports in that website(s)
- A user with view permissions cannot add other users, websites, or manage plugins

Managing websites

You can create unlimited users in Piwik as well as unlimited websites. This, of course, is not completely true. You are limited by the server resources that you have available and the skill your IT team has at clustering databases and web servers. Cloud hosting providers such as Amazon make some of your scaling easy by allowing you to add memory, space, and processing power on the fly. But I digress. Let's just say that some Piwik installations track thousands of websites.

Adding a website

So, as we said before, in the standard installation of Piwik only the Super User can add new websites and users. So let's add another site. If you are logged in as the Super User of your Piwik installation, click on the **Settings** link again in the top right-hand side corner of your Piwik interface. Then, choose the **Websites** tab.

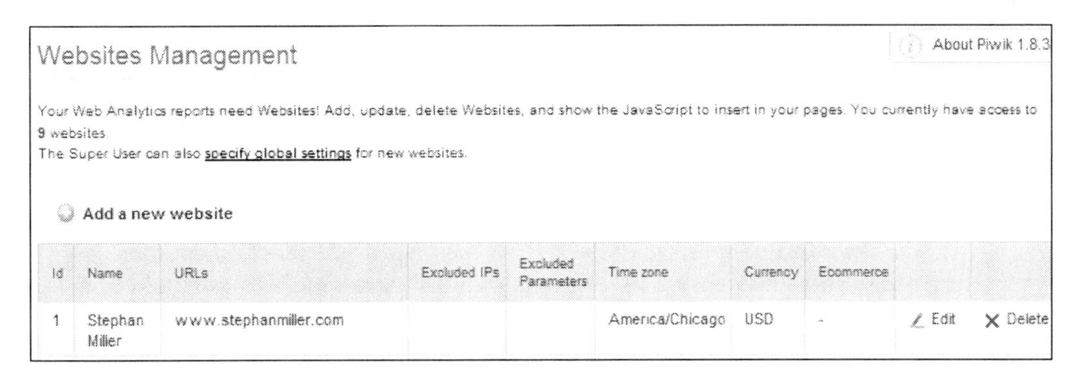

Now click on **Add a new website** and you will be greeted with a form appearing at the bottom of the table of your websites, as shown in the following screenshot. You may have to scroll horizontally, unless you have a super widescreen high resolution monitor.

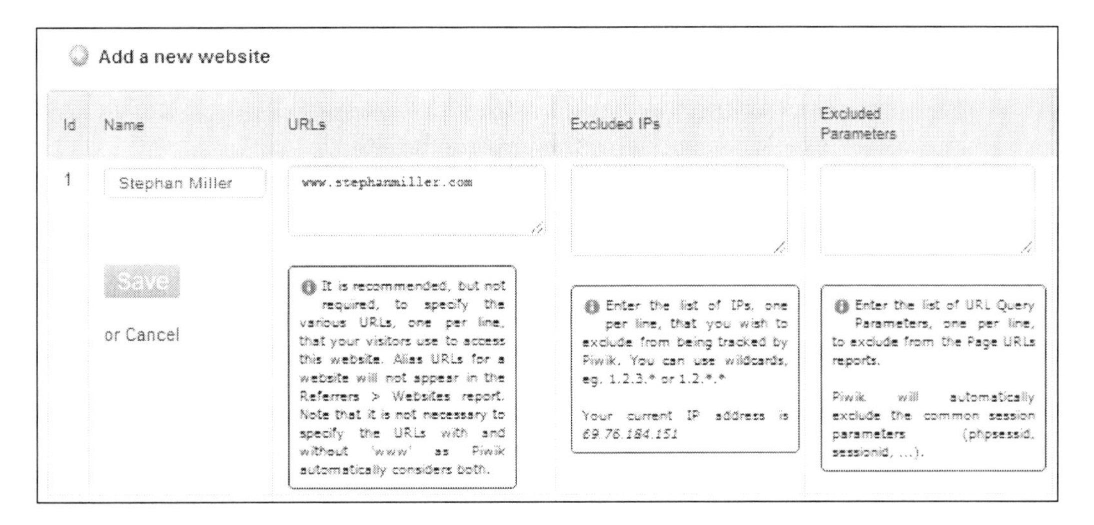

This form has several fields in it. They are as follows:

- **Name**: This can be the domain name of the website or another name you choose to use to identify the site you are tracking.
- Alias **URLs**: These are the domains and subdomains that will be tracked in this website account. You do have to add the subdomains separately for sites such as WordPress Multisite or any site you have wildcard subdomains for. This is so you can alternately choose to set up a website for the subdomain by itself. But Piwik will track the www and non-www version of your site as the same domain without entering both.

- **Excluded IPs**: This can be a list of IPs or IP ranges that you do not want to be tracked by the website. You can enter a range of IPs by using an asterisk as the wildcard character such as this: `192.168.*.*`.
- **Excluded Parameters**: This is the list of URL parameters that you wish to exclude from tracked URLs. Some websites still use session parameters instead of cookies to track their users across the website, and many fall back to session parameters in the URL when the visitor has blocked cookies. Adding these and other URL cluttering query parameters to this field will keep your **Actions** | **Pages** reports cleaner and free from duplicate URLs masquerading as unique ones.
- **Time Zone**: This is a drop-down form to select the time zone the reports will be using. It is the simple type, where you really only have to know a nearby city to select the correct time zone. Changing the time zone on an active site will only change the reports from the time of the change. All older reports will still be on the old time zone setting.
- **Currency**: This simply allows you to choose the currency symbol to display in the revenue column of your goals.
- **Ecommerce**: As we discussed in *Chapter 7, E-commerce Tracking*, this field enables or disables e-commerce tracking on the site.

Editing or deleting a website

To edit a website, you simply click on the **Edit** link at the far right-hand side end of the website's row. Again, you may have to scroll horizontally to get there.

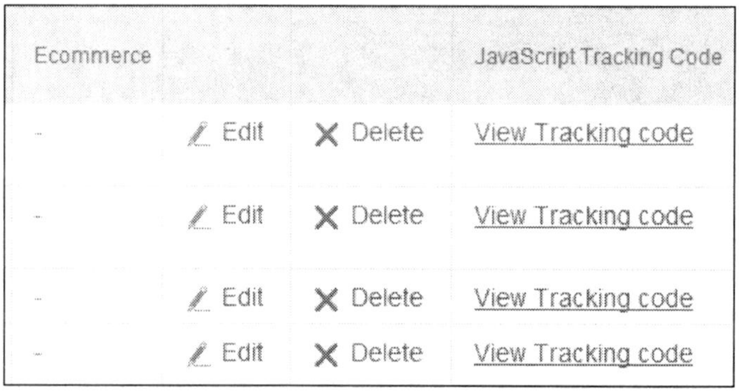

Ecommerce			JavaScript Tracking Code
-	Edit	Delete	View Tracking code
-	Edit	Delete	View Tracking code
-	Edit	Delete	View Tracking code
-	Edit	Delete	View Tracking code

The same form will open up with the current values already filled in. Then just click on the **Save** button to complete your edit. To delete a website, you simply click on the **Delete** link in its row. Deleting a website will delete everything about that site that has not been backed up, so be sure you really want to delete a site before you do.

Editing the global website settings

You may have noticed that when you went to add a website or edit a website in Piwik, another form opens up at the bottom of the page. This is the **Global website settings** form. This is shown in the following screenshot:

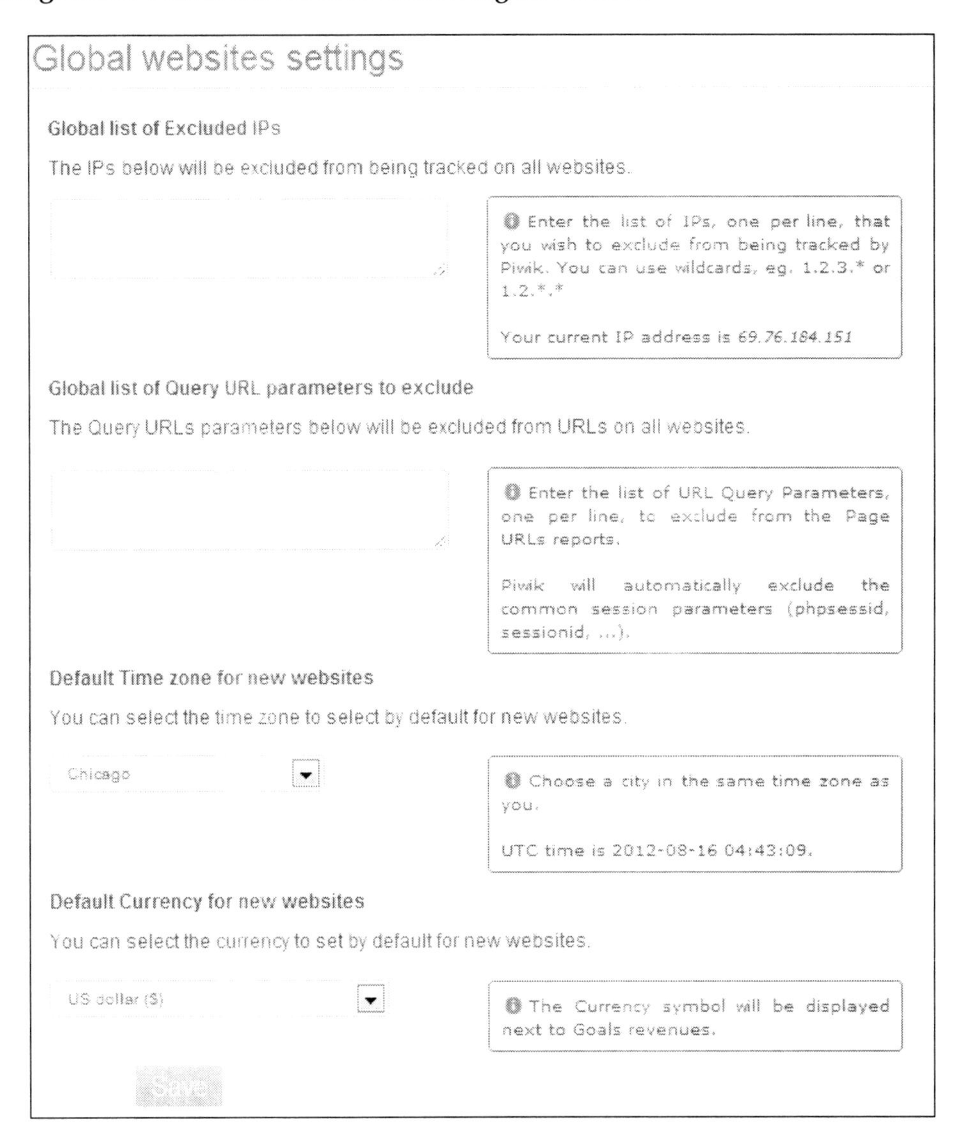

With it, you can add to the settings that apply globally to all websites being tracked, or by default on newly added websites. For currently tracked websites, you can add **Excluded IPs** and **Query URL parameters to exclude**. You can also change the default currency and time zone for websites created in the future.

Tracking multiple domains or subdomains with one website account

Previously, we mentioned the alias **URLs** field, where you can enter more than one domain or subdomain to be tracked. When you are tracking more than one site with the same website profile in Piwik, it may become hard to detect which page titles are referring to which websites. One way to make this easier is to use Piwik's `setDocumentTitle` function to add the domain or subdomain name to the page title itself.

```
<!-- Piwik -->
<script type="text/javascript">
  var pkBaseURL = (("https:" == document.location.protocol) ?
"https://$PIWIK_URL" : "http://$PIWIK_URL");
  document.write(unescape("%3Cscript src='" + pkBaseURL + "piwik.js'
type='text/javascript'%3E%3C/script%3E"));
</script>
<script type="text/javascript">
  try {
  var piwikTracker = Piwik.getTracker(pkBaseURL + "piwik.php",
$SITE_ID);
piwikTracker.setDocumentTitle(document.domain + "/" + document.title);
  piwikTracker.trackPageView();
  piwikTracker.enableLinkTracking();
  } catch( err ) {}
</script>
<noscript><p><img src="$PIWIK_URL/piwik.php?idsite=$SITE_ID"
style="border:0" alt="" /></p></noscript>
<!-- End Piwik Tracking Code -->
```

So let's say you have a domain and a subdomain that you are tracking with the same website account. One being `silver.holyhandgrenadesareus.com` and one being just `holyhandgrenadesareus.com`. And let's assume that the page title of each site's homepage is "Holy Hand Grenades Are Us". Now you shouldn't really name these the same for the sake of SEO, but let's just assume you did. Consider the following line in the previous code:

```
piwikTracker.setDocumentTitle(document.domain + "/" + document.title);
```

Without this line both page titles would show up the same in your Piwik reports. But because we have added this line, we will get `silver.holyhandgrenadesareus.com/Holy Hand Grenades Are Us` for the page title of one and `holyhandgrenadesareus.com/Holy Hand Grenades Are Us` for the page title of the other.

But this is not all we have to do. We have to make sure the cookies are set correctly for our subdomains, so we have to modify our code again and add a call to Piwik's `setCookieDomain` and `setDomains`. The first function will help set the correct cookie for us across our subdomains and the second function will make sure that download and click tracking data is handled by the same website in Piwik. Let's look at some code that uses these functions.

```
<!-- Piwik -->
<script type="text/javascript">
  var pkBaseURL = (("https:" == document.location.protocol) ?
"https://$PIWIK_URL" : "http://$PIWIK_URL");
  document.write(unescape("%3Cscript src='" + pkBaseURL + "piwik.js'
type='text/javascript'%3E%3C/script%3E"));
</script>
<script type="text/javascript">
  try {
  var piwikTracker = Piwik.getTracker(pkBaseURL + "piwik.php",
$SITE_ID);
  tracker.setCookieDomain('*.holyhandgrenadeareus.com');
  tracker.setDomains('*.holyhandgrenadeareus.com');
  piwikTracker.trackPageView();
  piwikTracker.enableLinkTracking();
  } catch( err ) {}
</script>
<noscript><p><img src="$PIWIK_URL/piwik.php?idsite=$SITE_ID"
style="border:0" alt="" /></p></noscript>
<!-- End Piwik Tracking Code -->
```

This is the same code as previously mentioned after we have added the two functions we need. We use an asterisk as a wildcard character so that `holyhandgrenadesarus.com`, `silver.holyhandgrenadesarus.com`, and any other subdomain we have on this domain will be tracked correctly.

Setting up an intranet as a website in Piwik

There may be a case when you have to set up a Piwik installation to track traffic on an intranet. And if you are given the task to set this up, you are in luck. Piwik will work for you. But the Piwik installation has to be on the intranet itself and you have to edit your Piwik configuration file, which is the `config.ini.php` file, that is located in the `config` folder of your Piwik installation. You will be adding these lines to the file. Anywhere is good. Order isn't important in the configuration file other than for your own ease of use.

```
[Tracker]
trust_visitors_cookies = 1
```

This will tell your Piwik installation that unique visitors will be based on cookies, even though all of your visitors may come from the same IP, operating system, and so on.

Turning Piwik into a white label analytics solution

If you plan on using your Piwik installation to host other user's analytics, you may want to remove the Piwik logo and name and replace it with your brand's logo. Fortunately, this is easy with Piwik. You can choose a logo that will be seen:

- At the top of analytics reports
- At the login screen
- In e-mails
- In PDF reports

The following are a few tips on creating your logo so it works and fits correctly in your Piwik interface:

- The logo should be a JPG, PNG, or GIF format file.
- The logo should have a white rather than a transparent background to blend in with the white background of Piwik. Uploading a transparent background image will not work and the transparent background will be turned black.
- The minimum height of this logo should be 110 pixels.

So let's customize our Piwik installation. First, click on the **Settings** link in the top-right corner of your Piwik interface and then choose **General settings**.

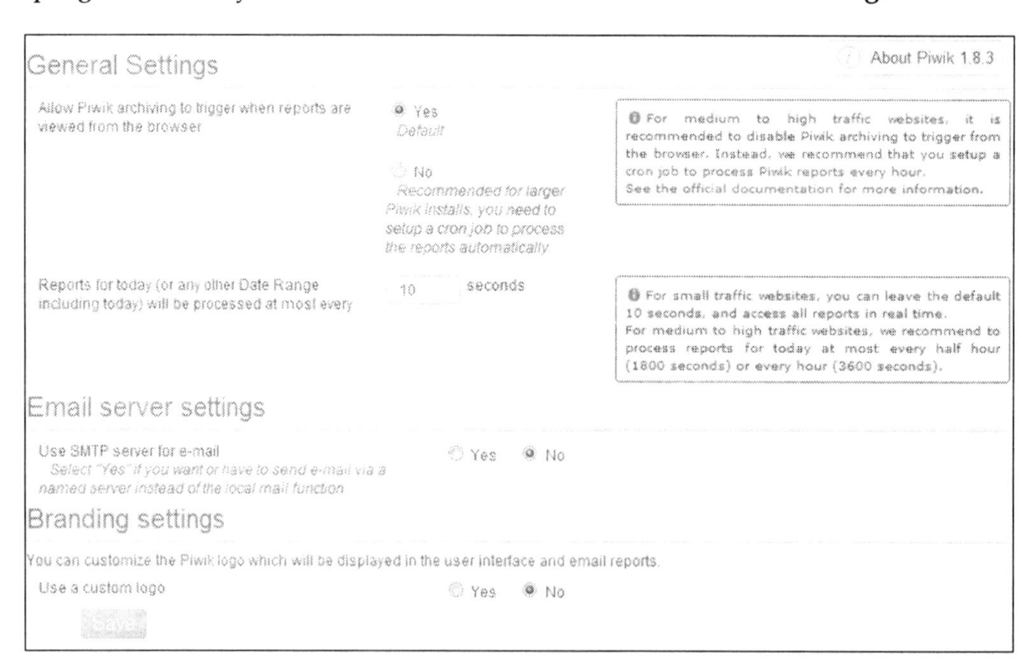

Once you get to the **General settings** page, you will notice a **Branding settings** heading about halfway down the page. Presently, the **Use a custom logo** radio button will be set to **No**. Once you choose **Yes**, a form to upload your logo will appear, as shown in the following screenshot:

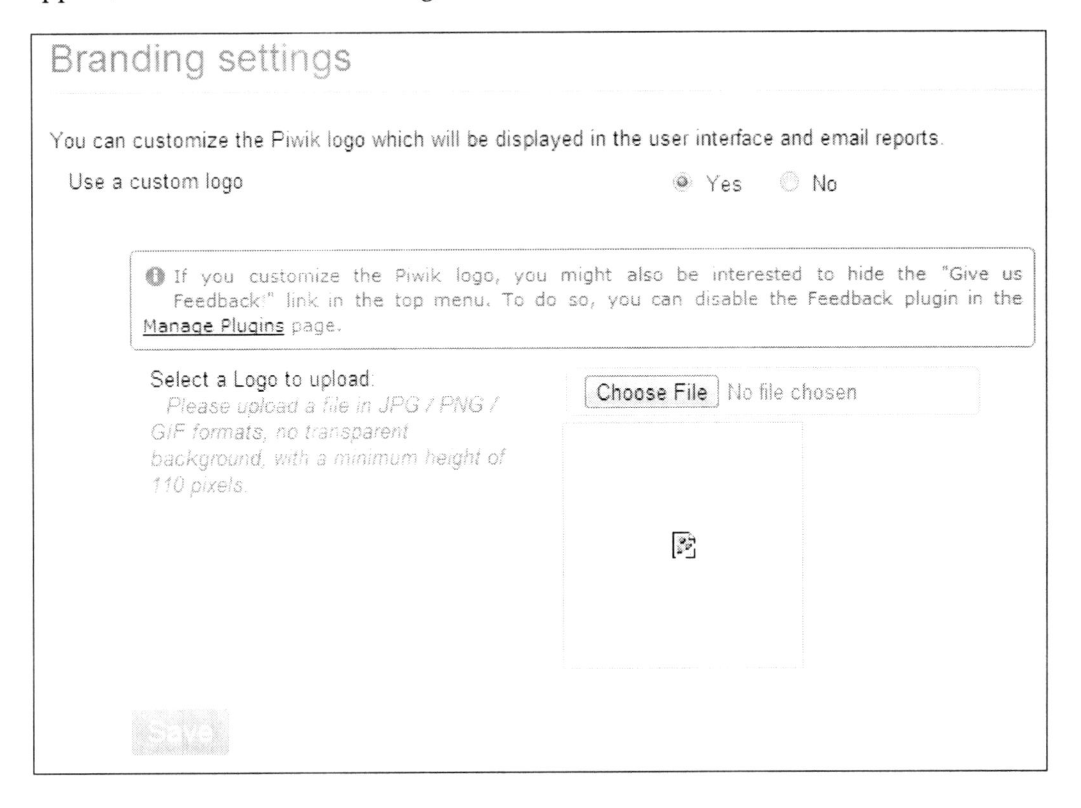

To upload a file from your local computer to your Piwik installation, click on the **Choose File** button. A file browser window will open for you to choose your image file, as shown in the following screenshot:

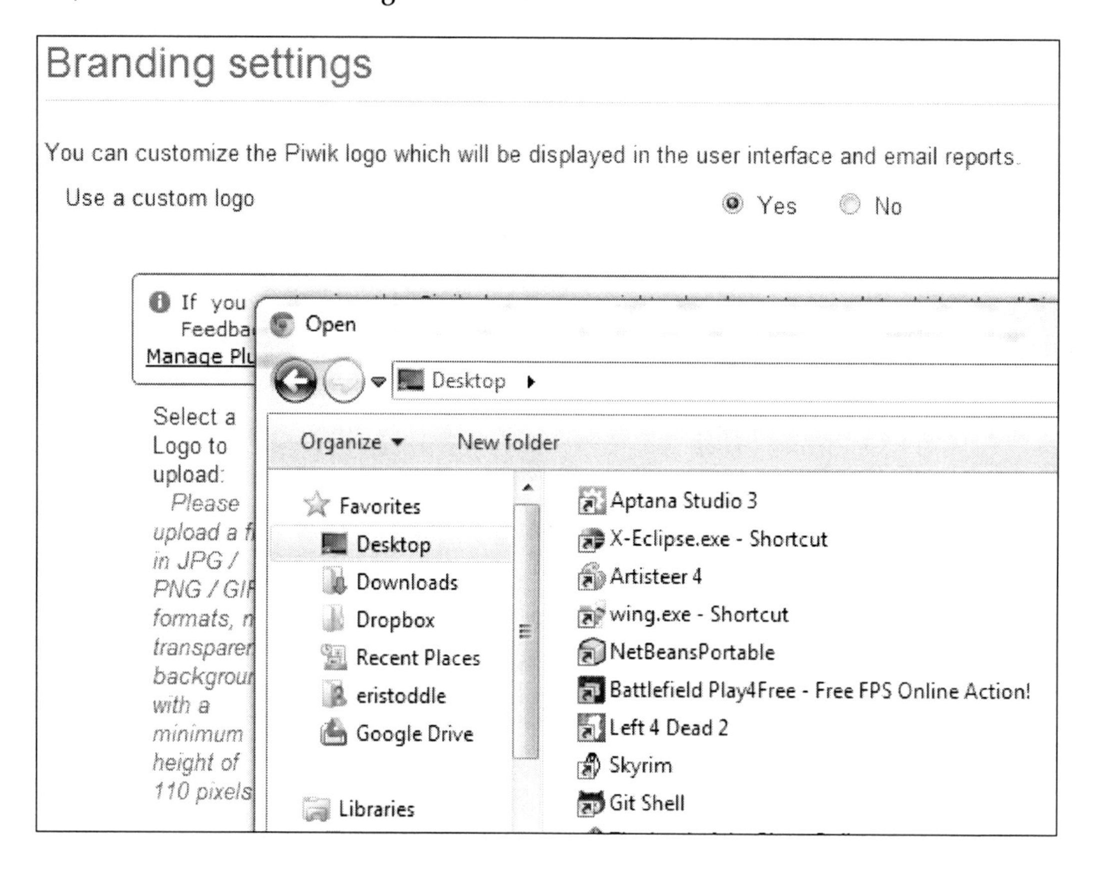

Browse to the location of your image file and select it in your file browser. Afterwards, your logo will show on the page. Hopefully, your logo designer is much better at coming up with a logo than I am.

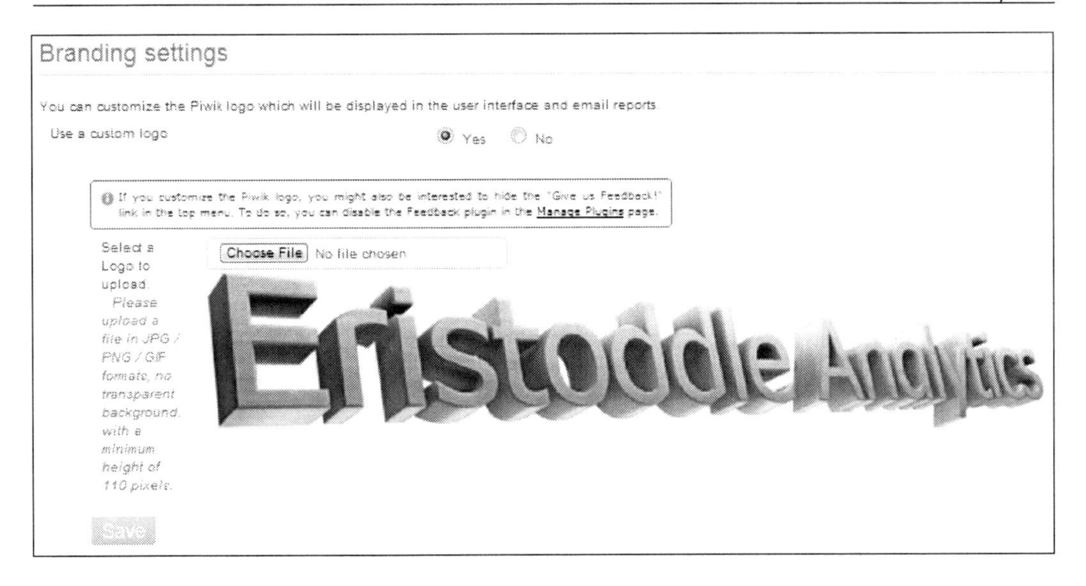

Then just click on **Save** and your logo now replaces the Piwik logo.

Any time you want to change your logo, just go back and switch it out. If you choose to go back to Piwik's logo, just go back to this page and set the **Use a custom logo** radio button to **No**.

Now, this is not a pure white label solution. The Piwik name and "Powered by Piwik" appear in documentation and various parts of your installation, but it will be hidden, for the most part, from standard users.

But another thing you might want to do on your white label Piwik installation is hide the "Give us Feedback!" link in the top menu, because this is for giving feedback on Piwik. To do this, we need to go to the **Plugins** section of the **Settings** menu. When you get there, scroll down until you find the **Feedback** plugin in the **Plugin** column.

ExamplePlugin	0.1	Example Plugin: This plugin shows how to create a very simple plugin, that exports two widgets in the Dashboard. (GPL v3 or later) By Piwik.	Active	Deactivate
ExampleRssWidget	0.1	Example Plugin: How to create a new widget that reads a RSS feed? By Piwik.	Active	Deactivate
ExampleUI	0.1	Example Plugin: This plugin shows how to work with the Piwik UI: create tables, graphs, etc. By Piwik.	Inactive	Activate
Feedback	1.8.3	Send your Feedback to the Piwik Team. Share your ideas and suggestions with us! By Piwik.	Active	Deactivate
Goals	1.8.3	Create Goals and see reports about your goal conversions: evolution over time, revenue per visit, conversions per referrer, per keyword, etc. Piwik allows for advanced Ecommerce Analytics tracking & reporting. Learn more about Ecommerce Analytics. By Piwik.	Active	Deactivate

At the right-hand side of the **Feedback** row, in the **Action** column, you will see a link that says **Deactivate**. Click on this link and the plugin is deactivated.

Allowing user sign up with the Piwik Signup plugin

One of the benefits to using an open source software solution is that many users are working together to make the software do as much if not more than any paid solution. Sometimes there may be features that most users of the software may not need, but a lot would like to have. In these cases, it is good to make sure that your software has a plugin system so that users can customize the installation to their needs.

As we saw in the previous section, Piwik does have such a plugin system. In fact, many of the features of your standard Piwik installation are plugins themselves and can be deactivated whenever you need, such as the **Feedback** plugin we just deactivated in the previous section. There are even some example plugins installed with Piwik to give developers something to start with.

Other plugins available for Piwik are listed on the official Piwik website. There is a list of some of these plugins as well as plugins for CMSs available at `http://piwik.org/faq/plugins/`. You can also find the long list of community submitted plugins at `http://tinyurl.com/8fzcr2n`.

One of the plugins available for Piwik is the `Signup` plugin. This plugin changes some of the rules that apply to our users. It allows anonymous users to sign up for an analytics account in your Piwik installation.

Installing a Piwik plugin

So let's add the `Signup` plugin to our white label Piwik installation. First you need to go to this thread at the Piwik Developer Zone, `http://dev.piwik.org/trac/ticket/1148`. You will see an **Attachments** section (as shown in the following screenshot) right after the first post on the thread.

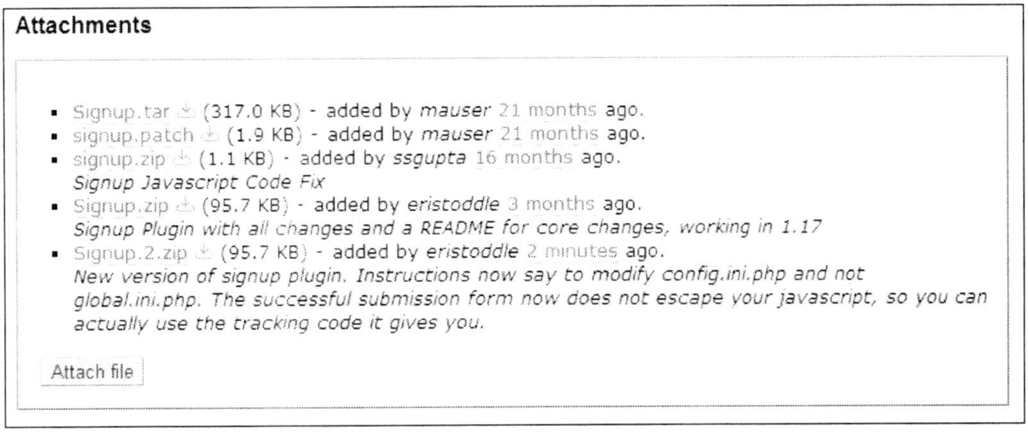

Attachments

- Signup.tar (317.0 KB) - added by *mauser* 21 months ago.
- signup.patch (1.9 KB) - added by *mauser* 21 months ago.
- signup.zip (1.1 KB) - added by *ssgupta* 16 months ago.
  Signup Javascript Code Fix
- Signup.zip (95.7 KB) - added by *eristoddle* 3 months ago.
  Signup Plugin with all changes and a README for core changes, working in 1.17
- Signup.2.zip (95.7 KB) - added by *eristoddle* 2 minutes ago.
  New version of signup plugin. Instructions now say to modify config.ini.php and not global.ini.php. The successful submission form now does not escape your javascript, so you can actually use the tracking code it gives you.

Attach file

Choose the bottom `Signup.2.zip` file. The file at the top is older and the others are patches for the older version. The file at the bottom is the file I actually put together for the book, so you wouldn't have to a lot of file editing. You will also get it in the code files for this book.

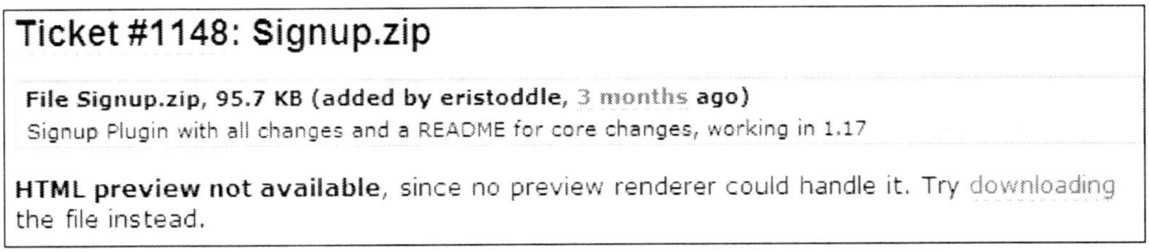

Ticket #1148: Signup.zip

File Signup.zip, 95.7 KB (added by eristoddle, 3 months ago)
Signup Plugin with all changes and a README for core changes, working in 1.17

HTML preview not available, since no preview renderer could handle it. Try downloading the file instead.

On this page, click on the link that says **downloading** and download the file to your computer. Once it is downloaded, unzip the folder. You should now have a **Signup** folder with a lib folder, template folder, `Controller.php` file, `README.md` file, `RegisterForm.php` file, and a `Signup.php` file inside of it.

Now that you have all the signup plugin files in their own folder, it is time to get out of your FTP software and upload these files to your Piwik server. You will be uploading the complete **Signup** folder to the plugins folder inside your Piwik installation, as shown in the following screenshot:

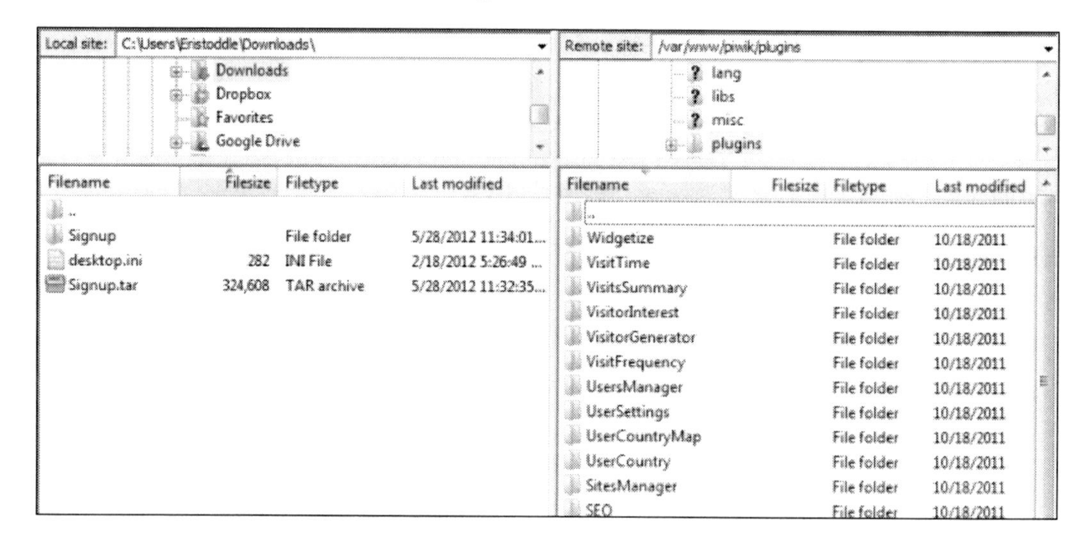

For many Piwik plugins, you don't need to edit any files in Piwik, but for this plugin, we are going to have to edit two files. So keep your FTP software open and find the `config.ini.php` file in the `config` folder of your Piwik installation. Open it in a text editor and scroll to the bottom of the file and add the following two lines:

```
[Signup]
enable_captcha = 0
```

This will turn CAPTCHAs off in your signup form. Alternately, you can set this to `1` to turn on CAPTCHAs. When you are done, save the file and upload it back to your Piwik installation.

Now find the `en.php` file in the `lang` folder of your Piwik installation. This file is the English language file for your Piwik installation. It replaces various variables in Piwik templates with the correct words according the language you chose for your installation. We are going to be adding the new variables we need for our `Signup` plugin to the array in this file. Open it in your text editor and scroll to the bottom of the file. The last line of code will be `);` and right before this line, add the following:

```
'Signup_InvalidWebsiteURL' => 'Invalid Website URL. Enter full URL
with http:// prefix.',
'Signup_Captcha' => 'Enter text from image above',
'Signup_InvalidCaptcha' => 'Invalid text from image.',
'Signup_Signup' => 'Sign Up',
```

```
'Signup_Intro' => 'Please fill this form to sign up for an account.',
'Signup_ProceedDashboard' => 'Proceed to Dashboard',
'Signup_CompleteMessage' => 'Sign up Complete!<br /><br />Make sure
your JavaScript code is entered in your pages, and wait for your
first visitors.<br /><br />You will receive an email with confirmation
shortly.',
'Signup_MailSubject' => 'Signup Complete',
'Signup_MailBody' => "Hi %1\$s!\n\nYou have successfully signed up for
an account. \n\nYour Username:\t%2\$s\nYour Password:\t%3\$s\nLogin
URL:\t%4\$s\n\nTo count all visitors, you must insert the JavaScript
code available inside your Dashboard: Settings > Websites > View
Tracking Code.\n\nSincerely,\nPiwik Open Source Analytics%5",
```

This will add our variables to the end of the array. Save this file and then upload it to your Piwik installation. This file edit adds the necessary text variables this plugin needs for buttons, messages, and e-mails.

Now your plugin is in place, but is not yet activated, so you need to go to the **Settings | Plugins** menu in Piwik to activate it.

SEO	1.8.3	This Plugin extracts and displays SEO metrics: Alexa web ranking, Google Pagerank, number of Indexed pages and backlinks of the currently selected website. *By Piwik*	Active	Deactivate
SecurityInfo	1.8.3	Based on PhpSecInfo from the PHP Security Consortium, this plugin provides security information about your PHP environment and offers suggestions for improvement. It is a tool in a multilayered security approach. It does not replace secure development practices nor audit the code/application. *By Piwik*	Inactive	Activate
Signup	0.1	Allows users to signup for a piwik account *By Maciej Zawadzinski, Clearcode*	Inactive	Activate

You will see the `Signup` plugin listed there in alphabetical order. Clicking on the **Activate** link on its row will turn on the `Signup` plugin.

How the user Signup plugin works

Now the `Signup` plugin does not put a direct link to the sign up page anywhere else in the Piwik interface. You must browse to it at the following URL: `http://YOUR_PIWIK_URL/index.php?module=Signup`.

This is where you replace `YOUR_PIWIK_URL` with the URL of your Piwik installation. There you will see a form that looks like the following screenshot:

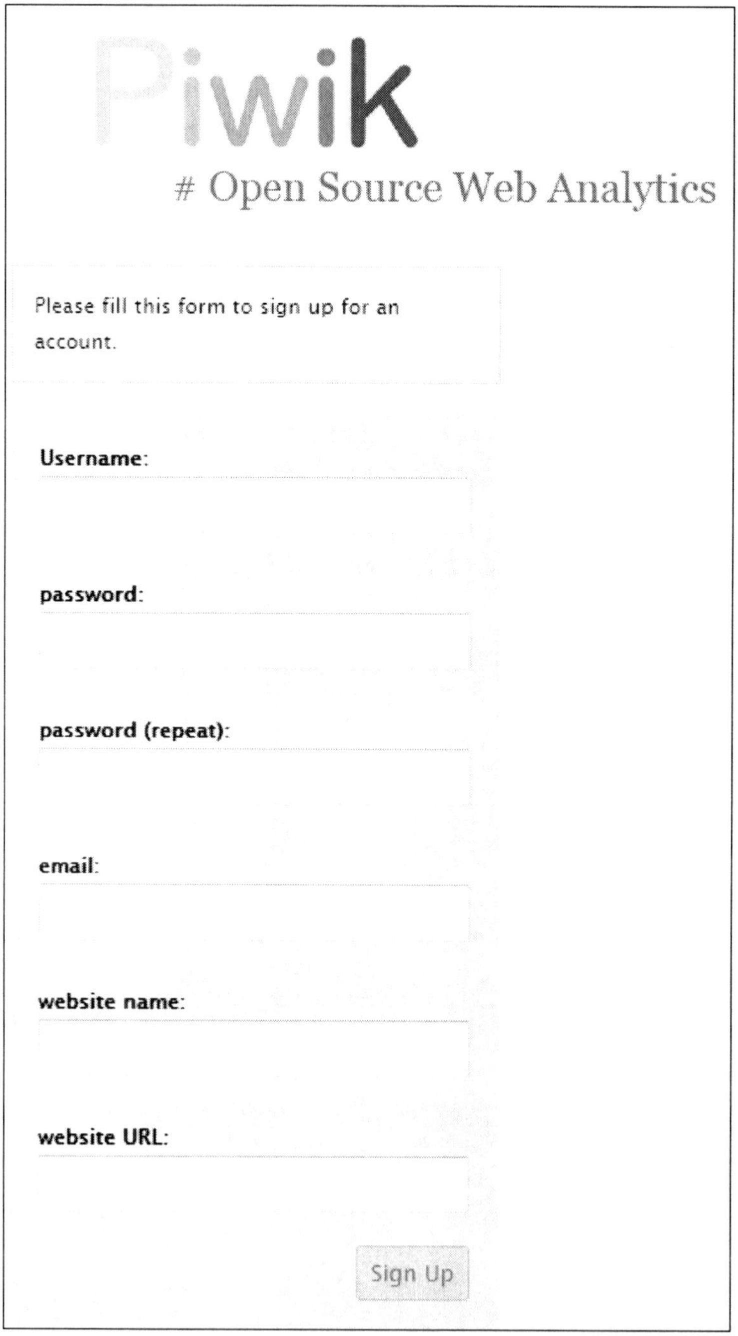

Piwik
Open Source Web Analytics

Please fill this form to sign up for an account.

Username:

password:

password (repeat):

email:

website name:

website URL:

Sign Up

You can test it out if you'd like. Just enter a new username, your password twice, your e-mail address, the name you will call your website in Piwik, and its URL. Click on the **Sign Up** button at the bottom and you will instantly have a new account, logged in, and you will be sent an e-mail with your account details.

Accounts created in this manner still give the Super User full access to the created user and website, so you can also log in with your super to see the new website and user you just created.

This `Signup` plugin has very basic functionality, but it will get the job done if you want users to sign up by themselves. Maybe as we learn more about Piwik, you will want to add the features you see necessary to the plugin.

Summary

After reading this chapter, you should be able to add and edit users and websites in Piwik. You also learned how to fine-tune the permissions that users get on a site-by-site basis. We also added a logo to our Piwik installation so that you can provide your own brand of website analytics. And finally, you learned how to install a Piwik plugin in order to let your users sign up for an account by themselves.

In the next chapter, we will dig down deeper in the Piwik analytics API to learn advanced tracking techniques.

9
Advanced Tracking and Development

So far, we have covered tracking goals, tracking events, tracking campaigns, and tracking e-commerce actions and some of this tracking might be considered fairly advanced. It definitely involved a bit more work than simply pasting JavaScript before your closing body tag. But we never really strayed that far from using JavaScript to do our tracking. In *Chapter 7*, *E-commerce Tracking* we used some PHP code to write the JavaScript code for us, but we were still using JavaScript.

There will be times where standard tracking just won't do the job. There may be pages or apps that will not allow or cannot execute the JavaScript code. That is why Piwik has more than JavaScript to offer. You can also track with images or use the tracking API. Image tracking may not be all that advanced and it is out of the norm but you have to think a little differently. With it, you can track visitors on sites such as eBay and Craigslist that don't allow JavaScript. The tracking API doesn't require JavaScript, so you can access it from other programming languages for use in non-standard web apps, phone apps, or desktop apps.

There may be some of you who want to change some of the functionality of Piwik through Piwik's plugin system to add features or different types of reports. The data is all in Piwik. If you don't see something you need in a report, maybe writing a plugin is the solution.

In this chapter, we will learn:

- How to use simple image tracking
- How to use advanced image tracking
- How to use the PiwikTracker.php API
- How to access the Piwik tracking API with any language
- How to debug your tracking
- How to write a Piwik plugin

Tracking visitors with image tracking

You may have noticed the `noscript` section at the bottom of your Piwik tracking code. We haven't gone over what this does in detail up to this point in the book.

```
<!-- Piwik -->
<script type="text/javascript">
varpkBaseURL = (("https:" == document.location.protocol) ?
"https://$PIWIK_URL" : "http://$PIWIK_URL");
document.write(unescape("%3Cscriptsrc='" + pkBaseURL + "piwik.js'
type='text/javascript'%3E%3C/script%3E"));
</script><script type="text/javascript">
try {
varpiwikTracker = Piwik.getTracker(pkBaseURL + "piwik.php", $SITE_ID);
piwikTracker.trackPageView();
piwikTracker.enableLinkTracking();
} catch( err ) {}
</script><noscript><p><imgsrc="$PIWIK_URL/piwik.php?idsite=1"
style="border:0" alt="" /></p></noscript>
<!-- End Piwik Tracking Code -->
```

Between the `noscript` tags is an HTML image tag, but it doesn't point to an image. It points to a PHP script that will load in the page like an invisible image and help you track visitors when a browser's JavaScript is disabled.

But you may find yourself needing to track visitors on someone else's website, and if that site doesn't allow JavaScript, you know beforehand that the code above is not going to work for you. The following are just some of the sites that you may want to add tracking to:

- MySpace
- eBay
- Craigslist
- LiveJournal

The only way you are going to accomplish this is using Piwik's image tracking functionality. We are about to learn that we can do a lot of complex tracking with this little fake image. First, let's look at the easy way of using image tracking.

Simple image tracking

Using simple image tracking is as easy as copying and pasting the code that Piwik gives you. If you are tracking a complete blog on LiveJournal or are running a lot of eBay auctions, you may want to create a website in Piwik for your image tracking purposes instead of mixing your image tracking into another website account. Although, if you have a business blog hosted on a free blog host and a business site that is closely related, it may not hurt to put the tracking under one account.

Let's get that image code. First, click on the **Settings** link in the top right-hand corner of the Piwik interface.

Then click on the **Websites** tab of the main menu on the **Settings** page.

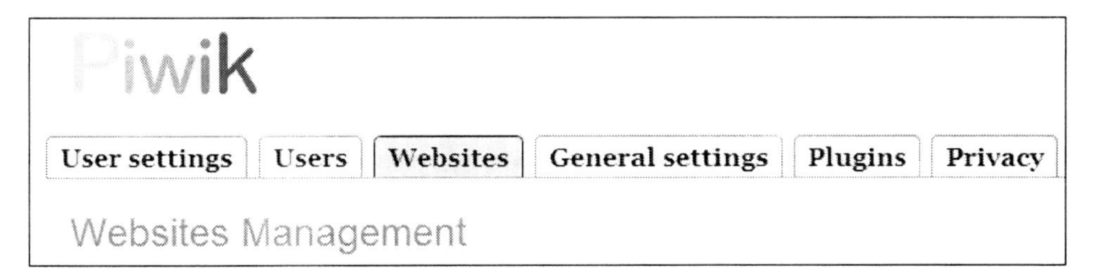

The image tracking code is in the same place as the standard JavaScript tracking code, so find your chosen site in the table and click on the **View Tracking code** link at the end of the row.

Currency	Ecommerce			JavaScript Tracking Code
USD	-	Edit	Delete	View Tracking code
USD	-	Edit	Delete	View Tracking code

On the tracking code page, you will see the **Image Tracker code** section right under the **Standard JavaScript Tracking code** section.

Standard JavaScript Tracking code

Copy and paste the following code in all the pages you want to track with Piwik.
In most websites, blogs, CMS, etc. you can edit your website templates and add this code in a "footer" file.

Here is the JavaScript Tracking code to include on all your pages, just before the </body> tag.

```
<!-- Piwik -->
<script type="text/javascript">
var pkBaseURL = (("https:" == document.location.protocol) ? "https://ec2-50-19-0-
18.compute-1.amazonaws.com/piwik/" : "http://ec2-50-19-0-18.compute-
1.amazonaws.com/piwik/");
document.write(unescape("%3Cscript src='" + pkBaseURL + "piwik.js'
type='text/javascript'%3E%3C/script%3E"));
</script><script type="text/javascript">
try {
var piwikTracker = Piwik.getTracker(pkBaseURL + "piwik.php", 1);
piwikTracker.trackPageView();
piwikTracker.enableLinkTracking();
} catch( err ) {}
</script><noscript><p><img src="http://ec2-50-19-0-18.compute-
1.amazonaws.com/piwik/piwik.php?idsite=1" style="border:0" alt="" /></p>
</noscript>
<!-- End Piwik Tracking Code -->
```

If you want to do more than tracking a page view, please check out the Piwik Javascript Tracking documentation for the list of available functions (for example: Tracking Goals, Custom Variables, Ecommerce orders, products and abandoned carts, etc.).

Click on the **Display Image Tracker code** link and that section of the page will expand.

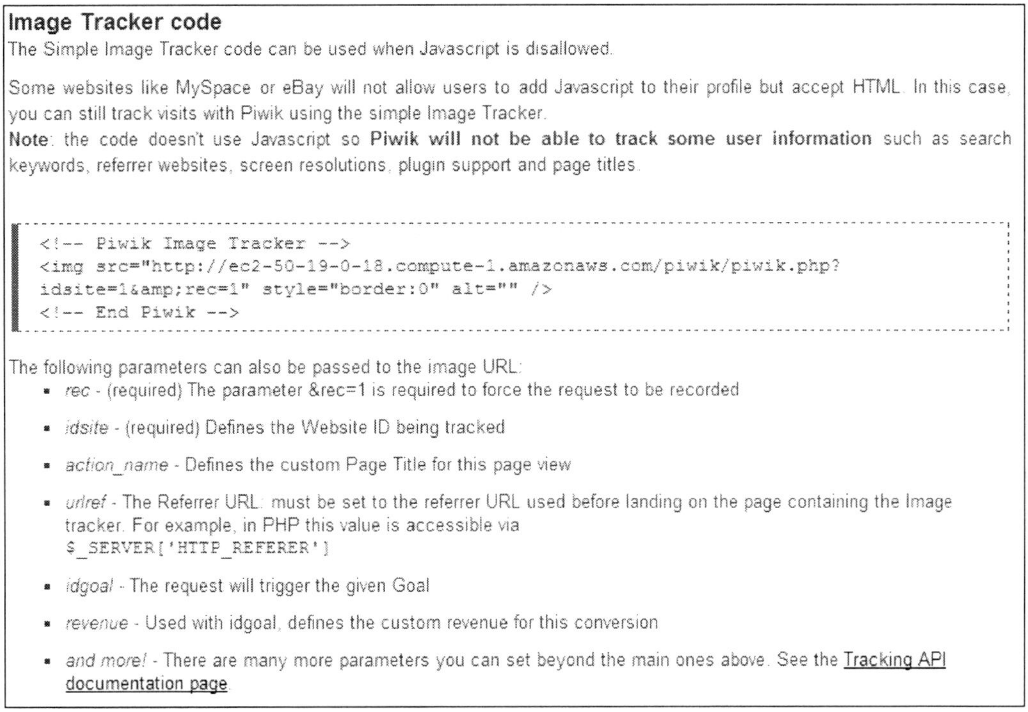

Image Tracker code

The Simple Image Tracker code can be used when Javascript is disallowed.

Some websites like MySpace or eBay will not allow users to add Javascript to their profile but accept HTML. In this case, you can still track visits with Piwik using the simple Image Tracker.
Note: the code doesn't use Javascript so **Piwik will not be able to track some user information** such as search keywords, referrer websites, screen resolutions, plugin support and page titles.

```
<!-- Piwik Image Tracker -->
<img src="http://ec2-50-19-0-18.compute-1.amazonaws.com/piwik/piwik.php?
idsite=1&amp;rec=1" style="border:0" alt="" />
<!-- End Piwik -->
```

The following parameters can also be passed to the image URL:

- *rec* - (required) The parameter &rec=1 is required to force the request to be recorded
- *idsite* - (required) Defines the Website ID being tracked
- *action_name* - Defines the custom Page Title for this page view
- *urlref* - The Referrer URL: must be set to the referrer URL used before landing on the page containing the Image tracker. For example, in PHP this value is accessible via `$_SERVER['HTTP_REFERER']`
- *idgoal* - The request will trigger the given Goal
- *revenue* - Used with idgoal, defines the custom revenue for this conversion
- *and more!* - There are many more parameters you can set beyond the main ones above. See the Tracking API documentation page.

In the blue section of the page, you will see **Image Tracker code** similar to this:

```
<!-- Piwik Image Tracker -->
<img src="http://YOUR_PIWIK_URL/piwik/piwik.php?idsite=YOUR_SITE_
ID&amp;rec=1" style="border:0" alt="" />
<!-- End Piwik -->
```

Here, `YOUR_PIWIK_URL` is the URL of your Piwik Installation and `YOUR_SITE_ID` is the ID of the website you are tracking.

You can take that bit of HTML and put it in your eBay auction or your MySpace page and start tracking.

Image tracking limitations

There are some limitations to image tracking. It just won't do everything that JavaScript tracking will do. It won't be able to track:

- Search keywords
- Referrer websites
- Screen resolution
- Browser plugin support
- Local time
- Cookie support
- Page titles

If you plan on using image tracking in e-mails, do know that most images in e-mails are blocked by e-mail clients unless the user chooses to view them, and if the only image in your e-mail is your fake tracking image, chances are people will not make that choice.

But you do have some wiggle room with image tracking, so let's look at just what you can do with it.

Advanced image tracking

So let's say you want to do something more with your image tracking. It's great to have standard tracking as it gives you a lot of information, but what if you want to trigger a conversion goal, set a page title, or track revenue?

Well, you can do that too, because like we said before, the image is not really an image, but a PHP script. It is actually Piwik's REST API endpoint. In other words you can send more parameters than just the site ID.

Let's look at our default image tracking code again.

```
<!-- Piwik Image Tracker -->
<img src="http://YOUR_PIWIK_URL/piwik/piwik.php?idsite=YOUR_SITE_
ID&amp;rec=1" style="border:0" alt="" />
<!-- End Piwik -->
```

It seems that the bare minimum parameters we need are `idsite` and whatever `rec` is. Well, `rec` is simply a parameter that triggers the request to be recorded. It is required and must be set to `1` to record the visit.

Another thing you should notice is that the URL is URL encoded. For example, the URL is `http://YOUR_PIWIK_URL/piwik/piwik.php?idsite=YOUR_SITE_ID&rec=1` instead of `http://YOUR_PIWIK_URL/piwik/piwik.php?idsite=YOUR_SITE_ID&rec=1`. All string parameters must similarly be URL encoded.

Adding page titles to eBay auction tracking

Let's say that now we're eBay power sellers. We have a lot of auctions going at once, a lot to ship out, a lot of questions to answer, and a backlog of feedback to give. We need better stats than a simple old page view counter, but eBay won't allow JavaScript.

So, we create a site in the backend of Piwik called "My eBay Store" and get our image tracking code. We can put the HTML snippet for Piwik image tracking just about anywhere in the auction body and eBay will allow it. We choose the bottom and edit all of our auctions to add the image tracker code. Seconds later, we can see the visits piling up on our eBay auctions. Things are good until we go to the **Actions | Pagetitlesreport** and see that our page titles are not defined.

This will not work. We have the Pages report which will list our page view data by URL. But that isn't going to help much with eBay's URLs. We need something to identify which auctions and merchandise are getting the most views, and which may need a little work to get more window shoppers without having to click on the links in the Pages report.

Luckily, we can add the `action_name` parameter to our image URL to set the page title for visits. Now we have a choice of what to use for our page title. We could use our actual auction title or we could use a shorter version of our auction title. If we are running similar auctions to test two or more different titles, using the full title only makes sense. If our auctions are a lot of liquidated merchandise and no two are the same, a full page title may just clutter up the interface and it may be better to use just a product name and a quantity if it is needed. We may want to put a dash in our page title and add the eBay auction ID to the end if we need to be sure.

So now we have a URL similar to the following code:

```
http://YOUR_PIWIK_URL/piwik/piwik.php?idsite=YOUR_SITE_
ID&amp;rec=1&amp;action_name=Lot of 4 Holy Hand Grenades
```

Then we remember something about URL encoding. The spaces in the `action_name` value are going to break our URL if we don't use it. Spaces are one of the characters that can't be used in a URL and must be replaced by a URL character code. The following table shows some of the more common characters that need to be replaced:

<table>
<tr><th>Character</th><th>URL Character Code</th><th>Character</th><th>URL Character Code</th></tr>
<tr><td><</td><td>%3C</td><td>`</td><td>%60</td></tr>
<tr><td>></td><td>%3E</td><td>;</td><td>%3B</td></tr>
<tr><td>#</td><td>%23</td><td>/</td><td>%2F</td></tr>
<tr><td>%</td><td>%25</td><td>?</td><td>%3F</td></tr>
<tr><td>{</td><td>%7B</td><td>:</td><td>%3A</td></tr>
<tr><td>}</td><td>%7D</td><td>@</td><td>%40</td></tr>
<tr><td>|</td><td>%7C</td><td>=</td><td>%3D</td></tr>
<tr><td>\</td><td>%5C</td><td>&</td><td>%26</td></tr>
<tr><td>^</td><td>%5E</td><td>$</td><td>%24</td></tr>
<tr><td>~</td><td>%7E</td><td>+</td><td>%2B</td></tr>
<tr><td>[</td><td>%5B</td><td>"</td><td>%22</td></tr>
<tr><td>]</td><td>%5D</td><td>space</td><td>%20</td></tr>
</table>

We see from the table that the character code for a space is `%20`, so we replace the spaces with `%20` and our image URL is now:

```
http://YOUR_PIWIK_URL/piwik/piwik.php?idsite=YOUR_SITE_
ID&amp;rec=1&amp;action_name=Lot%20of%204%20Holy%20Hand%20Grenades
```

This makes our tracking code look like this:

```
<!-- Piwik Image Tracker -->
<img src="http://YOUR_PIWIK_URL/piwik/piwik.php?idsite=YOUR_SITE_
ID&amp;rec=1&amp;action_name=Lot%20of%204%20Holy%20Hand%20Grenades
" style="border:0" alt="" />
<!-- End Piwik -->
```

Now we just create one for each of our auctions. We could also create templates for our auctions if we are relisting the same products over and over and don't want to worry about changing the image tracking code, unless we are adding the auction ID to the page title.

Tracking a goal with an image

Let's say that we have found this product on someone else's site that would be a perfect addition to the products on our own site. The company doesn't offer any wholesale pricing but they do have an affiliated program that pays pretty well and might add a little more income to our website.

The affiliated program allows tracking through the use of an image, which many affiliated programs do. We can add the URL to our Piwik image to our profile with the affiliated company and it will be added to the sales page that results from our unique affiliated link. We will be notified every time there is a sale. We could just use the standard image in the form like this:

```
http://YOUR_PIWIK_URL/piwik/piwik.php
```

This would only track each sale as a visit. It is a visit, but it is more importantly a goal, so we will need to add some GET parameters in the image URL to trigger a goal conversion.

The thing about image tracking without using any other code such as JavaScript or PHP to dynamically generate our data for us is that our tracking is set in stone. Once we put the image tag in place on the page, it will do the same thing for every visitor. In our eBay example previously, all we did was set a page title for Piwik so that we could analyze our results more easily. When we set a goal with the image, we have to be sure that the page we are adding the image to will only load when a conversion for that goal has occurred. In our case, we don't have to worry. We are adding the image to one page and it is the sales success page. Only goals make it there.

We discussed in *Chapter 4, Setting up and Tracking Goals*, how to set up goals in our Piwik installation, so we need to go there first and set up a goal for our affiliated sales. Once we have a goal set up in Piwik, we need to grab its ID to add to our Piwik image URL. So after you create the goal, stay on the **Goals Management** page and scroll down to the bottom where it says **View and Edit Goals** and click on the link as shown in the following screenshot:

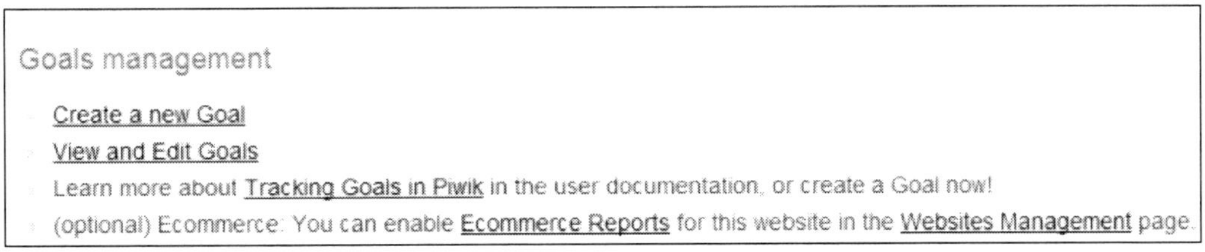

Goals management

- Create a new Goal
- View and Edit Goals
- Learn more about Tracking Goals in Piwik in the user documentation, or create a Goal now!
- (optional) Ecommerce: You can enable Ecommerce Reports for this website in the Websites Management page.

Clicking on the link will open up a table of your goals as seen in the screenshot below:

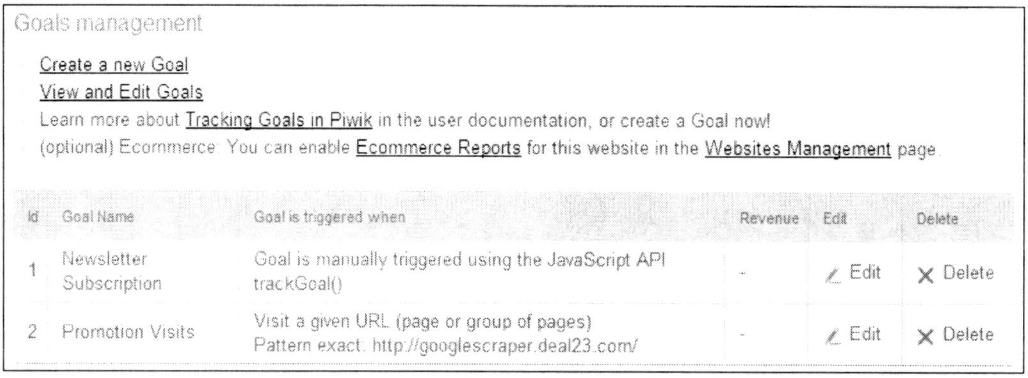

Goals management

Create a new Goal
View and Edit Goals
Learn more about Tracking Goals in Piwik in the user documentation, or create a Goal now!
(optional) Ecommerce: You can enable Ecommerce Reports for this website in the Websites Management page.

Id	Goal Name	Goal is triggered when	Revenue	Edit	Delete
1	Newsletter Subscription	Goal is manually triggered using the JavaScript API trackGoal()	-	Edit	Delete
2	Promotion Visits	Visit a given URL (page or group of pages) Pattern exact: http://googlescraper.deal23.com/	-	Edit	Delete

Just find the goal we created for our affiliated sales and grab the **Id** from the far left column. Now that we have this, we can create the image URL to trigger our goal conversion quite easily. The parameter we need to track our goal is `idgoal` and the final URL of our link would look something like this:

```
http://YOUR_PIWIK_URL/piwik/piwik.php?idsite=YOUR_SITE_
ID&amp;rec=1&amp;idgoal=2
```

That is, if the ID of our goal was 2. These are two simple examples of using Piwik's image and no other code to track various pages. There are many more parameters to choose from.

Parameter	Value
`rec`	(required) You must set this parameter to `1` if you want Piwik to track the visitor, like so: `&rec=1`.
`idsite`	(required) This is the ID of the website you are tracking in Piwik.
`action_name`	This parameter sets the custom page title for the page view which will be in the **Actions | Page titles report**.
`url_ref`	This is the referrer URL. Most likely, you will have to use PHP or some other programming language on site to set this value. In PHP this value is accessible with `$_SERVER['HTTP_REFERRER']`.
`idgoal`	This is the ID of your goal.
`revenue`	You can set this value if you want to track revenue along with your goal.

Tracking visitors with the PHP tracking API

Like we just learned, the image URL you use to add tracking to pages that don't allow JavaScript is actually the endpoint of Piwik's REST API. There is a lot more you can do with the REST API than just set page titles or track images, but I decided to save the code writing part for this section. You just can't expect to do everything by inserting an image in the page. Some data can only be captured dynamically.

There are options. If you don't want to or can't use JavaScript to do your dynamic tracking, you can use PHP. It will provide you with most of the tracking functions that the JavaScript tracker provides except for:

- Screen resolution
- Browser plugin support
- Local time
- Cookie support

`Piwik.org` even provides a tracking API available at the following URL: `http://piwik.org/docs/tracking-api/`. Just scroll down the page until you see **Click here to download the file PiwikTracker.php**.

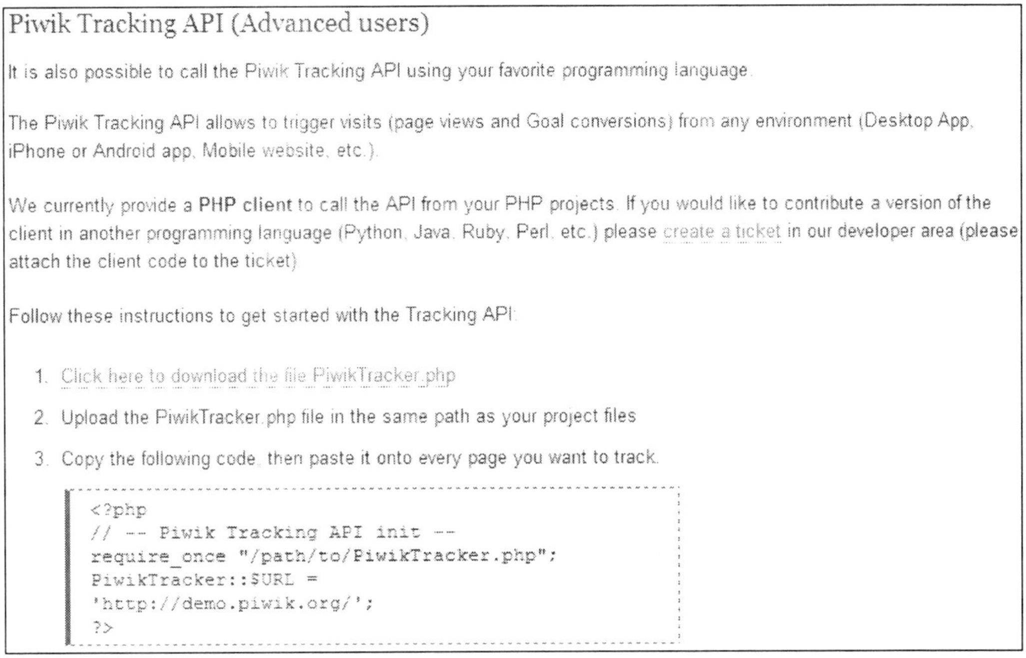

Piwik Tracking API (Advanced users)

It is also possible to call the Piwik Tracking API using your favorite programming language.

The Piwik Tracking API allows to trigger visits (page views and Goal conversions) from any environment (Desktop App, iPhone or Android app, Mobile website, etc.).

We currently provide a **PHP client** to call the API from your PHP projects. If you would like to contribute a version of the client in another programming language (Python, Java, Ruby, Perl, etc.) please create a ticket in our developer area (please attach the client code to the ticket)

Follow these instructions to get started with the Tracking API:

1. Click here to download the file PiwikTracker.php
2. Upload the PiwikTracker.php file in the same path as your project files
3. Copy the following code, then paste it onto every page you want to track.

```
<?php
// -- Piwik Tracking API init --
require_once "/path/to/PiwikTracker.php";
PiwikTracker::$URL =
'http://demo.piwik.org/';
?>
```

This API file will provide you with every function you need to track visitors using PHP including:

- Tracking Goals
- Tracking Events
- Tracking Campaigns
- Tracking E-commerce

The PHP API provides an easy to use set of functions that generate the call to Piwik's API. In other words, you don't have to worry about generating the long URL with boatloads of parameters. All you do is include the `PiwikTracker.php` file, use its functions, and it will generate all of this for you. We could write our Zen Cart plugin a completely different way using the PHP API now if we wanted to. So go download the file and open up your FTP software.

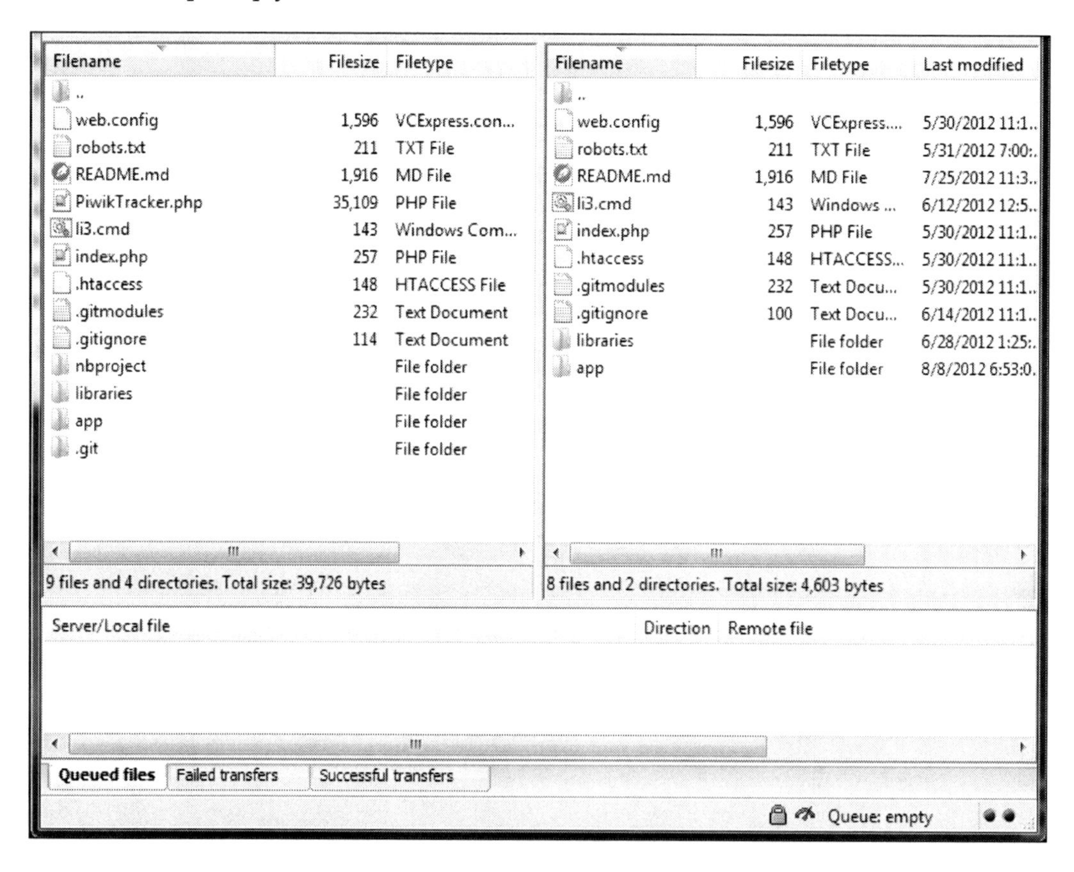

Now upload the `PiwikTracker.php` file to your website. Once it is uploaded, you need to include this file in every page you want to track. Here is an example of the PHP code you would use to do that:

```
<?php
// -- Piwik Tracking API init --
require_once "/PATH_TO/PiwikTracker.php";
PiwikTracker::$URL = 'http://YOUR_PIWIK_URL';
?>
```

Here, `PATH_TO` is the path to the location of your API file and `YOUR_PIWIK_URL` is the base URL of your Piwik installation. Now you are ready to start writing your tracking code.

There are actually two ways to do this. We could generate the HTML image tag using PHP and have a page load trigger our code, or we could make a request directly using PHP.

Generating the image tracker

The first way we are going to use the PHP tracker is to generate the URL to the Piwik REST API for use in an image tag. In the e-commerce plugin we wrote in *Chapter 7, E-commerce Tracking*, we used PHP code to generate the JavaScript we needed for the Piwik tracker.

This time, we are doing things a little differently. Firstly, there is no JavaScript involved, so we don't have to think in two languages at one time. Secondly, we only need to call the tracker object with parameters to generate the URL we need to put in our HTML image tag. All tracking happens when that URL is loaded in the browser. We don't have to worry about whether we need asynchronous code or if we called our functions in the correct order, before `trackPageView()`. Everything that is available in the JavaScript API can also be used in the PHP API.

Let's take a look at the Piwik JavaScript function that we would use to trigger Piwik to track a download link.

```
<a href="http://mywebsite.com/mydownload.zip" target="_blank" onClick
="javascript:piwikTracker.trackLink('http://mywebsite.com/mydownload.
zip', 'download');"> Download Me </a>
```

When we use this function, we have already added the Piwik JavaScript tracking code to our web site. When a visitor clicks on our download link, the Javascript `onClick` event executes `piwikTracker.trackLink` and this tells Piwik the file has been downloaded. But what if we send someone a link to the file in an e-mail? It's a file, it can't execute JavaScript.

We could use PHP. We will create a file called `mydownload.php` and use that for all of our links to the download whether on site or from an e-mail.

First, we need to make sure the `PiwikTracker.php` file is on our server and then make sure we add the code to include this file to the top of our `mydownload.php` file. The meta refresh tag is old school, but it works, so we are going to use it to redirect our visitor to the true download link. The following code snippet shows how our page looks like:

```
<?php
// -- Piwik Tracking API init --
require_once "/PATH_TO/PiwikTracker.php";
PiwikTracker::$URL = 'http://YOUR_PIWIK_URL';
?>
<!DOCTYPE HTML>
<html lang="en-US">
<head>
    <meta charset="UTF-8">
    <meta http-equiv="refresh" content="1;url=http://mywebsite.com/
mydownload.zip">
    <title></title>
</head>
<body>
    <?php
            // --Our Log Download Code --
            $download_url = str_replace(".php",".zip","http://".$_
SERVER['HTTP_HOST'].$_SERVER['REQUEST_URI']);
            echo '<imgsrc="'. str_replace("&","&amp;", Piwik_
getUrlTrackPageView( $idSite = {$IDSITE}, $customTitle = "MyDownload-
".$download_url)) . '" alt="" />';
    ?>
</body>
</html>
```

At the top of our file, we require the Piwik tracker file, which in this example is the root of our website. Below that you can see the meta refresh tag. We are going to let the page load for one second and then redirect the visitor to our download located at `http://mywebsite.com/mydownload.zip`.

Before it can redirect, the whole page has to load. At the bottom of the page we have the PHP code that will be generating our HTML image tag for tracking with Piwik.

```
<?php
            // --Our Log Download Code --
            $download_url = str_replace(".php",".zip","http://".$_
SERVER['HTTP_HOST'].$_SERVER['REQUEST_URI']);
```

```
        echo '<imgsrc="'. str_replace("&","&amp;",
Piwik_getUrlTrackPageView( $idSite = {$IDSITE}, $customTitle =
"MyDownload-".$download_url)) . '" alt="" />';
?>
```

The first line of PHP sets the download URL variable that we will be using in our call to Piwik. This is created from two variables that PHP has built in. You will be using these variables a lot with the PiwikPHP API.

- `$_SERVER['HTTP_HOST']`: This variable will give you the domain of the website where the current file is located. If the PHP file is `http://mywebsite.com/mydownload.php`, it will give you `mywebsite.com`.
- `$_SERVER['REQUEST_URI']`: This is the page on the domain that was requested from the server to load the current page. In other words, with the URL being `http://mywebsite.com/mydownload.php`, this variable would give us `/mydownload.php`, including the forward slash.

We join these two variables together and then to "`http://`" in order to create the full URL of the current page. The result is the following:

```
"http://".$_SERVER['HTTP_HOST'].$_SERVER['REQUEST_URI']
```

In this case, we actually didn't really need to do this. We already know what the URL is going to be and if we hardcoded the URL in the meta refresh, why are we dynamically generating a URL for our action URL? We are doing it just to learn. We will be using a lot of PHP server globals global variables with the PHP API and the two variables shown previosuly are the most common. It is best if we get familiar with them. After all, we don't even need the URL in this case, just the page title.

We then replace the `.php` in the URL we just created with `.zip`, using PHP's `str_replace` function. Again, this is overkill for what we are doing here, but this will create the URL for the actual download, which we store in the variable `$download_url`.

The next line of code prints out our final image tag and our URL to Piwik. We have already included the `PiwikTracker.php` file at the top of our current file, so it has access to all the classes and functions in the file. So we call `Piwik_getUrlTrackPageView`, which accepts the following parameters:

- `$idSite`: This is the ID of the site you are tracking in Piwik
- `$customTitle`: This is the page title that will appear in the **Action | Page titles report**

For our title, we are going to use a combination of `MyDownload-` and the URL we just created with PHP and of course, we replace `{$IDSITE}` with the ID of our site in our Piwik installation.

But before we print out the URL of the image to our page, we need to do one last thing to it. Use `str_replace` again to replace all of the ampersands with "&". I have probably drilled it into your head by now, but we need to URL-encode the URL. And finally we use `echo` to print our completed tag.

Since we have access to the whole `PiwikTracker.php` file, generating a complete image tag is unnecessary work, really. The bulk of this file is a PHP class of 1000 lines that will do about anything we need to do. We use one of the two functions at the bottom of the file that returns the completed URL for us.

```
function Piwik_getUrlTrackPageView( $idSite, $documentTitle = false )
{
    $tracker = new PiwikTracker($idSite);
    return $tracker->getUrlTrackPageView($documentTitle);
}
```

This function is using the `PiwikTracker` class to give us the URL. When a new `PiwikTracker` is created, we give it the site ID. That's all we need to do. Now we have an object that has all the functionality of the class. But this function only uses a very simplistic function in the class to track a page view. The other standalone function in the `PiwikTracker.php` file is as follows:

```
function Piwik_getUrlTrackGoal($idSite, $idGoal, $revenue = false)
{
    $tracker = new PiwikTracker($idSite);
    return $tracker->getUrlTrackGoal($idGoal, $revenue);
}
```

This is a function to track a goal that returns our URL. It again uses the `PiwikTracker` class to do so.

You may have noticed a pattern here. To create other complete URLs for our tracking purposes, we could just write a function like this. But like we said, with all this functionality, why use an image unless you have to. We can use an HTTP request to make a call to the Piwik API transparently. In the next example, we will be doing exactly that.

Making an HTTP request to the tracker

This time we will be using `PiwikTracker.php` to transparently make a call to Piwik to track a visitor and his actions. We don't have to output an image tag to our web page. Just let this bit of code do its work in the background. This will involve using the `PiwikTracker` class instead of simple functions from the file.

```
<?php

    require_once "/PATH_TO/PiwikTracker.php";

    //Set the id of your piwik site here
    $idSite = 1;
    $token_auth = 'your user token here';

    //Create a PiwikTracker Object
    $piwikTracker = new PiwikTracker($idSite, 'http://your_piwik_url.
com/piwik/');

    //Set token_auth - required for setVisitorId
    $piwikTracker->setTokenAuth( $token_auth );

    //Visitor Id from our site's user database
    $piwikTracker->setVisitorId( "33c31e01394bdc63" );


    // Sends Tracker request via http

    $piwikTracker->doTrackPageView('Get Page Title From DataBase
Here');

    // You can also track Goal conversions

    $piwikTracker->doTrackGoal($idGoal = 1, $revenue = 10);

?>
```

After you customize this snippet of code, you can include it in any PHP to track visits. We include our tracker file first. The ID of your site and your user token from Piwik are set at the top of the file. After that we create a new `PiwikTracker` object called `$PiwikTracker`. We instantiate this object by giving it the ID of our site and the URL of our Piwik installation.

The next line of code sets our unique visitor ID by calling the `setVisitorId` method. If we have an anonymous visitor come to our site, we could randomly generate a unique ID for them. In order to have this ID stick to the visitor as he goes from page to page, we would use PHP session variables. These are unique IDs generated by PHP that can then be appended to URLs as the visitor goes from link to link. Alternately, you could set a cookie to hold this value. If your visitor has signed up at your site and is logged in, you could store a unique ID in their account details and use this for a Piwik visitor ID. Another place where storing a unique ID that could stay more permanently with a visitor is in a phone application, where an ID can be generated when the application is installed and used for all tracking of its usage.

The next line of the code sends a request to Piwik to track the page view. When we call `doTrackPageView`, we give it the title of the page as a parameter. In pages dynamically generated by PHP, it shouldn't be too hard to access this variable and set it dynamically.

And at the end we track a goal with a revenue of $10. There are many more functions available in the tracker class. You can read about the complete functionality of the class at `http://piwik.org/docs/tracking-api/`.

Tracking visitors with other programming languages

If you decide not to use PHP to develop an application or website, there are still options available to you for using Piwik in your project.

Java

A Piwik user spent a lot of time converting all the functions in the `PiwikTracker.php` file into Java functions and released his Java Tracking client on the Piwik development forums. It's a Java class called `Piwiktracker.java`. You can find the current release of this API at the following link:

`http://dev.piwik.org/trac/ticket/2172`

Python

I do like Python. There is even an API for Piwik written in Python. This API is available on Github at the following link:

https://github.com/nkuttler/python-piwikapi

Silverlight

A Piwik tracking API for Microsoft Silverlight is also available on Github at the following link:

https://github.com/saintedlama/Piwik-Tracking

Flash

We touched a bit on how to using Piwik with Flash in *Chapter 6, Tracking Events*. We learned that Flash can interact directly with the JavaScript on the HTML page it is located on, though there is a big difference between `ActionScript2` and `ActionScript3`. With `ActionScript2`, you can use the `getURL` method to execute a Piwik function. With `ActionScript3`, you will have to reference the `flash.external.Interface` library to communicate with the Piwik JavaScript tracking code on the page.

Using Piwik's tracking API directly

The PHP, Java, or Python APIs for Piwik make tracking visitors and users where JavaScript can't be used, simple and easy by wrapping all calls to Piwik's API URL into simpler functions. We touched a bit on the tracking API when we manually created our image tracking code at the beginning of the chapter.

Since using the Piwik API only involves generating a URL and then making an HTTP request to it, you can easily track any application in any language as long as there is a way to access the Internet.

Of course, you will be generating a URL that looks something like the following URL:

```
http://mypiwik.com/piwik/piwik.php?action_name=Google%20Scraper%20
Footprint%20Finder&idsite=5&rec=1&r=055697&h=22&m=22&s=21&url=
http%3A%2F%2Fgooglescraper.deal23.com%2F&_id=8af038f1463fb845&_
idts=1340161706&_idvc=1&_idn=0&_refts=0&_viewts=1340161706&pdf=1&qt=1
&realp=0&wma=0&dir=1&fla=1&java=1&gears=0&ag=1&cookie=1&res=1600x900&r
and=0354510516
```

This is much longer than the URL we created for an image tracker. It has 25 parameters. The following table lists a few of them:

Parameter	Description
`idsite`	(required) This is the ID of the site in Piwik. In our example URL, our ID is `5`.
`rec`	(required) The parameter `&rec=1` is required to track. It is set up above in our URL.
`url`	(required) The URL is where the action is taking place. This can be the actual URL or a URL used to represent an action in a phone or desktop application. The URL-encoded URL in our URL above is `http%3A%2F%2Fgooglescraper.deal23.com%2F`. Now that was a mouthful.
`action_name`	(optional) This is the title of the page that shows up in the **Actions** | **Page**. You can also use this to categorize actions in an application. Slashes, "/", are handy for this. For example, creating a user in an app could set an `action_name` of `/user/create` and deleting a user, `/user/delete`. In our URL above, our `action_name` is `Google%20Scraper%20 Footprint%20Finder`, after being URL-encoded.
`_id`	(optional) This is a unique user ID. It requires a 16 character hexadecimal string. It is what allows Piwik to tell the difference between users. Without it, unique visitor tracking would not be accurate. Something you could use for this ID is the user's server session ID, or in an app, you could have your software create a unique ID as it is installed. That way each installation would be tracked as a unique user. The `_id` in our URL is `8af038f1463fb845`.
`rand`	(optional) Browsers proxy cache web pages so that they will load faster. Unfortunately, this means they may cache the result of your Piwik call. By setting the `rand` parameter, you create a unique URL each time the page loads, preventing this caching. The `rand` parameter in the URL above is `0354510516`.
`url_ref`	(optional) This is the URL of the referrer. If the referrer is a search engine, Piwik also parses it for the keywords the visitor used at the search engine. Our URL does not have a referrer because it was a direct visit.
`_cvar`	(optional) This is a JSON string containing the custom variables for the visit's scope. Our URL does not have a `_cvar` parameter. An example would be `_cvar={"1":["OS","iphone 5.0"],"2":["Piwik Mobile Version","1.6.2"],"3":["Locale","en::en"],"4":[ "NumAccounts","2"]}` which is part of a real tracking request used by the Piwik mobile app.

Parameter	Description
`_idvc`	(optional) This is the count of visits for the visitor and should be updated with each visit. In order to do this on a desktop or phone app, you would have to create this value and then store it in an app's database or in sessions, and add one to it with each new visit by the visitor. This value is used in the **Visitors** | **Engagement** | **Visits by visit number** report. Our URL has an `_idvc` parameter of `1`.
`_viewts`	(optional) This is the UNIX timestamp of the last time the visitor visited your site or app. This value is used to build the Visitors | Engagement | Visits by days since last visit report. Our URL above does not have this parameter, so it must not be from a returning visitor.
`_idts`	(optional) This is another UNIX timestamp, but it is set to the time of the first visit of the current visitor. In an app, for example, you can set this to the first time the user launches it. This value is used in the **Goals** | **Days to Conversion** report. In our URL, the `_idts` parameter is set to `1340161706`.
`res`	(optional) The resolution of the device, for example, 1280 × 1024. In our URL, the resolution of the visitor's screen is `1600x900`.
`h`	(optional) The current hour in the local time zone. This is in military time. The hour value in our URL is `22`.
`m`	(optional) The current minute in the local time zone. The minute value of our URL is 22.
`s`	(optional) The current second in the local time zone. The second value of our URL is 21.

That is a lot of information to pack into one URL and our example doesn't even use all the parameters available. You can see a complete list of all the parameters at `http://piwik.org/docs/tracking-api/reference/`.

There is a step you have to think of before you make your URL request with your given software. When you make your request, you should set the header, because Piwik uses these values too. The following values need to be set:

- **User-Agent**: This will tell Piwik the browser and operating system of the tracked visit
- **Accept-Language**: This will tell Piwik the language of the user which it can then use to determine the user's country

So the software you write that will be tracking with Piwik has to do the following four things:

- Gather the data needed for the call
- Generate the URL
- Generate the header
- Make the HTTP request

Debugging your tracking code

Now that you are dealing with custom APIs and more programming languages, the complexity of your application can grow and bugs pop up here and there in any software. Just in case your software is not perfect, you may want to know how to debug it.

If you run into more trouble then this short section can handle it. You will find that `Piwik.org` is a wealth of information on managing your Piwik installation and writing custom applications using Piwik, especially its FAQ section and its forum where there are plenty of other Piwik users willing to help.

All tracking calls to Piwik go through one file, `Piwik.php` in your Piwik installation directory. To turn on debugging, we will be setting the `PIWIK_TRACKER_DEBUG` global to `true`. By default, it is set to `false`, so you want to open the file up and edit it so it looks like the following:

```
<?php
/**
 * Piwik - Open source web analytics
 *
 * @link http://piwik.org
 * @license http://www.gnu.org/licenses/gpl-3.0.htmlGPLv3 or later
 * @version $Id: piwik.php 5485 2011-11-26 04:50:36Zvipsoft $
 *
 * @package Piwik
 */
$GLOBALS['PIWIK_TRACKER_DEBUG'] = true;
...
```

Setting this value to `true` will make Piwik load its error handler and exception handler and output its data to the debug log tables in the Piwik database.

To debug the requests that a tracked website is actually sending to your Piwik installation, you need to be able to see the request made by the tracker. It looks like the following:

```
http://mypiwik.com/piwik/piwik.php?action_name=Google%20Scraper%20
Footprint%20Finder&idsite=5&rec=1&r=055697&h=22&m=22&s=21&url=
http%3A%2F%2Fgooglescraper.deal23.com%2F&_id=8af038f1463fb845&_
idts=1340161706&_idvc=1&_idn=0&_refts=0&_viewts=1340161706&pdf=1&qt=1&
realp=0&wma=0&dir=1&fla=1&java=1&gears=0&ag=1&cookie=1&res=1600x900
```

The **Firebug** plugin available at `http://getfirebug.com/` for the **Firefox** web browser, which you can get at `http://www.mozilla.org`, makes this data much easier to read.

Once you have **Firebug** installed, just click on the **Firebug** button in the top-right corner of **Firefox** as shown in the following screenshot:

A panel will pop up at the bottom of **Firefox** and you will have to click on the **Net** tab.

Scroll down until you see **GET piwik.php** in the left column and click on the plus sign. Once this panel opens, click on the **Params** tab, and there you will see all the parameters in the URL in neat columns. With this information and our list of Piwik API parameters handy, we can make sure our tracker is sending in the correct data.

Piwik plugins

In *Chapter 7, E-commerce Tracking*, we wrote a plugin for ZenCart that added Piwik tracking where we needed in our store. In *Chapter 8, Piwik Website and User Administration*, we installed a plugin for Piwik. In this section, we will learn how a plugin is written.

First you must have an idea for a plugin; these usually come through using Piwik a lot and seeing a feature you might need or comparing Piwik to other analytical software and finding a feature that Piwik doesn't have yet. Some of Piwik's core functionalities came from plugins that were absorbed into the core. In fact, much of the core is composed of plugins that can be turned on and off in the **Settings | Plugins** menu. You can find examples of other third party plugins that have already been written by Piwik users by browsing to the following link:

`http://tinyurl.com/8fzcr2n`. There, you will find many types of plugins, some of which are as follows:

- **Funnel Analysis Reports**
- **Visitor Forecast**
- **Weekday Visits**
- **Adsense Earnings**
- **Search Engine Bot Tracking**
- **OpenID Login**
- **Hidden Tracking**
- **Quantcast Data Import**
- **Graphical Counter**

How Piwik works

Up to now, we have mainly been concerned with the data we send to Piwik. As far as we know, it's a magic black box that makes us pretty graphs. So before we start tearing into the internals of Piwik, we need to have an idea of how Piwik does what it does.

We just covered advanced API calls and every one of those calls go through `Piwik.php`. This file handles a lot of calls and it would be inefficient to process the data as it comes to Piwik. If Piwik did process the data instantly, it wouldn't be instant. Processing takes time and each millisecond stacks up. Any page being tracked would have to wait for the call to Piwik to send back a response to complete loading, so this data is stored in the database as it is.

The log data is not processed until you visit your Piwik dashboard or a crontab has processed it for you. Piwik then processes the data and archives the results in other tables in the database. Now this processed data is available for tables, reports, or API calls.

The anatomy of a plugin

Piwik stores data and presents it in different ways. When you get to the basics, that's all it does. Some plugins compute different types of statistics based on the current data. Some add new raw data, process it, and create statistics out of the results. Other plugins only add widgets that access remote data sources. Some only do things to the menus and interface or change the way Piwik is administrated as we saw with the plugin we installed so users could create their own accounts.

Piwik uses a hook system that allows plugins to intercept core events and modify their results. This is done by registering the plugin's functions with the event. Hook systems allow plugins to be turned off and on without any change to any core files.

Piwik's plugin system uses an MVC pattern which consists of a model which contains the model of the data, a view that displays the data, and a controller that matches requests to the model and view.

Without getting too much more into terminology, let me just say that Piwik comes with a few example plugins that you can use as the basis for your own. Browse to your `Piwik installation` folder and from there open the `Plugins` folder. In the `Plugins` folder, you should see the following folders:

- **ExampleAPI**: An example of a plugin that adds functionality to the Piwik API
- **ExampleFeedburner**: This plugin stores a Feedburner RSS URL in the Piwik database and accesses the Feedburner API to display feed stats in a widget
- **ExamplePlugin**: This plugin adds two widgets to the dashboard
- **ExampleRssWidget**: This plugin reads and displays an RSS feed
- **ExampleUI**: This plugin modifies Piwik's user interface

So let's take one of these plugins, modify it, and make it our own. We will create a simple one, don't worry. If you want to dig down deeper into Piwik's plugin hooks, please check out the documents on `Piwik.org`.

Writing a simple Piwik plugin

We are going to take the ExampleFeedburner plugin and turn it into an Alexa Traffic Graph widget. We could add data to the database to generate the widget but that is beyond the scope of this book.

First copy the ExampleFeedburner plugin and rename the folder AlexaWidget. Open up your new AlexaWidget folder and you will see a file in it called ExampleFeedburner.php. Rename this file to AlexaWidget.php and open it up in a text editor. At the top of the file, you will see a block of comments. We will be editing these, replacing any instance of ExampleFeedburner with AlexaWidget, until it looks like the following snippet:

```
/**
 * Piwik - Open source web analytics
 *
 * @link http://piwik.org
 * @license http://www.gnu.org/licenses/gpl-3.0.htmlGPLv3 or later
 * @version $Id: AlexaWidget.php
 *
 * @category Piwik_Plugins
 * @package Piwik_AlexaWidget
 */

/**
 *
 * @package Piwik_AlexaWidget
 */
```

The next line extends the Piwik class Piwik_Plugin. All plugins must extend this class to access the hooks available in Piwik. We will rename this class from Piwik_ExampleFeedburner to Piwik_AlexaWidget.

```
class Piwik_AlexaWidget extends Piwik_Plugin
```

This class originally had install and uninstall functions to add and remove the feed name from the database when activating or deactivating the Feedburner plugin. We won't need these functions, but we will be using the getInformation function to give Piwik info about it so we know what type of plugin we will be activating when we see it in Piwik.

```
class Piwik_AlexaWidget extends Piwik_Plugin
{
    /**
     * Return information about this plugin.
     *
```

```
     * @see Piwik_Plugin
     *
     * @return array
     */
    public function getInformation()
    {
        return array(
            'description' =>Piwik_Translate('My Alexa Widget'),
            'author' => 'Me',
            'author_homepage' => 'http://me.org/',
            'version' => '0.1',
        );
    }

}
```

You can also change the `author` and `author_homepage` values if you want. These are the values that Piwik outputs in the plugin table located at **Settings | Plugins**. The next function in the file is `Piwik_AddWidget`. This function tells Piwik to display your widget. It takes up to five parameters:

- The category of the widget. This is the category it falls under, when you choose to add a widget on the dashboard.
- The name of the widget.
- The widget's controller class name.
- The widget's controller function name.
- Custom parameters

We will be editing ours so it looks like the following:

```
Piwik_AddWidget('Example Widgets', 'Alexa Traffic Stats',
'ExampleAlexa', 'alexa');
```

We just added our widget to the `Example Widgets` menu. We could have chosen one of the other menus, such as `SEO` if wanted to, or create our own using the `Piwik_AddMenu` function.

Below this in our code is the `Controller` class of our plugin. We will be renaming this from `Piwik_ExampleFeedburner_Controller` to `Piwik_AlexaWidget_Controller`. It extends Piwik's `Controller` class. This controller function name is actually different from the function name we gave when we added the widget. Piwik expects the `Controller` class name to be wrapped with `Piwik_` and `_Controller`.

We will be simply giving the view our JavaScript from Alexa, so what we are going to do is take everything out of this class and add one `alexa` function back.

```
class Piwik_AlexaWidget_Controller extends Piwik_Controller
{

    /**
     * Simple alexa statistics output
     *
     */

    function alexa()
    {
            echo '<img src="http://traffic.alexa.com/graph?u=www.
stephanmiller.com&c=1&w=400&h=220&y=r&r=3m&b=e6f3fc" />';
    }
}
```

Just replace the URL in the HTML image code with your own and your widget is set. This is not exactly a complete widget. It doesn't have a template or view. We just echo our code out directly in the controller, which is fine if your plugin doesn't do much. It can simplify writing the Smarty templating code that Piwik uses if you don't really need it. In fact, if you can, delete the `Template` folder out of your `AlexaWidget` folder. At the end, we have one folder with one file in it. And it didn't take that long to write either.

Now we upload this folder to the `Plugins` folder of our Piwik installation. Then we browse to **Settings | Plugins** in our Piwik installation. Find **AlexaWidget** in the **Plugin** list and click on the **Activate** link in its row as shown in the screenshot below:

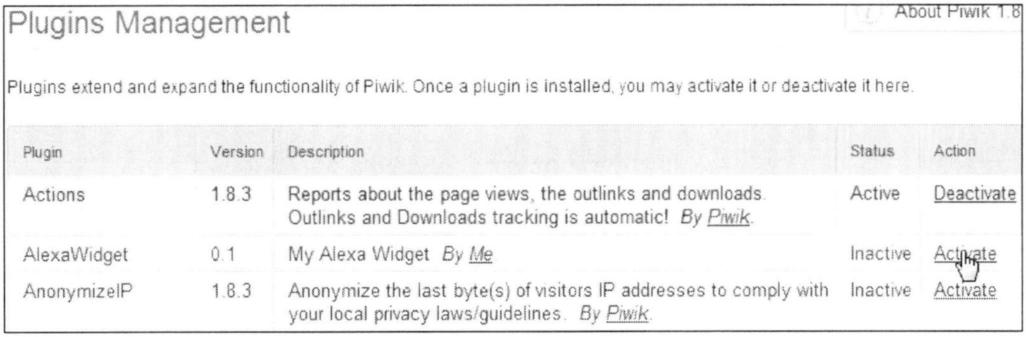

Plugins Management

About Piwik 1.8

Plugins extend and expand the functionality of Piwik. Once a plugin is installed, you may activate it or deactivate it here.

Plugin	Version	Description	Status	Action
Actions	1.8.3	Reports about the page views, the outlinks and downloads. Outlinks and Downloads tracking is automatic! *By Piwik.*	Active	Deactivate
AlexaWidget	0.1	My Alexa Widget *By Me*	Inactive	Activate
AnonymizeIP	1.8.3	Anonymize the last byte(s) of visitors IP addresses to comply with your local privacy laws/guidelines. *By Piwik.*	Inactive	Activate

Now go to your dashboard and add your widget there; it should look something like the following screenshot:

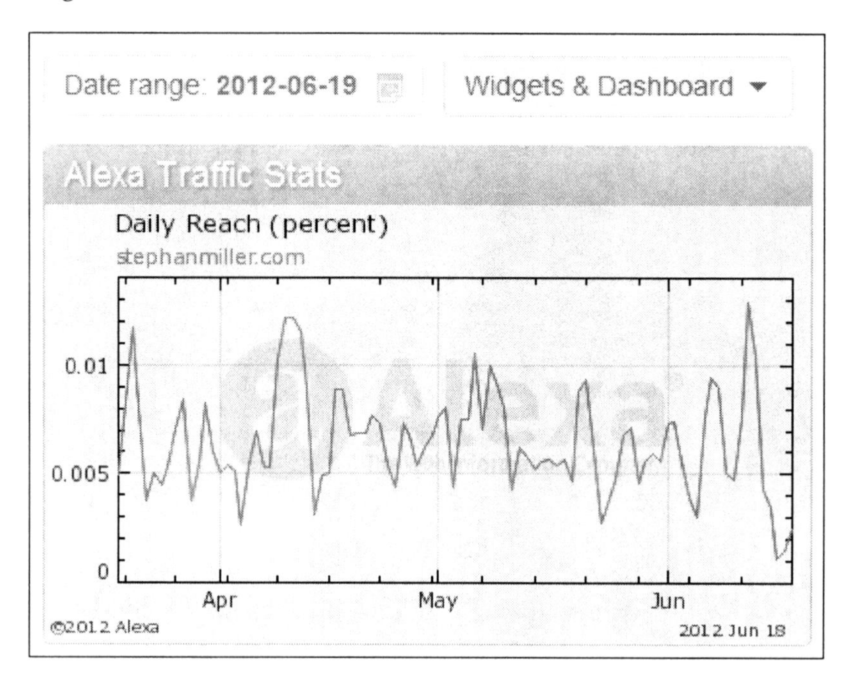

Since the size of the **Alexa** image is set by the URL we used, I made the previous widget look good by sizing my browser window perfectly, but it doesn't fit at any other resolution. A better plugin would have resized the image when the widget resized and would have grabbed the URL of the site being viewed out of Piwik's database. Now that you know the basics of a plugin, you can make those changes yourself. Maybe you could even dive into some Smarty templates.

Summary

After reading this chapter, you should have a good grasp on how Piwik and its tracking API works. You have learned how to access it through image tracking, through HTTP requests in PHP, and other languages. If something goes wrong, you know how to debug your tracking calls and fix the problem. Finally you learned how to extend Piwik by writing your own plugin.

In the next chapter, we will go beyond tracking and learn how to integrate Piwik and its data into other applications in various ways.

10
Piwik Integration

In the last chapter we learned how to send data to Piwik and that we can use any programming language we choose to do so. But the real magic comes in when we use Piwik's API to get the data back to use, analyze, and format however we want. We can do the same data manipulation inside Piwik by writing a plugin, another topic we covered, but you may have reasons you want to do this from the outside. You may want to simply display a widget from Piwik somewhere on your website to give your visitors an idea of your traffic. You may need to merge Piwik data with the inventory data for your e-commerce site to calculate when to order new products. Or you may want to do some heavy processing of the data available without bogging down the performance of your Piwik installation.

In this chapter, we will show you how to get the data back from Piwik so you can integrate it with other applications. The topics we will be covering are:

- Using plugins to integrate Piwik data
- Using Piwik Mobile
- Embedding Piwik widgets in other websites
- Using Piwik's analytics API
- Retrieving graphs from Piwik's API
- Using the Live! API
- Using segmentation with the Piwik API

CMS plugins

Some plugins that integrate Piwik into open source software do very little more than what our simple ZenCart plugin did. They make it possible to add Piwik's tracking code to the web platform's pages. But as Piwik's API gives you access not only to the tracking side but also to the analytics side of Piwik, a lot of plugins are written so you don't have to visit Piwik to get a breakdown of your stats. These plugins display this data for you and sometimes, in more advanced ways than you can see in Piwik itself.

A perfect example of this is the WP-Piwik Wordpress plugin. This plugin is available at `http://wordpress.org/extend/plugins/wp-piwik/`. Wordpress is the most popular CMS in use on the Internet. If you are familiar with Wordpress, you know how easy it is to install a plugin. You don't even have to use FTP. You can search for the plugin you need and install it in Wordpress's admin.

Well, the WP-Piwik plugin continues this ease of use by only needing the URL of your Piwik installation and your user API token. Once those are entered, the plugin will allow you to choose one of the sites listed at your Piwik installation from a menu, or to create a new website there on the fly, if you need it.

I use this plugin myself and when I installed it, I just thought it was an easy way to add tracking to my Wordpress blogs without having to edit my themes. But then I saw the dashboard widgets:

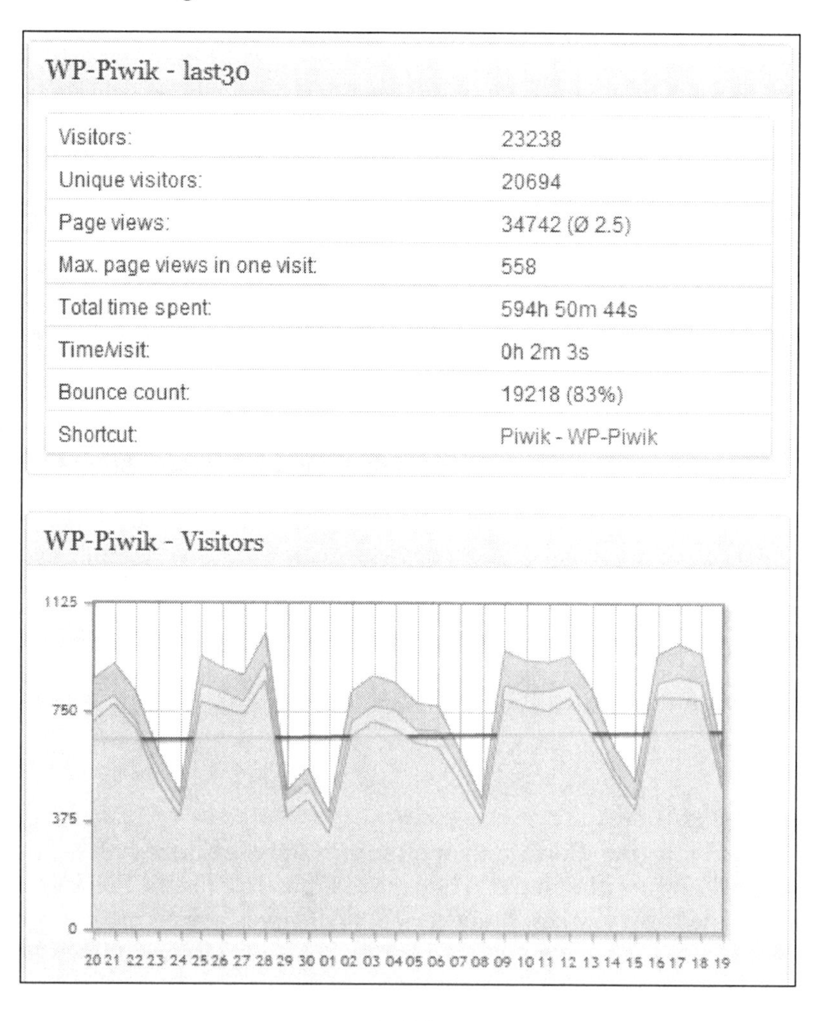

It gives you stats right there, after you log in to your blog. And notice the red line in the graph widget. That's the running average. This is something you don't get in Piwik itself and proves that you can do a lot more with the data you can access with Piwik's API than you may have imagined.

It's all in how you crunch it and later in this chapter, we will be doing our own analytics data crunching. But first, we will have a look at WP-Piwik's full dashboard page, just to give you some idea of what you can do with just data, PHP, and a graphing library. Here is a pie chart using Wordpress's built-in graphing library:

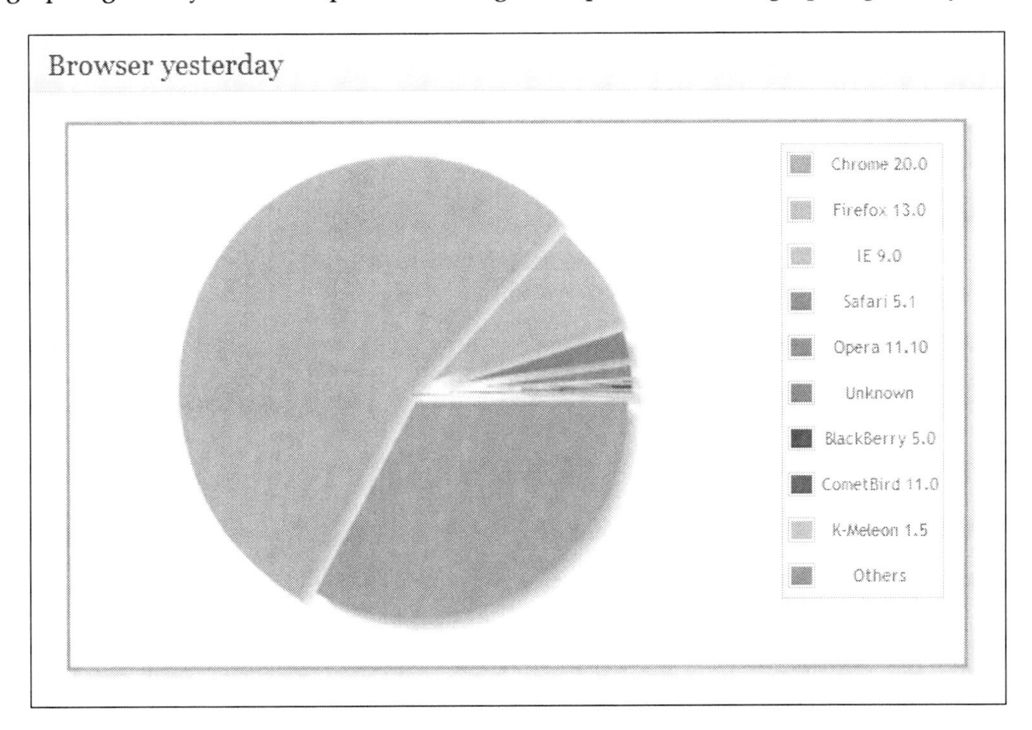

It is more efficient to access the data from Piwik and build your own graphs than pull the graph images from Piwik. The image files are too big.

This dashboard contains about a dozen widgets. In the following screenshot, we see the widget displaying the pages with the most visits:

Pages yesterday

Page	Unique	Visits
749 Free Classified Ad Sites List | Stephan Miller | Kansas City SEO - Web Developer	424	465
465 Bookmarking Sites List – Most Dofollow | Stephan Miller | Kansas City SEO - Web Developer	177	209
148 Free Press Release Sites List | Stephan Miller | Kansas City SEO - Web Developer	84	90
190 Free Blog Hosts | Stephan Miller | Kansas City SEO - Web Developer	38	44
Kansas City SEO, Web Site Developer - Stephan Miller	40	43

The WP-Piwik dashboard gives you just about everything you need to get a great overview of the traffic to your website and the actions occurring there. So if you have a Piwik installation and a Wordpress blog, this plugin will make tracking your blog a lot easier and you may not even need the rest of this chapter.

But that is not the only CMS that full-featured Piwik plugins have been written for. In fact, as of the writing of this book, the following platforms have Piwik plugins available:

- Drupal
- Joomla!

- Typo3
- DotNetNuke
- phpBB
- Magento
- Prestashop
- vBulletin
- Status.net
- SPIP
- MODx
- DotClear2
- Contao
- DokuWiki
- MediaWiki
- Gallery3
- Trac
- Sonar

And the list keeps going. Currently there are over 40 platforms you can instantly integrate with Piwik. Visit `http://piwik.org/integrate/` to see the current list of, as well as, view the links to CMS plugins for integrating Piwik into your web application.

Piwik Mobile

Mobile is becoming the Internet for a lot of people. With smart phones advancing every year with faster processors, more storage and better apps, many people don't need a computer for the Internet. They just use their phone. While some types of sites can use responsive design to account for both computer and phone resolutions, others don't really have the option. The information has to be presented in a different way. Piwik is a perfect example.

Piwik Mobile is Piwik's little brother. The Piwik Mobile app is available for both the Android and the iOS operating systems. The developers of Piwik Mobile kept the mobile app experience as close as possible to the web dashboard. You will find the same menus and look optimized for a mobile platform. And it uses the Piwik API to access its data. A screenshot of the **All Websites** menu of Piwik Mobile is as follows. This is on an Android phone.

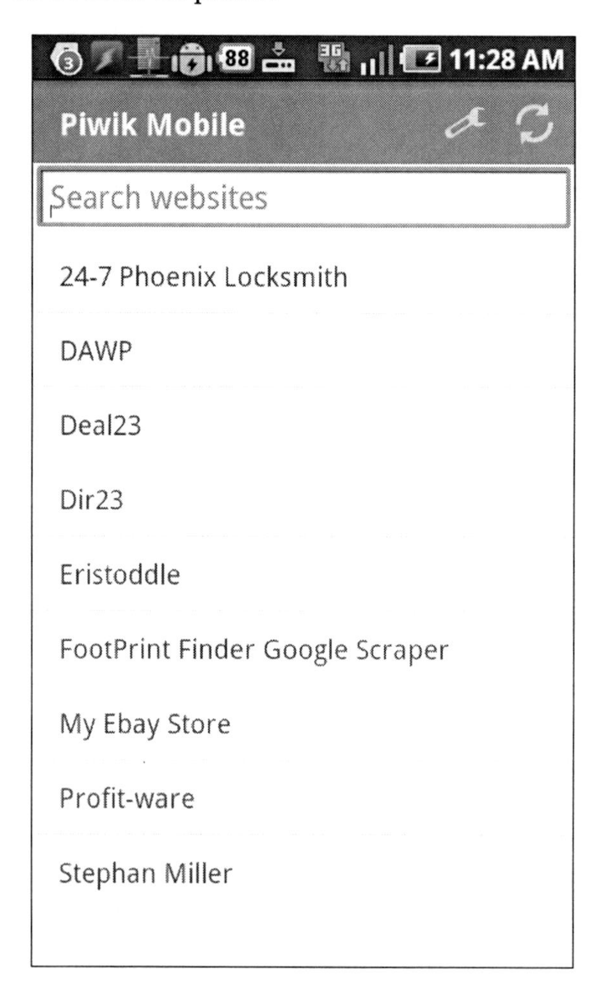

The following screenshot shows the **Visits Summary** screen of a website on the same Android phone. The iPhone interface is very similar.

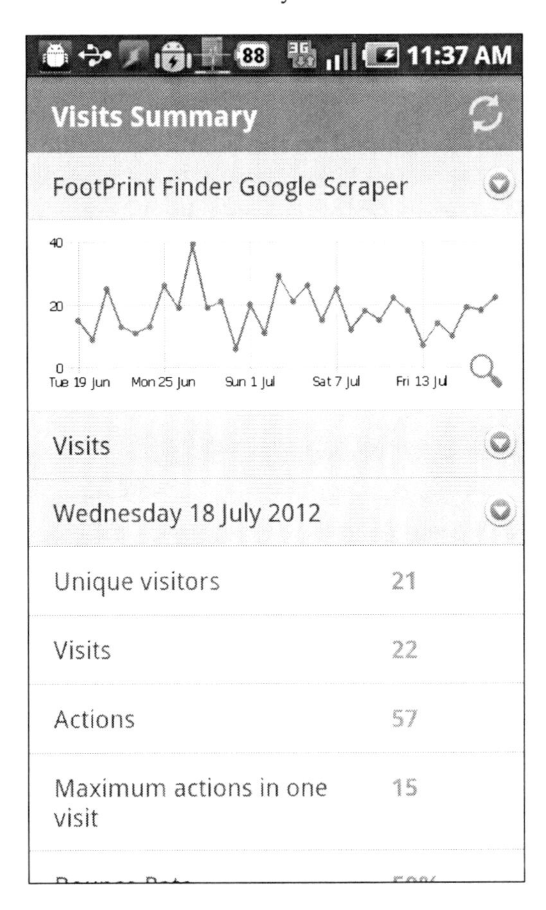

As you can see, the Piwik Mobile app is just a compact version of your Piwik website. With it, you can have your stats everywhere you go.

You can download the Piwik Mobile app from Google Play or the iPhone App Store. Once it is installed, it will require your Piwik URL and your access token to view your analytics data.

But there is more to this app than just a pretty display. It is also an open source project, one that you can either contribute to or use to create your own Piwik Mobile app with special reports only yours has. It would be great to be able to not only give your clients access to their stats online, but also a mobile app so they too can get their stats on the go.

The Piwik Mobile app was developed on the Titanium Mobile platform, available at `http://www.appcelerator.com/`. Titanium will build apps for both Android and iPhone and uses JavaScript as its scripting language. We won't get into detail about building a mobile app. But it is good to know that if you did need to build an app as a plugin to Piwik, 90 percent of the work is done for you. That can save a lot of time and money and make an app more feasible. You can read more about Piwik Mobile at `http://dev.piwik.org/trac/wiki/PiwikMobile`.

Embedding Piwik widgets

We haven't written any code so far in this chapter, but I bet you know it's coming. Let's get started with something easy. Then we can jump into the deep end. Embedding a Piwik widget in another page, such as the sidebar of your website, is easy. It is just like any other badge or widget you may add to your blog. Just generate the code right in your Piwik installation, paste the code where you want it on your site, and you are done. But there are a few details that mean the difference between a widget you can see and useless code.

Give your anonymous user rights

Piwik is going to give you the code you need, but first you have to make sure that your user named **anonymous** can see it, or else you may trick yourself. Because you are logged in to Piwik, you will be able to see the widget where you embedded it, but no one else will. So, go to **Settings | Users**:

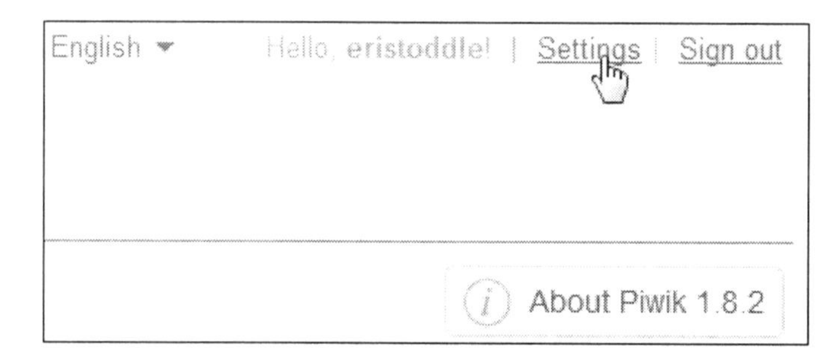

Choose the website account whose widgets you are going to embed. In this example, I choose my own:

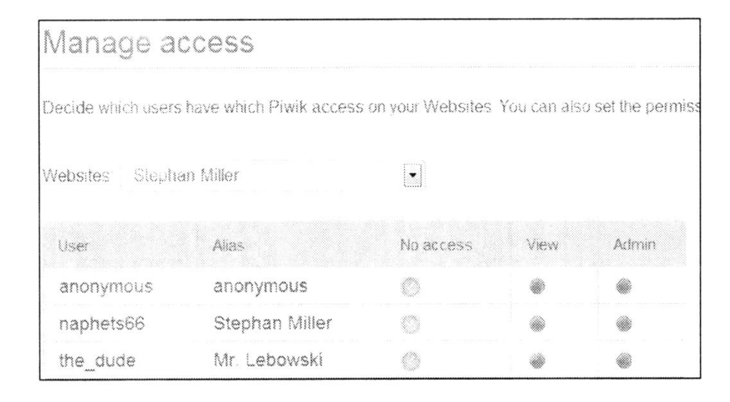

Click on the **View** button in the same row as **anonymous**. It should be red and clicking on it will turn it green. Once it is, you are ready to embed widgets that everyone can see.

But if you are going to embed Piwik on a password-protected page or private page, such as the admin section of your website, there is a second option. It requires you to create a new user in Piwik, and adding that user's `token_auth` to the widget URL. This exposes your `token_auth` to whoever can view the source, which is why it is recommended for a password-protected page. But you are not giving the anonymous user the right to view all your reports. When we get to our example, we will show this method too.

Choosing your widget

Now it is time to pick what we are going to embed. Click on the **Widgets** link in the top menu of your Piwik interface:

There are a few options when it comes to embedding a Piwik in another web page. All of them use IFRAMES to display the widget.

The Dashboard widget

This widget will display your dashboard as you have it set up in your Piwik installation. You can even choose the date and range of the reports in the widget. As it is your whole dashboard, using this widget would not be a good choice for a sidebar, but would be great for the admin side of your website, so that users get a view of the traffic without having to log in to a separate site.

Just double-click on the code at the end of the **Widgetize the full dashboard** paragraph and right-click with your mouse to copy.

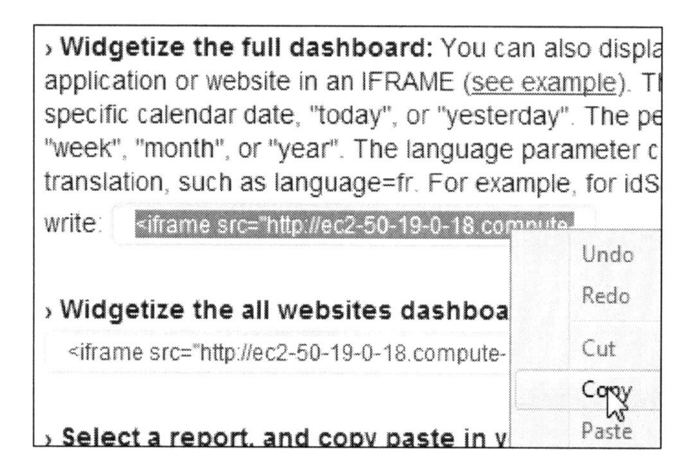

Now all you have to do is embed this in a web page:

```
<!DOCTYPE HTML>
<html lang="en-US">
<head>
  <meta charset="UTF-8">
  <title>Piwik Dashboard Widget</title>
  <style type="text/css">
        html, body { margin: 0; padding: 0; height: 100%; }
        iframe {
    position: absolute;
    top: 0; left: 0; width: 100%; height: 100%;
    border: none; padding-top: 32px;
    box-sizing: border-box; -moz-box-sizing: border-box; -webkit-box-
sizing: border-box;
        }
    </style>
</head>
<body>
```

```
<iframe src="http://YOUR_PIWIK_URL?module=Widgetize&action=ifram
e&moduleToWidgetize=Dashboard&actionToWidgetize=index&idSite=YOUR_
SITE_ID&period=week&date=yesterday" frameborder="0" marginheight="0"
marginwidth="0" width="100%" height="100%"></iframe>
</body>
</html>
```

You may notice some extra CSS in the header. That is necessary because this is a big widget and 100 percent height just doesn't work on some browsers, especially when JavaScript is involved. These styles make the IFRAME 100 percent of your browser's height, so you don't get a short widget that you have to scroll.

The All Websites widget

This widget will display the report you see when you click on the **Websites** link in the top menu of Piwik. It will display all of the websites you are tracking with visits, page views, revenue, and the evolution percentage of each site using either visits, page views, or revenue as the metric. This is the second widget choice on the page.

Again, the code to embed the widget is in the tiny textbox at the end the line:

› **Widgetize the all websites dashboard in an IFRAME** (see example)

<iframe src="http://ec2-50-19-0-18.compute-

Well, I promised I would show you how to convert at least one of these snippets to code that you will be using in the secure area of your website. So let's do it with this one. This concept will work with any one of the snippets from this page. Here is the original code:

```
<iframe src="http://YOUR_PIWIK_URL/piwik/index.php?module=Widgetiz
e&action=iframe&moduleToWidgetize=Dashboard&actionToWidgetize=ind
ex&idSite=YOUR_SITE_ID&period=week&date=yesterday" frameborder="0"
marginheight="0" marginwidth="0" width="100%" height="100%"></iframe>
```

Now you need to create a new user whose token you can use. So go back to **Settings | Users**, where we were just giving the **anonymous** user his/her rights. At the bottom of that page, you will see the **Add a new user** link. Go ahead and name the user what you want; we just want to use the user's token:

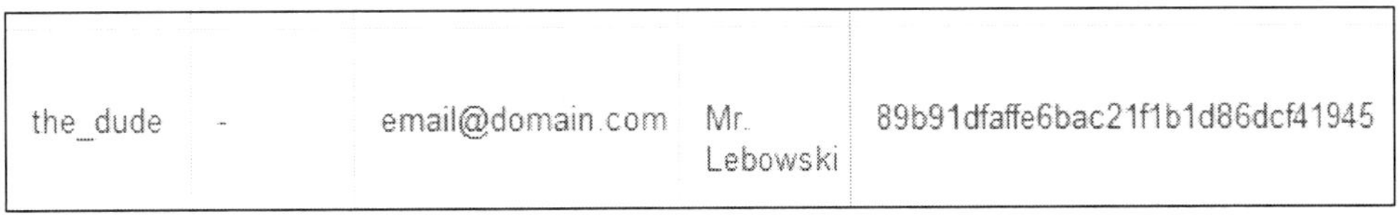

the_dude	-	email@domain.com	Mr. Lebowski	89b91dfaffe6bac21f1b1d86dcf41945

And as soon as you create the new user, there is the token you need. Grab that. It should look something like this: `89b91dfaffe6bac21f1b1d86dcf41945`. Now take the code that Piwik gave you for the widget and modify it so that it looks like this:

```
<iframe src="http://YOUR_PIWIK_URL/piwik/index.php?module=Widgetize&a
ction=iframe&moduleToWidgetize=Dashboard&actionToWidgetize=index&idS
ite=YOUR_SITE_ID&period=week&date=yesterday&token_auth=89b91dfaffe6ba
c21f1b1d86dcf41945" frameborder="0" marginheight="0" marginwidth="0"
width="100%" height="100%"></iframe>
```

All we did is added `&token_auth=89b91dfaffe6bac21f1b1d86dcf41945` to the URL in the source of the IFRAME.

Choose your own widget

Now the gigantic Dashboard widget may be great for your admin page, but for a sidebar widget, say for your top pages, you need something else. And Piwik lets you choose from any widget you see in your interface. Just scroll to the bottom and choose from one of the categories on the left-hand side of the page. You can even choose a live widget, so a visitor can watch themselves as they surf your website. Hey, who knows? It may add to the stickiness factor.

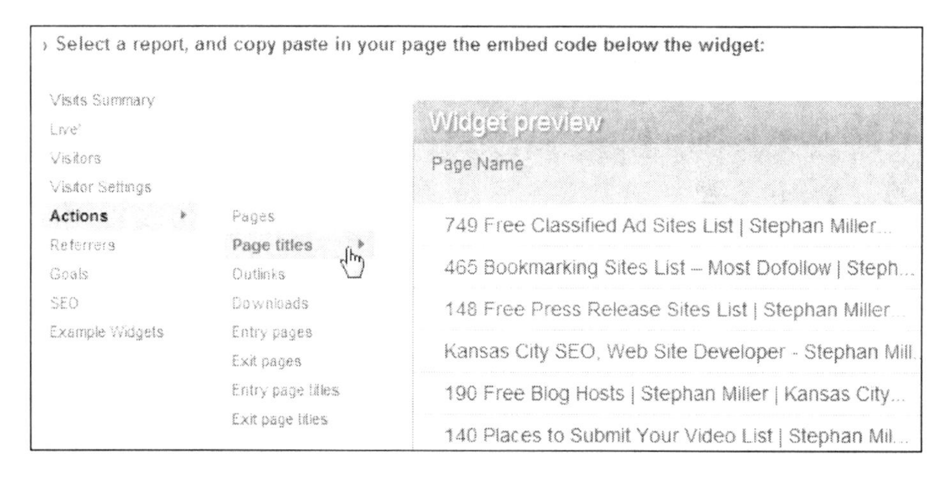

When you choose a category, you will see a list of the widgets available in the category. Hover over the widget you want and a preview of the widget will appear. At the very bottom of the page, you will see the **Embed Iframe** code. Just copy it to put on your page.

But you can also modify the code itself if you want to change what the widget displays.

```
<div id="widgetIframe"><iframe width="100%" height="350" src="http://
YOUR_PIWIK_URL/piwik/index.php?module=Widgetize&action=iframe&moduleTo
Widgetize=Actions&actionToWidgetize=getPageTitles&idSite=YOUR_PIWIK_ID
&period=day&date=yesterday&disableLink=1&widget=1" scrolling="no"
frameborder="0" marginheight="0" marginwidth="0"></iframe></div>
```

You can change the `date` parameter to:

- Today
- Yesterday
- A calendar date in YYYY-MM-DD format

You can change the `period` parameter also. Ours is "day". We have these choices:

- Day
- Week
- Month
- Year

And you can set the `language` parameter to display the widget in another language. This code does not have this parameter because it is using the default language. Piwik supports many languages. Here are some of the more common language codes:

Code	Language
en	English
fr	French
de	German
es	Spanish
it	Italian

We are going to change the code so that we see today's traffic, we see all the data for a whole month, and we want the widget translated into Spanish.

```
<div id="widgetIframe"><iframe width="100%" height="350" src="http://
YOUR_PIWIK_URL/piwik/index.php?module=Widgetize&action=iframe&mo
duleToWidgetize=Actions&actionToWidgetize=getPageTitles&idSite=YO
UR_PIWIK_ID&period=month&date=today&disableLink=1&widget=1&language=
es" scrolling="no" frameborder="0" marginheight="0" marginwidth="0"></
iframe></div>
```

Accessing Piwik's data

So far, we have looked at a couple of great examples of embedding Piwik in another application. And we have used the code that Piwik gives us to embed widgets on other web pages. But we haven't really looked at all that we can do with this analytics API. If we want to do a something a little bit different with the data, or use charts and graphs that are a different style to fit in with our project, we will need to do a bit more.

With the Piwik analytics API, you can programmatically request reports from Piwik. This API is very flexible and will return the data you request in the following formats:

- **XML**: Extensible Markup Language
- **JSON**: JavaScript Object Notation
- **TSV**: Tab Separated Values, for Excel
- **RSS**: Really Simple Syndication

With all of these data formats, you should find one you can use to get the data you need. So let's look at how we call this API. It's a lot simpler than you might think.

How to call the analytics API

A reference to the Piwik analytics API is built right into your installation of Piwik. Just click on the **API** link in the top menu to access it. This is the same page you visit to get your `token_auth`.

Below your `token_auth` is a listing of various parts of the Piwik analytics API.

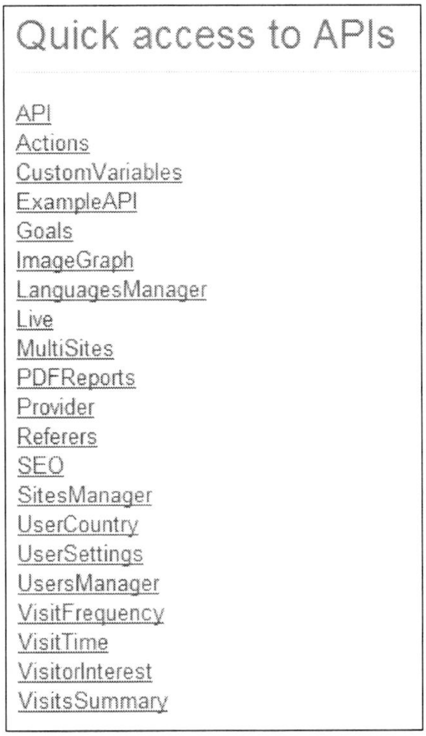

Quick access to APIs

API
Actions
CustomVariables
ExampleAPI
Goals
ImageGraph
LanguagesManager
Live
MultiSites
PDFReports
Provider
Referers
SEO
SitesManager
UserCountry
UserSettings
UsersManager
VisitFrequency
VisitTime
VisitorInterest
VisitsSummary

By clicking on one of these links, you will be taken to that section of the API reference. Just scroll down the page and you will see how extensive this reference is. There is so much you can do with this API, that we will only learn a small part of it in this chapter. So browse through it to get familiar with what it can do, but there is no need to memorize anything because this reference is always right where you need it.

Just like the Piwik tracking API, the analytics API has two ways you can call it. We will look at those now.

Calling the analytics API using REST

Most likely this will be the method you will be using. And as it is a REST API, you can call it in any language. So let's make a call with PHP. For this example, we are going to do it the easy way. We will get to more in depth examples later.

The first step is to go back to your Piwik dashboard if you are not already there and choose a site from the **Websites** drop-down menu. The second step is to click on the link to the API reference page again and get a URL for your call. We had to choose a site first, because the links on this page pertain to the current selected website. Once you are at the API page, click on the **Actions** link in the **Quick access to APIs** section. This will take you down to the **Module Actions** section:

Module Actions

The Actions API lets you request reports for all your Visitor Actions: Page URLs, Page titles (Piwik Events), File Downloads and Clicks on external websites.

For example, "getPageTitles" will return all your page titles along with standard Actions metrics for each row.
It is also possible to request data for a specific Page Title with "getPageTitle" and setting the parameter pageName to the page title you wish to request. Similarly, you can request metrics for a given Page URL via "getPageUrl", a Download file via "getDownload" and an outlink via "getOutlink".
Note: pageName, pageUrl, outlinkUrl, downloadUrl parameters must be URL encoded before you call the API.

- **Actions.get** (idSite, period, date, segment = '', columns = '') [Example in XML, Json, Tsv (Excel) , RSS of the last 10 days]
- **Actions.getPageUrls** (idSite, period, date, segment = '', expanded = '', idSubtable = '') [Example in XML, Json, Tsv (Excel) , RSS of the last 10 days]
- **Actions.getEntryPageUrls** (idSite, period, date, segment = '', expanded = '', idSubtable = '') [Example in XML, Json, Tsv (Excel) , RSS of the last 10 days]
- **Actions.getExitPageUrls** (idSite, period, date, segment = '', expanded = '', idSubtable = '') [Example in XML, Json, Tsv (Excel) , RSS of the last 10 days]
- **Actions.getPageUrl** (pageUrl, idSite, period, date, segment = '') [No example available]
- **Actions.getPageTitles** (idSite, period, date, segment = '', expanded = '', idSubtable = '') [Example in XML, Json, Tsv (Excel) , RSS of the last 10 days]
- **Actions.getEntryPageTitles** (idSite, period, date, segment = '', expanded = '', idSubtable = '') [Example in XML, Json, Tsv (Excel) , RSS of the last 10 days]
- **Actions.getExitPageTitles** (idSite, period, date, segment = '', expanded = '', idSubtable = '') [Example in XML, Json, Tsv (Excel) , RSS of the last 10 days]
- **Actions.getPageTitle** (pageName, idSite, period, date, segment = '') [No example available]
- **Actions.getDownloads** (idSite, period, date, segment = '', expanded = '', idSubtable = '') [Example in XML, Json, Tsv (Excel) , RSS of the last 10 days]
- **Actions.getDownload** (downloadUrl, idSite, period, date, segment = '') [No example available]
- **Actions.getOutlinks** (idSite, period, date, segment = '', expanded = '', idSubtable = '') [Example in XML, Json, Tsv (Excel) , RSS of the last 10 days]
- **Actions.getOutlink** (outlinkUrl, idSite, period, date, segment = '') [No example available]

Each API describes briefly what data it returns. The `Actions` API handles all the reports for visitor actions. Let's grab the same data we did with our top pages widget, but this time do it with the API so that we can create true HTML links on a page.

We are going to be using the `Actions.getPageTitles` call. And to make it even easier on this first try, we are going to choose the RSS example, which will return not only data, but data in HTML tables. So click on the link to the RSS example.

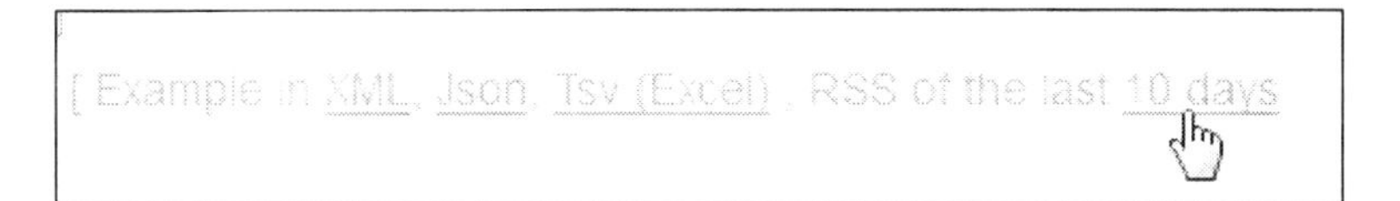

Although this URL is called an example, it is a true API call to Piwik with your `token_auth` and everything else. It should look something like the following:

```
http://yourpiwiksite.com/piwik/index.php?module=API&method=Actions.get
EntryPageTitles&idSite=1&period=day&date=last10&format=rss&token_auth=
2156e61de6286a2fe7faddf6ac181c96&translateColumnNames=1
```

We will get more into the parameters of these calls as we go on. But we can see the method parameter there in the URL, the ID of our site, the period, and the date. Getting a different set of data is as simple as modifying the parameters in this URL. If we want 30 days' worth of data instead of 10, we would just change the value of the date parameter from `last10` to `last30`. The advantage to the RSS format is that now you can take this URL and subscribe to it in your favorite feed reader to see the results. I use Google reader, and here is what the result looks like:

FootPrint Finder Google Scraper on 2012-07-18

by http://piwik.org

Label	Unique Pageviews	Unique visitors	Pageviews	Total time spent by visitors (in seconds)	Unique entrances	Entrances	Actions after entereing here	Total time spent by visitors (in seconds) after entereing here	Bounces	Unique exits	Exits	Avg. time on page	Bounce Rate	Exit rate
Google Scraper Footprint Finder	21	21	30	1011	20	20	46	1308	11	17	17	48	55%	81%
Free Google Scraper Download	7	7	12	203	-	-	-	-	-	1	1	29	0%	14%
Finding Backlink Footprints - Google Scraper Footprint Finder	3	3	3	11	1	1	2	5	0	1	1	4	0%	33%

We get all of this data from one URL. You can also access the API locally using the same API calls, with a few extra steps.

Calling the analytics API locally

If you do happen to have the script you want to use to access Piwik on the same server as your Piwik installation, you have another option you can use to access the Piwik API. It is a bit faster and more efficient, because you don't have to call out to another server for your data. You can call Piwik directly to get the data you need. It is pretty similar to developing a plugin for Piwik, although the plugin we wrote never accessed any of Piwik's data, it only added a widget.

Here is an example of a call you might make to Piwik locally. It retrieves the top keywords used to find a page. This is handy data to have when you are tweaking your site to move your listings higher in a Google search.

```
<?php
  define('PIWIK_INCLUDE_PATH', realpath('ReplaceWithThePathToYourPiwi
kFolder'));
  define('PIWIK_USER_PATH', realpath('PIWIK_INCLUDE_PATH'));
  define('PIWIK_ENABLE_DISPATCH', false);
  define('PIWIK_ENABLE_ERROR_HANDLER', false);
  define('PIWIK_ENABLE_SESSION_START', false);
  require_once PIWIK_INCLUDE_PATH . "/index.php";
  require_once PIWIK_INCLUDE_PATH . "/core/API/Request.php";
  Piwik_FrontController::getInstance()->init();
  $request = new Piwik_API_Request('
        method=Referers.getKeywordsForPageUrl
        &idSite=1
        &date=yesterday
        &period=week
        &url=http://www.stephanmiller.com/my-link-lists/92-free-
classified-ad-sites/
        &format=XML
        &token_auth=anonymous
  ');
  // Calls the API and fetch XML data back
  $result = $request->process();
  echo $result;
?>
```

First you must define where Piwik is located on your server. This is the full path to the folder that you have installed Piwik in. We then set the user path to that same variable. We also define a few boilerplate constants before we include the files from Piwik.

Then we include two files from Piwik. We load `index.php` to load everything necessary to access Piwik's functions and then `Request.php` from the API folder. We initialize an instance of Piwik's front controller and then it is time to make the request.

The only real parts of this code you have to worry about changing for any call you may make is the value of Piwik's `include` path at the top and the parameter that you initialize the `Piwik_API_Request` instance with. This parameter works just like a URL, with key and value pairs separated by ampersands(`&`). First we set the method we are going to call, which in our case is `Referrers.getKeywordsForPageUrl`. We want to know the keywords for a specific URL so that we can check their popularity and the page's rank in Google. Here is the API reference for this method:

```
Referrers.getKeywordsForPageUrl ( idSite, period, date, url )
```

So it doesn't matter what order we send the keys and values in this type of parameter. In our example, we set the ID of our site next, then the date. The `date` parameter can actually be a multitude of values like:

- YYYY-MM-DD
- A keyword like "today" or "yesterday"
- `lastX`, where `X` is how many days the report includes, including the current day (`&date=last30&period=day`) would return an entry for each of the last 30 days
- `previousX`, where `X` is how many periods before today (`&date=last4&period=week`) will return an entry for each of the 4 weeks before this week
- A range of dates when your period is set to range: `&period=range&date=2012-06-01,2011-07-04`

In our earlier example, we chose a range of yesterday. It doesn't matter if you are using the API locally or accessing it through a URL, the parameters have the same rules.

Next we have the `period` value. This is the range of dates we want to cover in the data we retrieve. There are a few different values you can use for period.

- **day**: For that specific day
- **week**: For the week the "date" is in
- **month**: For the month the "date" is in
- **range**: We have an example in the preceding list on how we can use range to set a specific range of dates

Again, the same rules apply for the URL-based API as well as when the API is used locally.

Next we have the `url` whose keyword we want. I put one of mine as the value of this parameter, because I was curious as to which keywords people were using to reach one of my most highly visited pages. You can replace it with one of your own. Just make sure that the id of the site and the URL refer to the same domain or it won't work.

Then we have the format, and there are a lot of formats available:

- **XML**: This stands for **Extensible Markup Language**. It is the format that both HTML and RSS are child of.
- **JSON**: If you want to do cross domain requests in AJAX and get JSON data, you can wrap the JSON data around a function call by using the `jsoncallback` parameter.
- **CSV**: This stands for **Comma-Separated Values**.
- **TSV**: This stands for **Tab-Separated Values**, similar to CSV but loads properly in Excel.
- **HTML**: Returns a table similar to the one in our RSS example.
- **PHP**: When you export the data in PHP format it is serialized by default (set `serialize=0` to get the raw PHP data structure). You can have a visual output of the data by setting `prettyDisplay=1`.
- **RSS**: This stands for **Rich Site Summary**, although there have been other interpretations of what it stands for. All you need to know is that it is one of the standard formats of a blog feed and can be subscribed to with a feed reader.
- **Original**: To fetch the original PHP data structure. This is useful when you call the Piwik API internally using the PHP code.

We chose good old XML for our example. And last but definitely not least, because your call won't work without it, we have the `token_auth` parameter which we just set to `anonymous`. The result of the call looks like this:

```
<?xml version="1.0" encoding="utf-8" ?>
<result>
  <row>Keyword not defined</row>
  <row>free classified websites</row>
  <row>classified sites</row>
  <row>free classified sites list</row>
  <row>free classified sites</row>
  <row>classified sites for free</row>
  <row>classified sites list</row>
  <row>free ad posting sites</row>
  <row>free classifieds list</row>
```

```
    <row>free classified websites list</row>
    <row>ad posting sites</row>
    <row>ads websites list</row>
    <row>classified ad sites</row>
    <row>classified ads sites</row>
    <row>classified ads website</row>
    <row>free add posting sites</row>
    <row>free classified ads</row>
    <row>free classified ad sites</row>
    <row>free classified websites list for ad posting</row>
    <row>list of ad posting websites</row>
    <row>list of classifieds sites</row>
    <row>list of free classified ads sites</row>
    <row>list of free classifieds</row>
</result>
```

This is a simple result. Most calls return more values in each row. Here is one row in a call to `Referrers.getKeywordsForPageUrl`:

```
<?xml version="1.0" encoding="utf-8" ?>
<result>
  <row>
    <label> Google Scraper Footprint Finder</label>
    <nb_visits>15</nb_visits>
    <nb_uniq_visitors>14</nb_uniq_visitors>
    <nb_hits>19</nb_hits>
    <sum_time_spent>228</sum_time_spent>
    <entry_nb_uniq_visitors>14</entry_nb_uniq_visitors>
    <entry_nb_visits>15</entry_nb_visits>
    <entry_nb_actions>23</entry_nb_actions>
    <entry_sum_visit_length>354</entry_sum_visit_length>
    <entry_bounce_count>10</entry_bounce_count>
    <exit_nb_uniq_visitors>12</exit_nb_uniq_visitors>
    <exit_nb_visits>13</exit_nb_visits>
    <avg_time_on_page>15</avg_time_on_page>
    <bounce_rate>67%</bounce_rate>
    <exit_rate>87%</exit_rate>
  </row>
</result>
```

Now that we know a few of the parameters we can use, the formats we can get our data in and the details of calling the Piwik API locally, we will now explore more of the data we can retrieve using the HTTP request API that most likely you will be using more often.

Including graphs

Another part of the Piwik analytics API are the graph images. These are API calls just like the rest we will be seeing, but they return a PNG image instead of data. A perfect example is a call to the official Piwik demo. We don't have to use any made up URLs. As it is an image, why don't we just create an HTML page with the following code so we can click on it to load in the browser:

```
<!DOCTYPE HTML>
<html lang="en-US">
<head>
  <meta charset="UTF-8">
</head>
<body>
<img src="http://demo.piwik.org/index.php?module=API&method=ImageGra
ph.get&idSite=3&apiModule=VisitsSummary&apiAction=get&token_auth=ano
nymous&graphType=evolution&period=day&date=previous30&width=500&heig
ht=250" alt="" />
</body>
</html>
```

The API call we use is `ImageGraph.get`. This method will accept a lot of parameters.

```
ImageGraph.get (idSite, period, date, apiModule, apiAction, graphType
= '', outputType = '0', column = '', showMetricTitle = '1', width =
'', height = '', fontSize = '9', aliasedGraph = '1', idGoal = '',
colors = '')
```

Notice that we have to call set `apiModule` and `apiAction` parameters for the data the graph will be using. We chose to get the visits summary in our example. We set our graph type to the evolution graph. There are other graph options, as follows:

- `evolution`: This is a line graph
- `horizontalBar`: This is a horizontal bar graph
- `verticalBar`: This is a vertical bar graph
- `pie`: This is a 2D pie chart

We can also define the `width` and `height` of the graph in pixels. We set our image size to 500 x 250. We know what the other parameters are from past examples. This is the resulting image:

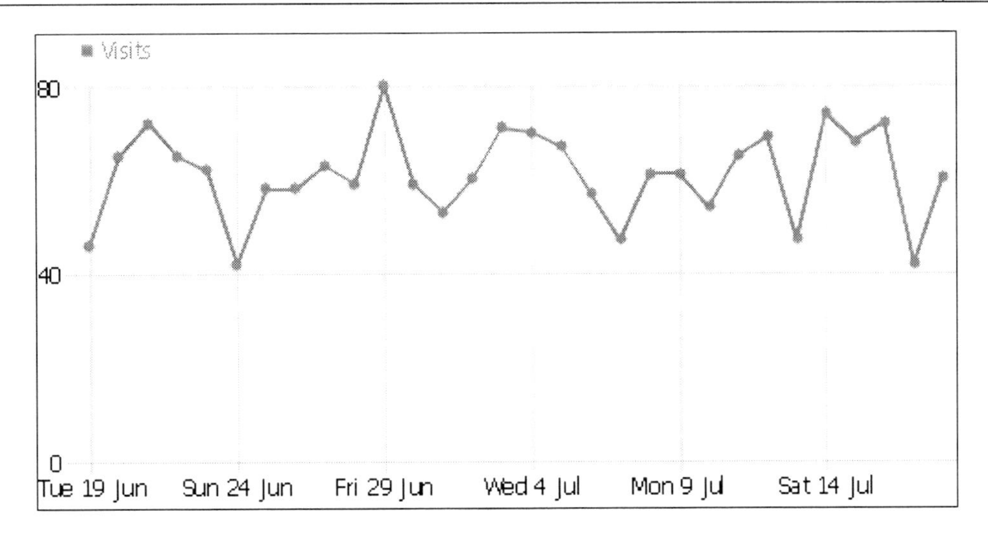

There are other features to the `ImageGraph` method. You can set the colors in the graph to your own custom colors using hexadecimal values. To make a really bright version of our graph we could use the following URL:

```
http://demo.piwik.org/index.php?module=API&method=ImageGraph.get&idSi
te=3&apiModule=VisitsSummary&apiAction=get&token_auth=anonymous&graph
Type=evolution&period=day&date=previous30&width=640&height=300&colors
=FF8000,8000FF,8000FF
```

The result will be as follows:

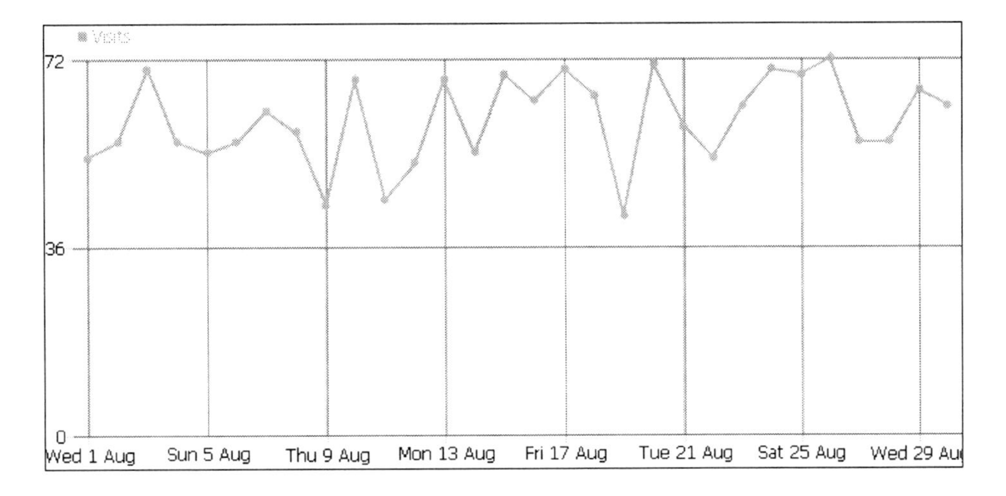

Using the Live! API

By using the Live! API remotely you can have a real time dashboard of your website traffic wherever you want it. Now we are going to be returning some simple data, not returning graphs. So let's create a simple PHP function that we can call any time we need to use it:

```
function piwik_data($stats_url) {
  $ch = curl_init($stats_url);

  curl_setopt ($ch, CURLOPT_HEADER, 0);
  curl_setopt($ch, CURLOPT_RETURNTRANSFER, 1);

  $result = curl_exec($ch);

  curl_close($ch);

  return $result;
}
```

There is not much to this function. It just takes a Piwik URL and gives us the data back. It doesn't even build the URL for us. What a rip off! But it will save a lot of time accessing our URLs and remembering the settings we need for PHP curl.

We will get to create the URLs in a second. First, let's look at the methods we have to work with:

- `Live.getCounters(idSite, lastMinutes, segment)`: This method will return a simple counter or whatever segment you choose (visits, number of actions, and so on). This is good for things like a "How Many Visitors are Online" widget for your blog or website.
- `Live.getLastVisitsDetails(idSite, period, date, segment, filter_limit, maxIdVisit, minTimestamp)`: This method will return extensive data from the last visitors to your site in real time.

So now, let's create a simple PHP file that will output a simple count of how many visits we have had in the last hour. Let's start with the URL:

```
http://YOUR_PIWIK_URL/piwik/index.php?module=API&method=Live.
getCounters&idSite=YOUR_SITE_ID&lastMinutes=60&format=json&tok
en_auth=anonymous
```

You will notice I chose the JSON format. PHP has simple functions to encode and decode JSON, JSON is a little less bulky than XML, and JSON works naturally with JavaScript. It's just a preference.

From this URL we get data that looks like this:

```
[{"visits":"15","actions":"25","visitsConverted":0}]
```

To turn this into something we can use in PHP, we can use the `json_decode` function. This will turn everything between the `[` and the `]` into an array and anything between { and } into an object. So let's look at the full code to see how this works:

```
<?php

function piwik_data($stats_url) {
  $ch = curl_init($stats_url);

  curl_setopt ($ch, CURLOPT_HEADER, 0);
  curl_setopt($ch, CURLOPT_RETURNTRANSFER, 1);

  $result = curl_exec($ch);

  curl_close($ch);

  return $result;
}

$data_url = 'http://YOUR_PIWIK_URL/piwik/index.
php?module=API&method=Live.getCounters&idSite=YOUR_SITE_ID&lastMinutes
=60&format=json&token_auth=anonymous';

$result = piwik_data($data_url);

$result_array = json_decode($result);

?>
<!DOCTYPE HTML>
<html lang="en-US">
<head>
  <meta charset="UTF-8">
  <title>Visitors in Last Hour</title>
</head>
<body>
<?php echo $result_array[0]->visits; ?>
</body>
</html>
```

You will notice our handy function at the top to return our data from Piwik. Then below that, we have our URL. We feed this URL to our function and store the result in the variable `$result`. We then convert the result into something we can use and store this in `$result_array`.

Down in the body of our page, we echo `$result_array[0]->visits`. The `0` selects the first object in the resulting array. There is only one object in this array. We then use `->` to select the member variable, `visits`, out of this object. If we received JSON exactly like the preceding code, our web page would only print out 15.

Segmentation

When using the Live! API earlier, we were given the option of a segment. Segmentation allows you take a slice of the visitors of your site, rather than all of them. You can think of it as a kind of filter.

The segment parameter can be applied to most of Piwik's API functions and segment values can be used together, so that you can narrow down your visitors to a very specific subset. First, let's take a standard URL for an API call to Piwik and modify it for our custom segment, so you can see how it's done. We will do a `Referrers.getKeywords` call:

```
http://YOUR_PIWIK_URL/piwik/index.php?module=API&method=Referrers.
getKeywords&idSite=YOUR_SITE_ID&period=day&date=today&format=JSON&tok
en_auth=anonymous
```

This URL will give us data on the keywords used to reach our site for today. But we can take this URL and modify it so that we can narrow down these keywords. Let's say that we know what our most popular keyword is and we don't want to see it in our report. We want the other keywords. To do so, we would modify this URL so it looks like this:

```
http://YOUR_PIWIK_URL/piwik/index.php?module=API&method=Referrers.
getKeywords&idSite=YOUR_SITE_ID&period=day&date=today&format=JSON&tok
en_auth=anonymous&segment=referrerKeyword!@Holy%20Hand%20Grenade
```

All we did was add the `segment` parameter and we join it to the segment we want to focus on with an equals sign, which is `referrerKeyword`. The keyword we want to filter out is "Holy Hand Grenade". In fact we don't even want other phrases that contain this phrase. The `!@` operator stands for "does not contain". Here is a table of the operators you can use. They give you a lot of flexibility.

Operator	Meaning	Example
`==`	Equals	`&segment=county==DE` Where the country equals Denmark
`!=`	Does not equal	`&segment=referrerName!=Bing` Where the name of the referrer is not Bing
`<`	Less than	`&segment=daysSinceLastVisit<2` Where the days since the last visit is less than 2
`<=`	Less than or equal to	`&segment=actions<=2` Where the actions the visitor made are less than or equal to 2
`>`	Greater than	`&segment=visitDuration>180` Where the visit duration is longer than 180 seconds or 3 minutes
`>=`	Greater than or equal to	`&segment=visitServerHour>=18` Where the time of the visit is greater than or equal to 6 PM
`=@`	Contains	`&segment=referrerKeyword=@free` Where the phrase does contain "free"
`!@`	Does not contain	`&segment= referrerKeyword!@ Holy%20Hand%20Grenade` Where the phrase does not contain "Holy Hand Grenade"

You can also combine segments together in two ways. One way is if you want to match one segment or another:

```
&segment=visitDuration>180,visitDuration<300
```

This will return the data where the visitor stayed between 3 and 5 minutes. A comma separates the two segments and even though they are the same, we have to name the segment again for the second value.

Another way to join segments is using the `AND` operator. For this we will use a semicolon:

```
&segment=country=IN;actions>2
```

This will give us the segment of our data for visitors from India who acted more than twice on our site.

Segments give you great flexibility for filtering your data. We only covered a few of the segments. You can find a complete list of segments you can use in your API calls here: `http://piwik.org/docs/analytics-api/segmentation/`.

The custom variable segments go all the way up to five because you can have up to five custom variables in Piwik. With these many ways to filter your data, you have an amazing tool to help you nail down the needs of specific visitors. To read more about Piwik segments, visit `http://piwik.org/docs/analytics-api/segmentation/`.

We haven't created anything too advanced yet. Piwik has a lot of methods in its API, including a Metadata API that gives you the ability to add users and websites remotely. The WP-Piwik plugin uses this API to dynamically add your blog to your Piwik installation without even visiting it, except for maybe your `token_auth`, because I doubt you have that one memorized. There is a lot to explore and try, enough for a whole book just on this topic. We can't cover everything, but let's look at a chopped down version of something I actually wrote for my own use that integrates Piwik data with another simple data source.

Creating a change log for your website with analytics feedback

I tried to put at least some useful examples in this book, real-world examples instead of toys, though I had to fall back on toys a few times. But when it comes down to dealing with the data side of Piwik, there are some tools I wish I had. Learning about software such as Piwik gives you the ability to take those dreams and make them a reality.

This example is actually a tool I will use. I have been building websites for a long time and tweaking them for the same amount of time to play the cat and mouse game with Google and the other search engines. I always knew it was a good thing to log these changes and then check your stats to see how these changes affected traffic and conversions.

Split testing is the best way to see the true effect the changes will have on your site. But split testing occurs after a visitor enters your site. You run two pages at the same time, sending some visitors to one and some visitors to another. Then you check the results to see which one converted better.

But I was interested more in how the changes in my site affected my rank in the search engines and my traffic. Conversions could be tweaked after traffic was there, so I just kept notes that simply had a date and the changes I made. And I thought, why not keep/write? a log, that marked changes in the same graph in which I saw visitors. So that is what I built.

Because we are learning about Piwik here, we are going to make the logging software as simple as we can. We are going to use a single PHP file to:

- Hold our form
- Write to a file to log our changes
- Retrieve data from Piwik
- Display that data

Okay, let's look over the code for each part separately, so that we can see how all of it fits together. First we need an HTML page with a form. We can call `index.php` and put it in a folder called `SiteLog`, because it will be creating a logfile also and you might as well keep the two files together for this example. At the top of the page, we will have this PHP code:

```
 //The url to your Piwik folder
$p_url = "";
//The id of your site in Piwik
$site_id = "";
//Your Piwik token_auth
$token_auth = "";

  function write_log($message) {
      $log_file = 'logfile.txt';

$fp = fopen($log_file, 'a') or exit("Can't open logfile!");

      $time = @date('Y-m-d');

      fwrite($fp, "$time:$message" . PHP_EOL);

  fclose($fp);
  }
```

At the top of the file, we have three variables we must set:

- Your Piwik URL
- The ID of your site in Piwik
- The `token_auth` for your Piwik account

You can fill these in now if you want. We won't be using them just yet. Let's look at the `write_log` function. It has one parameter, a message. The function opens a file in the same folder called `logfile.txt`. We will be appending to this file with every new log message that we want to save, so we open the file in append mode with the "a" parameter. Then we get the time from our server. Then we take our message and our time and write it to the file. As we always should we close the file. Our logfile will end up looking something like this after a few messages have been added:

```
2012-06-18:Added blogging widget
2012-06-24:Removed blogroll widget
2012-06-30:Removed eight categories
2012-07-04:Wrote link bait post
2012-07-11:Wrote guest post
```

That's our function for writing a log. There is not really much to it. So let's look at our form in the body of our HTML:

```
<div id="wrapper">
    <header>
      <h1>Website Log</h1>
    </header>
    <form action="" method="post">
      What Changed?: <input type="text" name="message" size="50"/>
      <input type="submit" name="mysubmit" value="Log Change" />
    </form>
    <h2>Website Log Chart</h2>
    <div id="visualization" style="width: 1000px; height: 600px;"></
div>
    <footer>
      <p></p>
    </footer>
</div>
```

We have one text field for input, which we have named `message`, and a `submit` button. We leave `form action` blank so it will post to itself. Now we need something to take the posted message and execute our `write_log` function. Once we do this, we will have a PHP file that will write a log for us:

```
<?php

  //The url to your Piwik folder
  $p_url = "";
  //The id of your site in Piwik
  $site_id = "";
```

```
  //Your Piwik token_auth
  $token_auth = "";
  function write_log($message) {
        $log_file = 'logfile.txt';

    $fp = fopen($log_file, 'a') or exit("Can't open logfile!");

        $time = @date('Y-m-d');

        fwrite($fp, "$time:$message" . PHP_EOL);

    fclose($fp);
    }

  if (isset ($_POST['message'])) {
    write_log($_POST['message']);
  }

?>
<!DOCTYPE HTML>
<html lang="en-US">
<head>
  <meta charset="UTF-8">
  <title>Website Log</title>
</head>
<body>
  <div id="wrapper">
    <header>
      <h1>Website Log</h1>
      </header>
      <form action="" method="post">
      What Changed?: <input type="text" name="message" size="50"/>
      <input type="submit" name="mysubmit" value="Log Change" />
    </form>
    <h2>Website Log Chart</h2>
    <div id="visualization" style="width: 1000px; height: 600px;"></
div>
    <footer>
      <p></p>
    </footer>
  </div>
</body>
</html>
```

To get the message to our function, all we had to do was add this bit of code to grab the POST variable and check that there is actually content in our log message.

```
if (isset ($_POST['message']) && strlen($_POST['message']) > 0) {
  write_log($_POST['message']);
}
```

If we have posted a message, it will run our write_log function. And if not, it only loads the rest of the page.

Now that we have something to write our log, we can use a similar function to read the logfile. It also parses our lines as it goes into an array.

```
function read_log() {
  $log_file = 'logfile.txt';

  $fp = fopen($log_file, 'r') or exit("Can't open logfile!");

  $log_rows = array();

  while(!feof($fp))  {
    $log_parts = explode(":", fgets($fp));
    if (count($log_parts) == 2){
      $log_rows[$log_parts[0]] = $log_parts[1];
    }
  }

  fclose($fp);

  return $log_rows;
}
```

To grab our Piwik data, we will use a slightly modified version of our PHP curl function that we wrote earlier. We just added json_decode to the function itself.

```
function piwik_data($stats_url) {
  $ch = curl_init($stats_url);

  curl_setopt ($ch, CURLOPT_HEADER, 0);
  curl_setopt($ch, CURLOPT_RETURNTRANSFER, 1);

  $result = curl_exec($ch);

  curl_close($ch);
  return json_decode($result);
}
```

Now I tried to keep it simple, so let's just take this next function at face value. It is slightly more complex than the rest, but it takes the data from both the logfile and the Piwik API and merges them into a multidimensional array so that all the data for one day can be accessed with the date. We need this because we are going to be using Google's Visualization library to draw our graph and we need our data in order. If you understand PHP, dig into it and figure out how it works.

```
function merge_data($p_url,$site_id,$token_auth){
    $stats_url =  $p_url."?module=API&method=VisitsSummary.
getVisits&idSite=".$site_id."&period=day&date=last30&format=JSON&tok
en_auth=".$token_auth;
    $log_data = read_log();
    $stats_data = piwik_data($stats_url);
    $merged_data = array();

    foreach ($log_data as $k => $v) {
      $merged_data[$k]['notes'] = trim($v);
    }

    foreach ($stats_data as $k => $v) {
      if (array_key_exists($k, $merged_data)) {
        $merged_data[$k]['visits'] = (int)$v;
      }else{
        $merged_data[$k]['visits'] = (int)$v;
        $merged_data[$k]['notes'] = null;
      }
    }

    return $merged_data;
  }
```

Here is how we generate our visits graph annotated with our log data. We put this in the header of our page. We loop through our merged data and print out in our JavaScript, converting the array into what our JavaScript needs to create the lines and tags.

```
<script type="text/javascript" src="https://www.google.com/jsapi"></
script>
<script type="text/javascript">
    google.load('visualization', '1', {packages:
['annotatedtimeline']});
    function drawVisualization() {
      var data = new google.visualization.DataTable();
      data.addColumn('date', 'Date');
      data.addColumn('number', 'Visits');
```

```
        data.addColumn('string', 'title1');
        data.addRows([
        <?php
          $data = merge_data($p_url,$site_id,$token_auth);
          foreach ($data as $k => $v) {
            echo "[new Date(";
            $date_array = explode("-",$k);
            echo $date_array[0].",".$date_array[1].",".$date_
array[2]."),";
            echo $data[$k]['visits'].",";
            echo "'".$data[$k]['notes']."'],";
          }
        ?>
        ]);

        var annotatedtimeline = new google.visualization.
AnnotatedTimeLine(
        document.getElementById('visualization'));
        annotatedtimeline.draw(data, {'displayAnnotations': true});
      }

      google.setOnLoadCallback(drawVisualization);
    </script>
```

Now we need to add the section of HTML that this JavaScript will use to actually display the graph:

```
<div id="visualization" style="width: 1000px; height: 600px;"></div>
```

I used Google Chart Tools for this script because you can include the JavaScript files from their remote source and we could still keep our project in one file. You can read more about Google Chart Tools at `https://developers.google.com/chart/`. The result of the log is shown in the following screenshot:

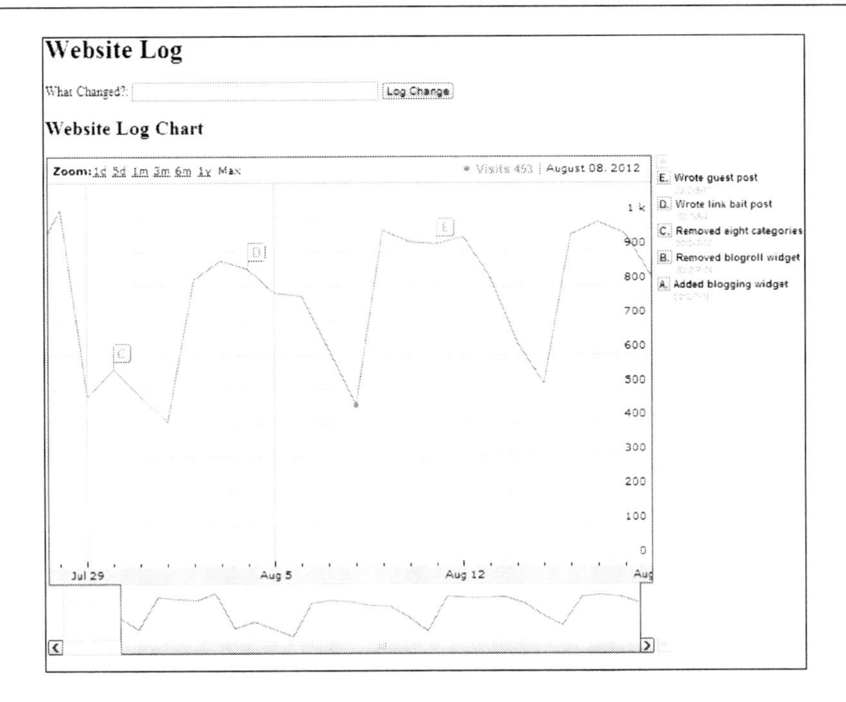

The log entries show up as the **A**, **B**, **C**, **D**, and **E** flags on the line graph and they are listed on the right-hand side.

The complete file is available with the code files for the book on the Packt website. To read more about the Analytics API, please visit `http://piwik.org/docs/analytics-api/`.

Summary

You now know how to embed widgets from Piwik into other sites by simply copying and pasting code from your Piwik installation. You have also learned how to use Piwik's Analytics API in various ways. We learned that we can retrieve graphs from Piwik, access real time visitor data and use segmentation to narrow down our results. We then built a standalone tool to match changes in our website to the visits logged in Piwik.

We have now reached the end of the book, other than the two appendices. You should now have a good understanding of how you can use Piwik to track visitor data on your website. For more information on Piwik, please visit `http://www.piwik.org`.

Tracking API Reference

This appendix is for extended reference to the Piwik tracking API which was covered in depth in *Chapter 9, Advanced Tracking and Development*, of this book.

The Piwik tracking API

The Piwik tracking API allows you to track websites and apps where JavaScript won't do the job. It can be accessed through any type of programming language using an HTTP request.

Variables

The URL to your Piwik installation must be set first. You can set this in the following manner:

```
PiwikTracker::$URL = 'http://yourwebsite.org/piwik/'
```

Methods

The Piwik tracking API gives you access to all the methods that are available in the JavaScript tracker.

Constructor __construct

This method builds a `PiwikTracker` object.

```
PiwikTracker __construct (int $idSite, [string $apiUrl = false])
```

These variables indicate the following:

- `int $idSite`: This variable determines the site ID to be tracked
- `string $apiUrl`: For example, if this variable is set to `http://example.org/piwik/` or `http://piwik.example.org/`, it will overwrite `PiwikTracker::$URL`

addEcommerceItem

This method adds an item in the e-commerce order and should be called before `doTrackEcommerceOrder()`, or before `doTrackEcommerceCartUpdate()`. You will call this method for each item that gets added to the cart. The SKU parameter is the only required parameter and every other parameter is optional and should be set to false if unknown or unneeded.

```
void addEcommerceItem (string $sku, [string $name = false],
[string|array $category = false], [float|int $price = false], [int
$quantity = false])
```

These variables indicate the following:

- `string $sku` (required): This is the SKU parameter, the product identifier.
- `string $name` (optional): This is the product name.
- `string|array $category` (optional) : This is the product category, or array of product categories (up to five categories can be specified for a given product).
- `float|int $price` (optional): This indicates the individual product price (supports integer and decimal prices).
- `int $quantity` (optional): This is the product quantity. If not specified, this will default to 1 in the reports.

disableCookieSupport

By calling this function, you can disable cookies in the application using the Piwik tracking API.

```
void disableCookieSupport ()
```

doTrackAction

This method tracks a download or an outlink.

```
string doTrackAction (string $actionUrl, string $actionType)
```

These variables indicate the following:

- `string $actionUrl`: This is the URL of the download or outlink
- `string $actionType`: This indicates the type of the action, either download or link

doTrackEcommerceCartUpdate

This method will update the monetary value of a shopping cart Piwik is tracking. It is called after one or more calls to `addEcommerceItem()`.

```
void doTrackEcommerceCartUpdate (float $grandTotal)
```

- The `float $grandTotal` variable indicates the cart grand total (typically the sum of all items' prices)

doTrackEcommerceOrder

This method tracks an e-commerce order. It is called after you have called `addEcommerceItem()` for each item in the order.

```
void doTrackEcommerceOrder (string|int $orderId, float $grandTotal,
[float $subTotal = false], [float $tax = false], [float $shipping =
false], [float $discount = false])
```

These variables indicate the following:

- `string|int $orderId` (required): This is the unique order ID. This will be used to count the order only once in the event even if the order page is reloaded several times. `orderId` must be unique for each transaction, even on different days, or the transaction will not be recorded by Piwik.
- `float $grandTotal` (required): This is the grand total revenue of the transaction (including tax, shipping, and so on).
- `float $subTotal` (optional): This is the subtotal amount, typically the sum of items' prices for all items in this order (before tax and shipping costs are applied).
- `float $tax` (optional): This is the tax amount for this order.
- `float $shipping` (optional): This is the shipping amount for this order.
- `float $discount` (optional): This is the discounted amount in this order.

doTrackGoal

This method records a goal conversion.

```
string doTrackGoal (int $idGoal, [float $revenue = false])
```

These variables indicate the following:

- `int $idGoal`: This is the ID of the goal to record a conversion
- `float $revenue`: This is the revenue for this conversion

doTrackPageView

This method tracks a page view.

```
string doTrackPageView (string $documentTitle)
```

- The `string $documentTitle` variable is the page title as it will appear in the **Actions** | **Page** titles report

enableBulkTracking

This method enables the Piwik tracking API's bulk tracking feature. Using it causes each tracking action to be stored until the `doBulkTrack` method is called.

```
void enableBulkTracking ()
```

doBulkTrack

This method sends all tracking data that has been stored in bulk. It is used along with `enableBulkTracking()`.

```
string doBulkTrack ()
```

getAttributionInfo

This method will return the attribution information that has been stored in a Piwik cookie.

```
string getAttributionInfo ()
```

getBaseUrl

This method will return the base URL of your Piwik installation.

```
void getBaseUrl ()
```

getCustomVariable

This method will return the current custom variable stored in a Piwik first part cookie.

```
array|false getCustomVariable (int $id, [string $scope = 'visit'])
```

These variables indicate the following:

- `int $id`: This is the custom variable integer index to fetch from cookie. This should be a value from 1 to 5.
- `string $scope`: This is the custom variable scope. The possible values are `visit` and `page`.

getRequestTimeout

The method will give you the maximum time in seconds that the `PiwikTracker` object will wait for a response from Piwik. By default, it is set to 600 seconds.

```
void getRequestTimeout ()
```

getTimestamp

This method returns the current timestamp, or the forced timestamp/datetime if it was set.

```
string|int getTimestamp ()
```

getUrlTrackAction

This method will track an action.

```
string getUrlTrackAction (string $actionUrl, string $actionType)
```

These variables indicate the following:

- `string $actionUrl`: This is the URL of the download or outlink.
- `string $actionType`: This is the type of the action. It can be either `download` or `link`.

getUrlTrackGoal

This method will track a goal.

```
string getUrlTrackGoal (int $idGoal, [float $revenue = false])
```

These variables indicate the following:

- `int $idGoal`: This is the ID of goal to record a conversion
- `float $revenue`: This is the revenue for this conversion

getUrlTrackPageView

This method will track a page view.

```
string getUrlTrackPageView ([string $documentTitle = false])
```

- The `string $documentTitle` variable is the page view name as it will appear in Piwik reports.

getVisitorId

This method will return the visitor ID from a visitor's first party Piwik cookie. If it is called programmatically, it will return the random visitor ID assigned to the visit.

```
string getVisitorId ()
```

setAttributionInfo

This method sets the attribution information to the visit. This must be a JSON encoded string that would most likely be retrieved from the JavaScript API: `piwikTracker.getAttributionInfo()` and that you have JSON encoded via `JSON2.stringify()`.

```
void setAttributionInfo (string $jsonEncoded)
```

- The string `$jsonEncoded` variable is the JSON encoded array containing attribution information

setBrowserHasCookies

With this method, you tell Piwik whether or not the user's browser supports cookies.

```
void setBrowserHasCookies (bool $bool)
```

- The `bool $bool` variable holds a `true` or `false` value

setBrowserLanguage

This method will set the browser language.

```
void setBrowserLanguage (string $acceptLanguage)
```

- The `string $acceptLanguage`: For example, `fr-fr`

setCustomVariable

This method sets a custom variable in the visit or page scope.

```
void setCustomVariable (int $id, string $name, string $value, [string
$scope = 'visit'])
```

These variables indicate the following:

- `int $id`: This is the custom variable slot. The ID ranges from 1 to 5.
- `string $name`: This is the custom variable name.
- `string $value`: This is the custom variable value.
- `string $scope`: This is the custom variable scope. The possible values are `visit` or `page`.

setDebugStringAppend

This method will append a custom string at the end of the tracking request for debugging purposes.

```
void setDebugStringAppend (string $string)
```

setEcommerceView

This method triggers an e-commerce product or category page view. It has to be called before you call `doTrackPageView` in order to be counted.

```
void setEcommerceView ([string $sku = false], [string $name = false],
[string|array $category = false], [float $price = false])
```

These variables indicate the following:

- `string $sku`: This is the product SKU being viewed.
- `string $name`: This is the product name being viewed.
- `string|array $category`: This is the category being viewed. On a product page, this is the product's category. You can also specify an array of up to five categories for a given page view.
- `float $price`: This specifies the price at which the item was displayed.

setForceVisitDateTime

This method will override the current `datetime` so you can set it manually. The time is in UTC and can only be used by a super user using the `setTokenAuth` method.

```
void setForceVisitDateTime (string $dateTime)
```

- The `string $dateTime` variable is the date with the format "Y-m-d H:i:s", or a UNIX timestamp

setIp

This method overrides the IP address. Allowed only for the super user, must be used along with `setTokenAuth()`.

```
void setIp (string $ip)
```

- The `string $ip` variable contains the IP string, for example, 130.54.2.1

setLocalTime

This method sets local visitor time.

```
void setLocalTime (string $time)access: public
```

- The `string $time` variable is in the HH:MM:SS format

setPlugins

This method sets visitor browser supported plugins.

```
void setPlugins ([bool $flash = false], [bool $java = false], [bool
$director = false], [bool $quickTime = false], [bool $realPlayer
= false], [bool $pdf = false], [bool $windowsMedia = false], [bool
$gears = false], [bool $silverlight = false])
```

These variables indicate the following:

- `bool $flash`: This is set to `true` if Flash is enabled
- `bool $java`: This is set to `true` if Java is enabled
- `bool $director`: This is set to `true` if Director is enabled
- `bool $quickTime`: This is set to `true` if Quicktime is enabled
- `bool $realPlayer`: This is set to `true` if RealPlayer is enabled
- `bool $pdf`: This is set to `true` if PDF support is enabled
- `bool $windowsMedia`: This is set to `true` if Windows Media is enabled
- `bool $gears`: This is set to `true` if Google Gears is enabled
- `bool $silverlight`: This is set to `true` if SilverLight is enabled

setRequestTimeout

This method sets the maximum number of seconds that the tracker will spend waiting for a response from Piwik. By default it is set to 600 seconds.

```
void setRequestTimeout (int $timeout)
```

- The int `$timeout` variable is an integer value representing the seconds of timeout

setResolution

This method sets user resolution width and height.

```
void setResolution (int $width, int $height)
```

- `int $width`: This is an integer value of width in pixels
- `int $height`: This is an integer value of height in pixels

setTokenAuth

For those tracking API methods that require special authentication, by either an admin or a super user, this method will allow you to set the `token_auth`.

```
void setTokenAuth (string $token_auth)
```

- The `string $token_auth` variable is the 32 chars `token_auth` string

setUrl

This method sets the current URL being tracked.

```
void setUrl (string $url)
```

- The `string $url` \variable is the raw URL (not URL encoded)

setUrlReferrer

This method sets the URL referrer.

```
void setUrlReferrer (string $url)
```

- The `string $url` variable is the raw URL (not URL encoded)

setUserAgent

This method sets the user agent, used to detect OS and browser. If this method is not called, the user agent will default to the current user agent.

```
void setUserAgent (string $userAgent)
```

- The `string $userAgent` variable bears values; for example, Mozilla/5.0 (iPad; U; CPU OS 3_2_1 such as Mac OS X; en-us), AppleWebKit/531.21.10 (KHTML, such as Gecko), and Mobile/7B405

setVisitorId

This method will set the visitor ID manually. Only the super user is allowed to use it and it must be used with `setTokenAuth`.

```
void setVisitorId (string $visitorId)
```

- The `string $visitorId` variable bears a 16 hexadecimal character visitor ID; for example, 33c31e01394bdc63

B
Analytics API Reference

This appendix is for extended reference to the Piwik analytics API which was covered more in depth in *Chapter 10, Piwik Integration*.

The Piwik analytics API

The Piwik analytics API allows you to access all the data remotely that is available in Piwik's interface. With it you can embed Piwik's data in another application using any programming language, or you can manipulate the data for reports and graphs not available in Piwik itself. Complete documentation of the Piwik analytics API is available at `http://piwik.org/docs/analytics-api/reference/` or at the **API** link in any live Piwik installation.

Module API

This API provides metadata on all the other API methods. In other words, calling a function in the Module API will tell you what methods are available for you to use and will give you human-readable information on these methods. The following are some examples of its methods:

- A list of all API methods using `getReportMetadata`
- A list of metrics that each one of the previous methods will return along with their readable name, when you use `getDefaultMetrics` and `getDefaultProcessedMetrics`
- A list of all the segments that you can use with functions that support segments using `getSegmentsMetadata`

You can read more about the methods available in the Metadata API at `http://piwik.org/docs/analytics-api/metadata/`.

Module Actions

The Actions API will give you information on all of your visitors' actions such as page titles, clicks on external links, and file downloads.

The `getPageTitles` method will return all of your page titles and the standard metrics available to that method.

You can also request the data for a single page title by using `getPageTitle`, by setting the `pageName` parameter to the page title you choose.

Some more of the methods available are `getPageUrl`, which will give you metrics for a specific page URL, `getOutlink`, which will give you outlink data, and `getDownload`, which will give you the downloaded files' data.

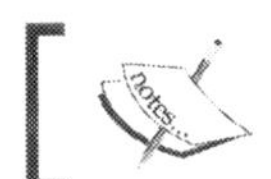

The `pageName`, `pageUrl`, `outlinkUrl`, and `downloadUrl` parameters must be URL encoded before you call the API.

You can find out more about all of the functions available in the Actions API by visiting `http://piwik.org/docs/analytics-api/reference/#Actions`.

Module CustomVariables

The CustomVariables API lets you access reports for your CustomVariables names and values. It has only two functions shown as follows:

```
CustomVariables.getCustomVariables (idSite, period, date, segment
= '', expanded = '').
CustomVariables.getCustomVariablesValuesFromNameId (idSite,
period, date, idSubtable, segment = '').
```

Module ExampleAPI

The ExampleAPI is useful to developers building a custom Piwik plugin. It is essentially a toy API created to help you learn. You can read more about it at `http://piwik.org/docs/analytics-api/reference/#ExampleAPI`.

Module Goals

The Goals API gives you control over your goals. You can use `updateGoal` to change a goal's details, `deleteGoal` to remove a goal, and `addGoal` to create a new goal. And if you want to list the goals for one or more websites, you can use the `getGoals` method.

Another feature is that this API provides access to your e-commerce tracking data. You can retrieve a list of products purchased on your site by using `getItemsSku`, `getItemsName`, or `getItemsCategory`. These methods will return a list of products that have been purchased on your site along with supporting metrics.

You can explore more of the Goals API by visiting `http://piwik.org/docs/analytics-api/reference/#Goals`.

Module ImageGraph

The ImageGraph API will return PNG graphs for any Piwik report that supports them. In your request, you can specify these graph types as line plot, vertical bar chart, or 2D/3D pie chart. You can also specify the width, height, font size, and even the colors of the graph being returned.

You can read more about the ImageGraph API at `http://piwik.org/docs/analytics-api/reference/#ImageGraph`.

Module LanguagesManager

The LanguagesManager API lets you translate the data you receive from Piwik into any one of the 40+ languages that Piwik supports.

For more information on the LanguagesManager API, please visit `http://piwik.org/docs/analytics-api/reference/#LanguagesManager`.

Module Live!

The Live! API will give you real-time information about your visitors. You can also use segmentation with this API to drill down your data to very specific subsets. The `getLastVisitsDetails` method will give you a massive amount of detail on each of your visitors. By adding the parameter `&segment=`, you can use segmentation to filter the visits that have been returned by any valid criteria.

The `getCounters` method will return a simple count of visits, actions, or converted visits for your chosen time period.

Here are the two methods available in the Live! API.

```
Live.getCounters (idSite, lastMinutes, segment = '').
Live.getLastVisitsDetails (idSite, period, date, segment = '',
filter_limit = '', maxIdVisit = '', minTimestamp = '').
```

Module MultiSites

The MultiSites API will return the key metrics from all the websites you are tracking in Piwik. It only has one method, listed as follows

```
MultiSites.getAll (period, date, segment = '')
```

Module PDFReports

The PDFReports API gives you remote control over Piwik reports. With it, you can generate, download, email, or schedule reports.

To learn more about the PDFReports API, please see `http://piwik.org/docs/analytics-api/reference/#PDFReports` and `http://piwik.org/docs/email-reports/`.

Module Provider

The Provider API lets you access reports for your visitors' Internet providers such as Comcast, Road Runner, and Cox. It has only one method:

```
Provider.getProvider (idSite, period, date, segment = '')
```

Module Referers

The Referers API will give you data on the referrers that visitors used to find your website. It will return data on websites, search engines, keywords, and campaigns.

An example widget that uses the referrer API is available at `http://tinyurl.com/9b8z8hz`.

You can read more about the Referers API at `http://piwik.org/docs/analytics-api/reference/#Referers`.

Module SEO

The SEO API returns a list of SEO data on your URL. It will give you Google PageRank, Yahoo! backlinks, Yahoo! indexed pages, Alexa Rank, and domain name age. Here is its one method:

- `SEO.getRank (url)`

Module SitesManager

The SitesManager API lets you control your websites in Piwik remotely. You can create, update, and delete the websites that your Piwik installation tracks as well as retrieve data on the configuration of those sites.

You can read more about all the methods available in the SitesManager API at `http://piwik.org/docs/analytics-api/reference/#SitesManager`.

Module UserCountry

The UserCountry API will return reports about your visitors' countries and continents.

You can read more about this API at `http://piwik.org/docs/analytics-api/reference/#UserCountry`.

Module UserSettings

The UserSettings API will return reports about your visitors' browsing environment including the browser they use, their operating system, plugins they have installed in their browser, their screen resolution and their screen type.

You can learn more about all the methods available in this API at `http://piwik.org/docs/analytics-api/reference/#UserSettings`.

Module UsersManager

The UsersManager API allows you to control Piwik users remotely. You can add, delete, update or get information about the users that have access to your Piwik installation.

To find out more about these methods and others available in the UsersManager API please visit `http://piwik.org/docs/analytics-api/reference/#UsersManager`.

Module VisitFrequency

The VisitFrequency API lets you access a list of metrics related toreturning visitors. It has one method:

```
VisitFrequency.get (idSite, period, date,
segment = '', columns = '')
```

Module VisitTime

The VisitTime API lets you access reports by hour (server time), and by hour (local time) of your visitors. It has only these two methods:

- `VisitTime.getVisitInformationPerLocalTime (idSite, period, date, segment = '')`
- `VisitTime.getVisitInformationPerServerTime (idSite, period, date, segment = '', hideFutureHoursWhenToday = '')`

Module VisitorInterest

The VisitorInterest API gives you visitor engagement reports.

You can find out more about this API at `http://piwik.org/docs/analytics-api/reference/#VisitorInterest`.

Module VisitsSummary

The VisitsSummary API lets you access the core web analytics metrics.

To read about all the methods you can use with this API, please see `http://piwik.org/docs/analytics-api/reference/#VisitsSummary`.

Index

Symbols

A

E

F

G

H

I

J

K

L

O

P

Q

R

S

T

U

V

W

Z

Thank you for buying
Piwik Web Analytics Essentials

About Packt Publishing

Packt, pronounced 'packed', published its first book "*Mastering phpMyAdmin for Effective MySQL Management*" in April 2004 and subsequently continued to specialize in publishing highly focused books on specific technologies and solutions.

Our books and publications share the experiences of your fellow IT professionals in adapting and customizing today's systems, applications, and frameworks. Our solution based books give you the knowledge and power to customize the software and technologies you're using to get the job done. Packt books are more specific and less general than the IT books you have seen in the past. Our unique business model allows us to bring you more focused information, giving you more of what you need to know, and less of what you don't.

Packt is a modern, yet unique publishing company, which focuses on producing quality, cutting-edge books for communities of developers, administrators, and newbies alike. For more information, please visit our website: `www.packtpub.com`.

About Packt Open Source

In 2010, Packt launched two new brands, Packt Open Source and Packt Enterprise, in order to continue its focus on specialization. This book is part of the Packt Open Source brand, home to books published on software built around Open Source licences, and offering information to anybody from advanced developers to budding web designers. The Open Source brand also runs Packt's Open Source Royalty Scheme, by which Packt gives a royalty to each Open Source project about whose software a book is sold.

Writing for Packt

We welcome all inquiries from people who are interested in authoring. Book proposals should be sent to author@packtpub.com. If your book idea is still at an early stage and you would like to discuss it first before writing a formal book proposal, contact us; one of our commissioning editors will get in touch with you.

We're not just looking for published authors; if you have strong technical skills but no writing experience, our experienced editors can help you develop a writing career, or simply get some additional reward for your expertise.

CPSIA information can be obtained at www.ICGtesting.com
Printed in the USA
LVOW050609171012

303116LV00005B/5/P

9 781849 518482